for
rk
and the celebration of
your maverick family.
Best Wishes,
Sue

CREATIVE MAVERICKS:
BEACONS OF
AUTHENTIC LEARNING

Cover illustration by Sam Burr

CREATIVE MAVERICKS: BEACONS OF AUTHENTIC LEARNING

Sue Haynes

To order additional copies of this book, contact:
Xlibris Corporation
1-888-795-4274
www.Xlibris.com
Orders@Xlibris.com
30466

CONTENTS

Part II

Part III

Dedicated to my three maverick sons:
Michael, Adam, and Matt

Acknowledgments

From the start, the writing of this book has been a shared journey. I began with interviewing creatively gifted adults who had struggled with schooling before actualizing their gifts. I then researched writings on learning disabilities, ADD, visual/spatial learners, the Indigo Children, and highly creative individuals. During the writing of my facilitation chapter, I reflected on my revelatory work with maverick learners. Finally, as I became clearer about the role creatively gifted individuals play in bringing forth qualities of authentic learning, I interviewed teachers who sought to encourage all learners to be true to their inner agendas.

I am grateful for the amazing stories from the following creatively gifted adults: Fred Johnson, Peter Williams, Carolyn Williams, Emily Poole, Emily Bracale, Jonathan Bagley, Helen Farrar, Bob Keteyian, David Lamon, Matt Williams, Cathy Kozaryn, Sandy Heimann, Linden O'Ryan, Isabelle Mancinelli, Matt Haynes, Gary Sites, Emma Coffin, Soos Valdina, Mida Ballard, Margret Baldwin, Ashley Bryan, Bob Chaplin, Heather Rowe, Jennifer Westfall, Lesley Horvath, Francoise Gervais, Judith Brown, and Sarah Fraley.

I am grateful for the inspiring reflections from the following teachers: Lisa Plourde, Cathy Kozaryn, Adam Haynes, Sherri Clixby, Jill Farley, Phyl Brazee, MaryAnn Wheeler, Jane Disney, and Megs Metz.

I am grateful to the following friends and colleagues who have cheered me on and offered support: Marie Greene, for donating her time to transcribe many of the interviews; Sylvia Matteson, who encouraged me to take risks; Ann Bohrer, for her helpful response to story writeups; Emily Bracale, for our clarifying dialogues about authentic teaching and learning; Amy Davis, Bob Keteyian, and Phyl Brazee, for their suggestions and enthusiastic responses to sections of the book; Kate Montgomery, editor at Heinemann Publishing, and Janet Gore, editor at Great Potential Press, for their enthusiasm for my project and helpful suggestions.

I am grateful to my three maverick sons, Michael, Adam, and Matt, who challenged me to believe in the potency of creative vision against all odds.

Finally, I am grateful to Sandy Heimann, who has traveled with me on this project from its inception supporting me, both personally and through intuitive readings, on every aspect of the book. Without her ongoing feedback about the relevancy of my work, I doubt I would have had the will to sustain six years of writing this book.

Preface

We all know that what will transform education is not another
theory or another book but a transformed way of being in the
world. In the midst of the familiar trappings of education—
competition, intellectual combat, obsession with a narrow range
of facts, credits, credentials—we seek a life illumined by spirit
and infused with soul.

—Parker Palmer

Over the past thirty years of teaching, I have had the privilege of working
with a unique population of learners who, in their struggle with and often
resistance to standardized education, have revealed a quality of learning that
stems from a deeply sourced creative vitality. I term this population of learners
"creatively gifted." These maverick learners explore the frontiers of possibilities
"outside of the box." In their resistance to paying tribute to superficial and
often bogus learning agendas, they have become for me beacons of authentic
learning—a level of learning which has the potential to enliven, empower,
and even transform us. As I bring forth their struggles, their triumphs, and
their wisdom in this book, I hope to add their inspirational voices and visions
to our current dialogue about educational transformation.

The qualities of authentic teaching and learning that I share in this book
through my teaching experiences, through the personal stories of creatively
gifted learners, and through the reflections of teachers who engender authentic
learning cannot be translated into a scope and sequence curriculum. These
qualities transcend the culturally conditioned, functional self. They are sourced
from the "bejeweled self" of our innermost being and flower on their own
timetable of unique expression.

I believe that the purpose of education is to awaken and support this
bejeweled treasure within us and to infuse its creative vitality and wisdom

into our functional personality. E. T. Clark, (1991) in his chapter "The Search for a New Educational Paradigm: The Implications About New Assumptions About Thinking and Learning," discusses this larger perspective of educational goals:

> Acknowledging both the intuitive and the cognitive aspects of learning, these new assumptions recognize the fullness and richness of learning that can only be expressed through words like understand, appreciate, enjoy, know, and believe. Indeed it is because of the multidimensionality of these experiences that behaviorists refute them as unmeasurable. But in rejecting what these words represent, we are in danger of rejecting both the multidimensionality and potentiality of human learning. (p. 22)

This new paradigm of teaching and learning will focus on inward awareness and growth. External goals will be regarded as serving this awareness and growth, not as end points in themselves. The role of the teacher within this new paradigm changes radically:

> Once we acknowledge a new set of assumptions regarding the innate capacities of students, we find a new role for the teacher emerging. From being a dispenser of information and knowledge, the teacher becomes a gardener whose responsibility is to nurture growing children so that the innate potential of each organism is allowed to blossom and bear fruit. (Clark, 1991, pp. 26-27)

In writing *Creative Mavericks: Beacons of Authentic Learning*, I join with other new paradigm educators in bringing forth a visionary conceptualization of human potential and the tenets of teaching and learning that support its fruition. *Creative Mavericks* consists of three sections: Section One includes "Who is the Creatively Gifted Learner," which explores the attributes of highly creative learners, and "Seeing Through a Different Lens:Facilitating the Creatively Gifted Learner," which describes my teaching; Section Two, "Heartsongs: The Struggles and Triumphs of Creatively Gifted Learners," includes the stories of twelve individuals who share reflections on their schooling and the fruition of their creative empowerment; Section Three, "Implications of Education for Creatively Gifted Learners:Awakening Passion and Authenticity in All Learners," further explores the conditions which foster learning empowerment through the reflections of nine innovative classroom teachers. These teachers reveal that the passion and creative expression so evident in highly creative learners are seeded within all learners and can be awakened by teaching which honors the core uniqueness of each individual.

PART I

Who Is the Creatively Gifted Learner?

What lies before us and what lies behind us
are small matters compared to
what lies within us,
And when we bring what is within us
out into the world,
miracles happen.

—Henry David Thoreau

And the Beat Goes On

I knew I was in for it again when the drumming went on for more than three months. My son, Matt, at age two and a half, had recently discovered a professional drum set in the basement of a neighbor's house. When we persuaded our neighbor to give him a demonstration, Matt was mesmerized.

Over the ensuing days and continuing on for a year, Matt created drum sets in every setting of his life. In the kitchen he pulled out pots, pans and bowls for the drums and large spoons and other utensils for the drumsticks. In his room at "nap time," he dumped out all of his buckets of toys, grabbed some tinker toy sticks and thumped away. I would hear a syncopated rhythm repeated over and over followed by, "One, two, three, let's do it again!" When we camped out the summer he turned three, he relished utilizing tree stumps and found sticks. At his nursery school orientation that fall, he made a beeline for a set of small wooden color circles. He secured some Q Tips and began drumming out his beat. One of the teachers came over and asked him to name each of the colors. He lay down the Q Tips and correctly complied; as she left, he reclaimed the Q tips and picked up his beat. That year in nursery school his teachers said they could follow Matt's path through the two rooms of the school each morning by tracking a variety of abandoned drum set creations.

For a while, his father and I thought we might have a budding musician on our hands. Matt's beats were never random; they were deliberate and quite rhythmical. But when we gave him a real snare drum for Christmas, he mostly ignored it, focusing on his own creations instead. Thinking that it was the drum *set* concept that particularly enticed him, we gave him a fairly sturdy toy drum set for Christmas the following year that had all the bells and whistles. Matt mostly ignored that as well. We finally realized that it was the *inventing* of adaptations on a theme that obsessively drove him. And as the drumming faded out, a new obsession took its place—a passionate exploration of drawing that went on for years.

Matt is the youngest of my three sons. His oldest brother, Michael, had baffled me for years with his obsessive, atypical behaviors. Michael also demonstrated strong interests at an early age, first with Tinker Toy constructions, then Lego constructions, then cartooning. I remember Michael at age three, in singleminded oblivion, walking through a room filled with guests to procure some Tinker Toys to work out a new idea. When we traveled, we would take along his latest "fix" so he wouldn't become completely distraught. So Matt's emerging obsession at two and a half did not come as a complete surprise; I had already become seasoned, although I had had a hiatus with my middle son, Adam. Today, Adam is a highly creative film writer, and although he, too, was quite creative as a child, he adapted more flexibly to life and was not so clearly driven.

I greeted Matt's obsessive drumming with a mixture of admiration and despair. Although I had come to embrace his brother Michael's passions as "magnificent obsessions," I had felt challenged by Michael's difficulty with fitting in—to the family, his peer group, and much of school learning. While I prepared myself to similarly embrace Matt's driven creativity with affectionate admiration, I also steeled myself for his tough road ahead in the school culture of prescriptive agendas and standardization.

If I had only known then what I know now about what I have come to term "creatively gifted learners," I would have felt more confident and hopeful. I have currently accrued over thirty years of experience with highly creative learners through both parenting and teaching. With masters degrees in both special education and literacy, I have been in a position to work with a wide range of learners who are struggling in the education system. In the process of seeing them through a different lens, one that honors and delights in their divergent, atypical, creative learning styles, I have been able to support the growth of their learning prowess. My passionate honoring of creative learning orientations has been honed in by parenting my own children and by teaching a parade of highly creative learners who have marched through my life in a variety of settings: elementary schools, a high school, a college, and adult education as well as within my home where I do private tutoring.

It's as if the universe placed a sign on my door, "Creative learners inquire within."

Descriptors of Highly Creative Learners

Creative children look twice, listen for smells, dig deeper, build dream castles, get from behind locked doors, have a ball, plug in the sun, get into and out of deep water, sing in their own key.
—Paul Torrance

Who is the creatively gifted learner? My highly creative students have exhibited two particular attributes that are primary in my definition. The first attribute is a passion (at times obsessive passion) to explore what is personally fascinating, in conjunction with a need to learn through creative initiative. My son Matt was fascinated with the concept of drum sets and, at a very young age, spent a year exploring a variety of adaptations on this concept employing creative initiative in every arena of his life.

The second primary attribute delineating a creatively gifted learner is a drive to be true to one's emerging inner agendas, in conjunction with resistance to complying with others' agendas when they don't resonate. Highly creative learners, deeply sensitive to their intuitive knowing and imagination, source their learning from within. For example, my son Michael experienced anguish over learning to read through a reading curriculum that required him to learn skills-in-isolation applied to nonsensical texts (example from SRA's *A Pig Can Jig:* "A cat can pat. The fat cat sat. Pat! Pat! Pat!"). However, his reading took off in full flight when he became inspired by and determined to read *Mad Magazine*, a satirical match for his own highly developed satirical wit. He progressed in reading rapidly when his strong desire released him from strict adherence to the controlled vocabulary of his reading instruction. Michael exclaimed to me one day, "I can read a word I've never seen," as he integrated his strong language prediction into his scan of the print information in his beloved *Mad Magazine*. Michael, age thirty-three, continues to explore satire through books, films, and writing. Driven to be true to the development of his particular creative abilities, Michael learned to negotiate the opportunity to explore his satirical talent in all areas of curriculum.

E. Paul Torrance,(1970) in his book *Encouraging Creativity in the Classroom,* asserts,

> Honesty is the very essence of the creative personality . . . Genuine creative achievement requires that an individual be able to make independent judgment and to have the courage to stick to his conclusions and to work toward their achievement, even though he may be a minority of one at the beginning. (p. 20)

In Jane Pirto's (1998) book, *Understanding Those Who Create,* she quotes Theresa Amabile, a social psychologist who has done some of the major work on motivation for creativity:

> Six terms used in the field of social psychology are: *intrinsic* and *extrinsic motivation*; *field dependence* and *field independence*; and *inner locus of control* and *outer locus of control.* People who produce the most creative works, according to the work Amabile and her colleagues have done, have intrinsic motivation, are field independent and have inner loci of control. To have intrinsic motivation is to proceed in the work for the love of the work itself, and not for fame or glory. To have field independence is to proceed with confidence and individuality rather than wanting to be liked and wanting to please. To have an inner locus of control is to do what you do because you need or want to do it, not because someone else has given you an assignment to do it. (p. 354)

Highly creative individuals source their original learning from their authentic core.

A great variety of creative behaviors manifest from these primary energies of personal passion and authenticity. Isabelle Allende (2000), novelist, journalist, and playwright, said the following in an interview for *Modern Maturity*:

> Creativity is not a single quality but stands for a group of related abilities, such as fluency, originality and flexibility. Since my childhood I have been creative in weird ways. When I see a gadget,

say a blender, I imagine how I can use it for something else. I'm always trying to get things to do what they're *not* supposed to do. That's what creativity is; it's not always something to do with the arts or writing. It has to do with the way you carry your life. (p. 41)

T. W. Taylor (1967), a contributor to *Creativity: Its Educational Implications,* states,

> A creative mind continually reaches toward new designs, new patterns, new insight; there is an almost endless freshness in its inexhaustible powers. One new design is replaced by another, and then still another. (p.172)

Dorothy Briggs, in her book *Your Child's Self Esteem* (quoted in Jenkins,1986), describes the characteristics she feels distinguish creative youngsters:

> Creative children tend to be independent, rather unconcerned with group pressures or conformity, and disinterested in what other people think of them. They retain their capacity to wonder and question and see things afresh. They are flexible, imaginative, spontaneous, and playful in their approach to problems. They are highly receptive to their senses; they tend to see more, feel more, and drink in more of what is around them. Creative youngsters are equally open to themselves and what is going on within. In short, they are highly responsive to both their inner and outer worlds. Such children are willing to risk paying attention to intuition and trying the new. It requires a certain degree of confidence and security to work with the disorganized, the complex, the inconsistent, the unknown and the paradoxical. (pp. 88-89)

My highly creative learners have continually amazed me with the depth of their commitment to exploring areas of strong personal interest. The depth and complexity of their learning explorations go far beyond any imagined standards of learning goals for their age, and yet they often struggle with the more simplistic, prescribed (and often personally irrelevant) agendas of their schooling. They are compelled to explore and bring forth their original ideas through projects of infinite variety and scope. They thrive as highly evolved learners when given time, support, and encouragement for their personal agendas.

Charles Schaefer, in his book *Developing Creativity in Children: An Idea Book for Teachers* (quoted in Jenkins, 1986), discusses the following characteristics of creative children, some of which, he says, appear at the earliest years:

> Sense of wonder; heightened awareness of the world
> Openness to inner feelings and emotions
> Curious, exploratory, adventuresome spirit
> Imagination
>> Imagination is the power of forming mental images of what is not actually present to the senses; or of creating new images by combining previously unrelated ideas.
> Intuitive thinking
>> Intuitive thinking is the solving of problems without logical reasoning. The intuitive thinker is open to hunches and is able to make good guesses.
> Independent thinker
> Personal involvement in work
>> The creative person identifies with a task so that he becomes totally absorbed in and dominated by his work. He enthusiastically engages in tasks that are personally meaningful and satisfying.
> Divergent thinker
>> As opposed to convergent thinking, which seeks one right answer, as determined by the given facts, divergent thinking is defined as the kind that goes off in different directions . . . that seeks variety and originality, that proposes several possibilities rather than seeking one right answer.
> Predisposition to create
>> Tendency to express things in an original, idiosyncratic way rather than considering how things are supposed to be or always have been expressed.
> Tendency to play with ideas (pp. 89-90)

A high degree of sensitivity to both their inner as well as their outer worlds is a quality of creatively gifted learners described again and again by those who have studied highly creative people. At the beginning of this section, I put forth passion and authenticity as the two overriding qualities of all the creative behavioral descriptors. Passion is obvious to the attentive observer when witnessing the total absorption of creative people who are involved in work of riveting interest. Less obvious, perhaps, is the authenticity of their involvement—authentic because it is sourced from their inner core, their unique originality—uninfluenced by outside agendas and input. I am always inspired by the beauty of this devotion to authenticity, which sometimes comes at great cost to the creative individual who may be penalized and sharply criticized for continually leaping outside the lines. Dan Millman (1993), in his book *The Life You Were Born to Live*, postulates:

> Although many of us don't consciously recognize or acknowledge that we even *have* a specific life purpose, our subconscious knows what we are here to do; it reaches out to us, sending messages through our dreams, intuitions, and innermost longings. The call of our destiny manifests as our deepest drives and abilities—the hidden forces behind our personality. (p. xiv)

Creatively gifted learners are both conscious of and driven to be true to this inner awareness.

The Inner Knowing

You've seen a herd of goats
going down to the water.
The lame and dreamy goat
brings up the rear.
There are worried faces about that one
but now they're laughing,
because look, as they return
that goat is leading!
There are many different kinds of knowing.
The lame goat's kind is a branch
that traces back to the roots of presence.
Learn from the lame goat,
And lead the herd home.
—Rumi

While our society often celebrates the gifts of highly creative adults, it is often mystified by and disparaging of highly creative children who are noncompliant with cultural standards. George Kneller (1965) (cited in Jenkins, 1986) explains some of the uncomfortable traits of creative children:

> For instance, they are often difficult to handle, being more independent; they are less friendly and communicative, being more self-absorbed; they are often less studious and orderly, being more interested in their own ideas than in assigned work. Being interested in ideas rather than presentation, their work can be untidy and slapdash. They are likely to get involved in tasks and resent having to stop and move on to another subject.

> These and other "unattractive" characteristics, cause many teachers and parents to squelch the creative child, thus accounting for the great decline in creativity as a child moves up in school and into adulthood. Thus, an enormously valuable human resource is lost to the world. (pp. 92-93)

When I begin working with highly creative learners, who have experienced a great deal of frustration in school, I sense their longing for creative initiative within their overt resistance—a longing to give full expression to their deeply sensed learning agendas. These agendas are often not accommodated within, or are in conflict with, their school curriculum. Some of the learners I work with have become so frustrated that they initially resist any of my attempts to facilitate their authentic learning. Some, who have experienced a great deal of failure, have come to believe that they are inherently flawed, and they discount their unique learning abilities as somehow not being "real" learning. As I honor their inner agendas and their creative initiative, their learning prowess and joy inevitably blossom.

In his book *In the Mind's Eye: Visual Thinkers, Gifted People with Learning Difficulties, Computer Images, and the Ironies of Creativity,* Thomas West (1997) writes that some highly talented people succeed only beyond the culture of schooling. Referring to Winston Churchill, he wrote:

> The boy who spoke poorly, in time, came to deliver some of the most forceful and memorable speeches of his time. The boy who was disorganized, in time, became the man who was one of the foremost planners and leaders of an era. And the boy who was slow to develop in time advanced well beyond all his peers, by pressing energetically forward long after most others would have passed the baton." (pp. 165-166)

"There are many different kinds of knowing," says Rumi, the thirteenth-century Sufi poet, in his poem about the lame goat. Our culture and educational systems have most strongly valued and stressed left-brained analytical thinking. In his book *Hare Brain Tortoise Mind How Intelligence Increases When You Think Less,* Clay Claxton (1997) advocates less analytical thinking and free reign on creative thinking. "He argues . . . that the mind works best when we trust our unconscious or 'undermind'—a cool, intelligent resource that needs only time and receptivity to function." (flap of book) Describing the "undermind" as a tortoise mind, he writes:

> It is often less purposeful and clear-cut, more playful, leisurely or dreamy. In this mode we are ruminating or mulling things over; being contemplative or meditative . . . Some mysteries can *only* be penetrated with a relaxed, unquesting mental attitude. (p.2)

Countering Western society's fixation on the rational, he says:

> The individuals and societies of the West have rather lost touch with the value of contemplation. Only active thinking is regarded as productive. Sitting gazing absently at your office wall or out of the classroom window is not of value. (But) Einstein, it is said, would frequently be found in his office at Princeton staring into space. (p. 4)

Celebrating the "undermind," he writes:

> Wisdom arises from a friendly and intimate relationship with the undermind. One must be willing, like Winnie the Pooh, 'to allow things to come to you,' rather than like Rabbit, 'always going and fetching them.' Wisdom comes to those who are willing to expand their sense of themselves beyond the sphere of conscious control to include another centre of cognition to which the consciousness has no access . . . (p. 195)

My highly creative students have needed lots of "spirit space" for the gestation of their ideas. Their focused energy of productivity has been interspersed with times of quiet reflection and/or wonderful tangents of thought.

I believe that highly creative children are often seen as the lame and dreamy goat of Rumi's poem—the one who brings up the rear. But "the lame goat's kind is a branch that traces back to the roots of presence." Coleman Barks, a translator of Rumi's poems, described "the presence" in a conversation with Bill Moyers (PBS program "Poetry: The Language of Life"). He said that for him "the presence" referred to what William James called "the oceanic feeling." Barks said, "It's a total waking up. We all know there are marvelous moments of eternity that just happen." The creatively gifted, attuned to their inner reality and compelled to be true to its leadings, can, especially when supported, shine forth with authentic learning—learning sourced from a truly awakened consciousness. Through our support of highly creative learners, we are promoting an enlarged definition of intelligence and human functioning, an expanded understanding of personal and cultural potential.

Spinning Straw into Gold: About Learning Challenges

> Einstein used the most sophisticated mathematics to
> develop his theories, but often his sums would not come out right.
> He was a daydreamer who played fancifully with images in his mind,
> but in the process he created an objective image of the universe
> that transformed forever our view of physical reality. Einstein had
> trouble learning and remembering facts, words, and texts, but
> he was teacher to the world. He was slow to speak, but, in time,
> the world listened.
> —Thomas West, p. 129

When I work with highly creative students, I am entranced and amazed by their learning talents, which have often been masked by their struggles to perform certain school-based learning tasks. The individuals I work with are often diagnosed as "learning disabled" in one or a number of the academic areas of reading, writing, and math. As I take my focus off of their "disabilities" and onto their richly sourced, creative learning orientation, I witness their empowerment, not only in spite of, but sometimes *because* of, their difficulties. Sally Smith (1991), in her book *Succeeding Against the Odds,* writes:

> Educators have long been puzzled by students who fail in school
> and yet go on to achieve greatness. Gustave Flauber, William Butler
> Yeats and F. Scott Fitzgerald were all extremely poor students. Hans
> Christian Anderson, that spinner of magnificent fairy tales, could
> not read and so had to dictate his stories to a scribe. Thomas Edison,

the most prolific inventor of all time, could neither understand a lecture nor write a readable sentence. Woodrow Wilson, perhaps the most intellectually gifted of all American presidents, was called "backward" because he didn't learn to read until he was eleven. Nelson Rockefeller, who became governor of New York and then vice president of the United States, struggled all his life to read and to spell. He became an extraordinary extemporaneous speaker in part because he could not read fluently." (pp. 1 and 20)

Many creative learning behaviors are indicative of right-brained rather than left-brained functioning. Barbara Meister Vitale (1982), in her book, *Unicorns Are Real, A Right Brained Approach to Learning,* describes the modes of consciousness of the right and left brain hemispheres. Some of her descriptors are:

Left Hemisphere	Right Hemisphere
linear	holistic
logical	intuitive
verbal	nonverbal
temporal	nontemporal
abstract	analogic (a bent towards analogy)

Howard Gardner (1983), in his book *Frames of Mind, the Theory of Multiple Intelligence,* extensively describes seven intelligences. Five of these intelligences are right-brained and are not traditionally recognized in education.

The two left-brain intelligences are:

Linguistic intelligence and logical-mathematical intelligence

The five right-brained intelligences are:

Musical intelligence
Visual-spatial intelligence
Bodily-kinesthetic intelligence
Interpersonal intelligence
Intrapersonal intelligence

Examples of professions drawing upon these intelligences are the following:

Linguistic: poet, writer, public speaker, lawyer
Logical-mathematical: mathematicians, scientists
Musical: composers, musicians
Visual-spatial: the arts, engineering
Bodily-kinesthetic: dancers, athletes, actors
Interpersonal: political and religious leaders, teachers, therapists
Intrapersonal: novelist, wise elder

Because our schools have traditionally stressed the left hemispheric modes of intelligence, and have either not recognized or disparaged against the right hemispheric modes, creatively gifted learners, with unusual, skewed strengths in their right hemispheric processing, can often experience difficulties when asked to function in a traditional learning setting. Their right hemispheric talents, which will enable them to flourish as adults in a wide variety of endeavors, often go unrecognized and unsupported in their schooling. In his book *In the Mind's Eye: Visual Thinkers, Gifted People with Learning Difficulties, Computer Images and the Ironies of Creativity,* Thomas West discussed the enigma of talented individuals with learning difficulties:

> (They) . . . may have been so much in touch with their visual-spatial, right-hemispheric modes of thought that they have had difficulty in doing orderly, sequential, verbal-mathematical, left-hemispheric tasks in a culture where left-hemispheric capabilities are so highly valued. (p. 19)

West postulates that they succeed as adults not because of compensation but,

> ". . . because they could not fully compensate . . . Ironically if they had been able to compensate fully, they might not have been able to do anything out of the ordinary." (p. 19)

He goes on to explain (quoted in Freed and Parsons, 1997):

> In other words, the complex traits referred to as "learning difficulties" or "dyslexia" may be in part the outward manifestation of the relative strength of a different mode of thought, one that is

available to everyone to one degree or another, but one that a few children (and adults) find difficult to suppress. (p. 31, 32)

And

. . . Some of the best writers have a great deal of difficulty with words. Perhaps this difficulty is an essential element of their power. Perhaps these writers are drawing on something that is not directly rooted in words but rather in something that is other than words, beyond or underneath words. Perhaps they are drawing on elements of thought that are more primitive and more powerful than words. Perhaps if they worked with greater facility on the level of words, alone, their words would be less moving and less powerful. (p. 157)

In a PBS production of Willa Cather's book *Song of the Lark,* Thea, the main character, has left her rural home to study with a master pianist in Chicago. She made some progress with her playing but could not seem to fulfill her desired goal. After a dinner evening with her teacher and his wife, during which she was asked to entertain them with a song, her teacher told her:

Your gift was fighting us. Once you find your way to your gift, you will find peace.

Her teacher was telling her that he believed that her gift was her voice, not the piano.

I believe we are all asked to be true to our talents. And my observation is that the creatively gifted are *compelled* to be true to their authentic calling. My son Michael was destined to explore his satirical lens on life; he was literally unable to produce any kind of school-assigned writing that required him to be "realistic." He always managed to twist his assignments into marvelous satirical adaptations. In high school, he translated his talent fully enough to earn the respect of a number of his teachers, who both appreciated his delightful wit and recognized his sophisticated understanding of the subject at hand—far beyond the basic grasp required.

Rather than viewing their obstacles as disempowering, one can view them as steering the creatively gifted towards honoring their destinies. Their obstacles can be like the straw in the story of *Rumplestiltskin,* which has the potential to be turned into gold—or the irritating grit the oyster transmutes into a pearl.

Our Cultural Canaries

If I want to do it, if I like to do it,
I can.
Robert, a "learning disabled,"
creatively gifted eighth grader

When I worked for a year with a team of special educators at our local high school, I attended a number of PET (pupil evaluation team) meetings in which I heard over and over again, "What is this student's learning style: visual, auditory or kinesthetic?" Identifying sensory strengths or weaknesses has never been helpful for me in guiding my work with my highly creative learners, learners often identified as learning disabled and/or ADD (Attention Deficit Disorder) or ADHD (Attention Deficit Hyperactivity Disorder). I have operated from the premise that the core of my students' learning needs stems from their need to be engaged with authentic learning—learning that feels personally interesting and relevant, learning that gives them creative initiative to explore and express their self-determined learning agendas. I believe that if my learners have the opportunity to become engaged in an authentic way, they will automatically utilize whatever learning channel works for the experience at hand. They will also utilize multiple areas of intelligence, as needed, to complete their organizing vision.

My students have often been given labels that focus on their "disabilities" and failure-set behaviors observed within a school curriculum that denies them access to their natural learning. As I have noted previously in this chapter, many so-called learning disabled individuals have emerged into extremely high functioning, talented adults. While they couldn't succeed in the culture of schooling, they have achieved enormous success in the wider playing field of life. How might they have flourished in school as well if given the opportunity to learn in a way conducive to their creative learning needs?

The deficit model of special education, with its labeling system of disabilities, too often skews our perceptions of learners to their dysfunctions (within a system requiring a *particular* kind of learning), which can mask their gifted strengths. In an article in *Language Arts*, Phyllis Brazee (1991), a holistic educator, writes:

Many special educators today are not satisfied with the medical model. One of the biggest problems with it is that it is medical. A "learning disability," for example, is talked about as if it were a discernible disease, a discrete condition. Actually, it is just an intellectual construct invented by professionals for the purpose of professional discussion. Even the experts can't agree on what a learning disability is. (p. 356)

Another deficit label frequently discussed in our schools today is ADD (or ADHD). AD(H)D describes a collection of behaviors that interfere with learning engagement. Some of the characteristics are:

> Attentional issues
> Difficulty sustaining tasks
> Procrastination
> Poor organizational and planning skills
> Hyperactivity and impulsivity
> Daydreaming
> Distractibility
> Poor frustration tolerance

As with the confusion over a clear definition of a learning disability, a great deal of confusion exists over what constitutes AD(H)D. The behavior characteristics that constitute the diagnosis are evident in many learners on a continuum. What level of hyperactivity or distractibility connotes the label? And what *underlies* these behaviors on an individual basis?

In his book, *The Myth of the ADD Child: 50 Ways to Improve Your Child's Behavior and Attention Span Without Drugs, Labels or Coercion,* Thomas Armstrong (1995) suggests that we reinvision the negative behaviors of AD(H)D in a positive light. He writes:

Instead of thinking of your child as:	Think of him as:
hyperactive	energetic
impulsive	spontaneous
distractible	creative
a day dreamer	imaginative
inattentive	global thinker with a wide focus
unpredictable	flexible

argumentative	independent
stubborn	committed
irritable	sensitive
aggressive	assertive

(p. 256)

Armstrong's positive spin on the behavior characteristics indicative of possible AD(H)D, also well describes the creatively gifted learner.

In *Right-Brained Children in a Left-Brained World,* Jeffrey Freed and Laurie Parsons (1997) also write about the strengths as well as the struggles of learners with ADD characteristics. They refer to Dr. Armstrong's research on the few studies that have looked at the positive aspects of ADD:

> One showed that kids who are labeled hyperactive or ADD have huge reserves of energy. Another indicated that kids labeled ADD tell more novel stories than so-called normal kids. New research is also finding that children with ADD are more likely to be gifted. (pp. 31 and 32)

Freed and Parsons also refer to the premise of Edward Hallowell, MD, and John Rately, MD(1995), authors of *Driven to Distraction: Recognizing and Coping with Attention Deficit Disorder from Childhood Through Adult,* that ADD is a syndrome not of "attention deficit" but of "attention inconsistency," that kids who have symptoms of ADD in the classroom can show tremendous focus on a project that interests them at home and that perhaps their difficulties in the left-brained arenas are also strengths. Attention inconsistency is a hallmark of creatively gifted learners who have difficulty connecting with agendas that do not feel compatible with their internally sourced authenticity and who reveal intense connection to those learning situations that encourage exploration of their personal interests and passions.

Bonnie Cramond (1995), in her article "The Coincidence of Attention Deficit Hyperactivity Disorder and Creativity," asserts that there may be a misdiagnosis of ADHD in many cases of highly creative learners.

> A review of the literature indicates that there are striking similarities between the behavioral manifestations of Attention Deficit Hyperactivity Disorder (ADHD) and creativity . . . Of particular concern is the fact that the defining characteristics of ADHD,

inattention, hyperactivity, and impulsivity, are also key descriptors in biographies of highly creative individuals. (p. 1x)

Through my own experience with teaching atypical learners, I agree that for many of my students who might be labeled AD(H)D, I perceive a creative learning orientation as the *modus operandum* of their functioning. I see the strengths of the typically cited AD(H)D behavior characteristics, and I understand the crucial significance of the learning context that either disparages against or encourages and supports these strengths. As I sit beside my highly creative learners, I sense a waxing and waning of their focus as we explore learning that both does and doesn't resonate with their inner agendas. As I invite these learners into experiences that relate to their personal interests and invoke their creative expression, I witness their joyful, focused absorption in the place of their previous distractibility. Constance Weaver (1994), a holistic educator who edited the book *Success At Last Helping Students with ADHD Achieve Their Potential*, states that in her book:

> Most of the chapters demonstrate that while behavioral approaches may control behavior and lead to greater academic performance in the short run, approaches that respect the learner as a self-determining individual achieve significantly greater success in generating changed behavior patterns in the long run. (p. xi)

In her introduction, she writes,

> Situational demands can have a profound effect upon ADHD behaviors. For example, research clearly demonstrates that children with ADHD have great difficulty attending to tasks that they find boring, such as completing dittos and worksheets. They find it much easier to attend to tasks they find stimulating and meaningful. (p.9).

> What students with ADHD need is what students with learning disabilities—and indeed, *all* students—need: not a fragmented, skills-oriented curriculum, but a curriculum that keeps language and learning whole and meaningful, that offers students choice and ownership of learning, and that supports learners in taking more responsibility for their own learning and their behavior. (p.11)

In a chapter by Weaver's son John, who was diagnosed with ADHD, he states, "One of the things that greatly helped me was having assignments that encouraged creativity or at least allowed it." (p. 47) My suspicion is that perhaps a majority of learners with identified AD(H)D characteristics are highly creative and that, as Constance Weaver asserted, all learners could benefit from support for personally relevant learning.

In a conversation I had with Jim Conlon, director of the Sophia Center (a wisdom school in Oakland, California, which inspires its learners to "evoke what lies deeply within"), he suggested the term "cultural canaries" to describe those who are diagnosed as "learning disabled" but are actually highly creative individuals. "Perfect," I thought. Like the canaries used in coal mines to warn, through their demise, when toxic gas threatens life-giving oxygen, the struggles of the creatively gifted in the face of regimented, left-brain-dominated curriculums are a harbinger of what is dying in the culture: the passion for learning and creative expression sourced from our authentic core. If we can support what highly creative learners are attempting to bring forth in their original learning agendas, we can support what learning and teaching are essentially about—"to evoke what lies deeply within."

Parker Palmer (1999), a writer and traveling teacher who works independently on issues in education, spirituality, and social change, writes, in *The Heart of Learning, Spirituality in Education*, about confronting the familiar trappings of traditional education: competition, intellectual combat, obsession with a narrow range of facts, credits, and credentials. He asserts:

> I think, at heart, that we are seeking to find life-giving forces and sources in the midst of an enterprise which is too often death dealing:education. It may seem harsh to call education death-dealing, but I think we all have our experience of that sad fact. (p. 16-17)

> . . . education at its best—this profound human transaction called teaching and learning—is not just about getting information or getting a job. Education is about healing and wholeness. It is about empowerment, liberation, transcendence, about renewing the vitality of life. It is about finding and claiming ourselves and our place in the world. (pp. 18-19)

E. Paul Torrance (1970) declares,

> In some ways, one of the most fundamental creative needs is to be different, to be an individual, to be oneself. This is not for the sake of being different, but because the creative person has to be different in order to attain his potentialities. Rarely, however, do we respect the child's need to be an individual. We are more concerned about "appearing to be" than about "being." Even when one is different in ways which are defined as socially desirable, he finds himself under pressure. He may work too hard and learn more than he should. He may be too honest, too courageous, too altruistic, or too affectionate. He may be too adventuresome, too curious, or too determined. Parents do not want their children to be considered different or peculiar, and teachers endeavor to make children conform to behavioral norms or become socially well-adjusted. (p. 21)

Creatively gifted, maverick learners, a "misfit" for standardized education (that is influenced by a culture largely focused on the measurable, the controllable, and the objective) can, when supported, thrive in authentic learning *and* being and "lead the herd home."

Seeing Through a Different Lens: Facilitating the Creatively Gifted Learner

And so a child went forth every day,
And the first object he look'd upon, that object he became,
And that object became part of him for the day, or a certain part of
the day, Or for many years or stretching cycles of years.
The early lilacs became part of this child, And grass and white and
red morning-glories, and white and red clover, and the song of the
phoebe-bird, And the Third-month lambs and the sow's pink-faint
litter, and the mare's foal and the cow's calf,
And the noisy brood of the barnyard or by the mire of the pond-side,
And the fish suspending themselves so curiously below there, and the
beautiful curious liquid, And the water-plants with their graceful flat
heads, all became part of him.

—Walt Whitman

Case Study: Christina

Christina, a fourth-grade student in a small outer island school off the coast of Maine, had just about given up. She felt intense frustration with her classroom work; she felt like a complete failure as a learner. Christina's teachers knew that she was bright, despite her specific learning difficulties, but they felt powerless to ease her frustration and dispel her belief that she was stupid. Even an assessment affirming her high IQ did nothing to alter her belief.

At a PET (Pupil Evaluation Team) meeting following her testing, Christina was identified as "learning disabled" in the areas of reading, writing, and math. I was asked to work with her one afternoon a week in my capacity as special education teacher. After talking with her teachers and working with Christina during our initial session, I expressed my belief that she was, in fact, "creatively gifted." Applying the lens of "creatively gifted" is the first step I take in revaluing a highly creative, troubled learner. Along with seeing Christina's obvious challenges with her school work, I could see, on another level, Christina's highly creative orientation in all aspects of her learning.

Christina loved to draw, and her pictures displayed wonderful lines, perspectives, colors, details, and expressions. She was, in fact, driven to progress artistically, engaging in and exploring drawing at any given opportunity. I allowed Christina to draw as we worked together to honor her talent and fuel her energy and focus for our task at hand. I also arranged for Christina to have an art mentorship with the teacher aide Gail (who is an artist). Christina's weekly visit to Gail's home continues, two years later, to be the highlight of her week.

In our work with reading, writing, and math, I gave Christina choices of the resources we used, the topics we would explore, and our formats for practice. Creatively gifted learners have intense need for ownership in every aspect of their learning, and their strong intuitive ability makes them excellent choice-makers in line with their learning needs. I have always been amazed to see these learners sort through a considerable pile of book choices, for example, rapidly prioritizing them into "maybe now," "at some future time," and "let go." Their intuitive tuning fork often knows just what will work for them.

The first book Christina chose for our reading was Anne Lindbergh's *The Worry Week*, which is about three girls who connive to stay alone at their beloved vacation home on an island off the coast of Maine while their parents go away to a funeral. Allegra, who tells the story, is the middle sister, a similarity to Christina's position in her own family as the middle daughter sandwiched between an older sister and younger twin sisters. To increase Christina's confidence in reading, I encouraged her to draw upon her rich language sense and fabulous prediction, along with sharing helpful ideas for structural analysis of the print information. Most importantly, however, I reveled in her personal identification with the characters and the situations in the story and her deep understanding of the themes. Christina's rich bonding with stories continued through books with sophisticated themes, like David's growth of self-identity in A. Holm's *North to Freedom* (about the escape of a young boy from a concentration camp and his awakening from a deadened state of existence) and Cusi's journey to embrace his ordained destiny in *The*

Secret of the Andes by A. Clark. These are the kinds of books Christina chose and delighted in—stories which resonated with her deep sensitivities and perceptions.

To encourage and support Christina's enjoyment of the stories we read, I engaged her in spontaneous conversations about our responses, refraining from questioning that would assess a mere mentalized understanding. Christina's personal connection to the stories would lead her to argue sometimes with the characters. One day, while we were reading *The Secret of the Andes*, she became impatient with Cusi when he got sidetracked from his life mission by seeking a family of his own to live with. She commented, "I think he should try to find out who he is rather than trying to find a family." She also commented at this juncture of his traveling, "I miss Chuto." Chuto was Cusi's teacher who was waiting for his return in the hidden valley of their home. When we watched the PBS video, *The Incas,* following our reading, Christina transformed this rather dry documentary exclaiming, "That's Cusi's mother's hut," and "That's his llama, Misty." When I shared her responses with her art mentor Gail, she commented, "And for her, they really were."

In writing, I encouraged Christina to brainstorm a story idea that would spark an "organizing vision" compelling enough to encourage her risk-taking. Her previous attempts at writing had frustrated her related to her challenges in spelling, punctuation, and penmanship. Christina had also found it difficult to engage with writing assignments that were not in tune with personal relevance or interest.

I invited Christina to write on my portable computer to bypass her transcription angst, and while this novelty helped, she was still unable to find an appealing idea. In order to start *somewhere*, I suggested that she continue on with a piece she had written for her school newspaper about a young Russian girl immigrating to this country in the mid 1800s. Reluctantly, she began, placing the girl in Texas. Plodding along, she wrote a few lines each week with many pleas for typing help from me.

One day, Christina had her main character escape from her chores to travel with a friend to a nearby creek. At the creek the girl saw a man. "Or was it a boy?" I suggested. "Oh yes," she said, "a young black boy who had escaped from a cruel master." Fueled by this compelling idea, Christina set off with full wind in her sails. Christina has a strong sense of social justice, and this story gave her a creative opportunity to explore and express this. "Natasha's Adventures," the story of how a young girl helped an abused slave boy connect with the underground railroad, became a beautifully illustrated little book. Christina's transition from writer's angst to empowered author was a beautiful unfolding as she began to reenvision herself as a capable author and illustrator.

Christina and I still had the potential tedium of math facts and spelling words to work on. Within my developmental approach, I assessed where Christina had become stuck foundationally in both subjects. In math, she was not using number sense in computation and thus had difficulty learning her facts. Often with identified "learning disabled" students, this difficulty is deemed a short-term memory problem; however, it is my experience that a creatively gifted learner generally does not retain memory for any fact isolated from personal understanding or relevance. One must ask, "Memory in what context?"

For math computation work, we cocreated games to practice number sense. First, we reviewed the "10 + any number" rule and doubles. I also had Christina develop a fluent sense of counting up and back by two's on odds and evens. Once Christina was fluent in counting by twos and had learned the "10 + any number" rule and doubles, I taught her how to quickly figure out almost any addition fact by beginning with doubles or + 10 and adding or subtracting 1 or 2 as necessary (for example 9 + 7 is 10 + 7 - 1 and 8 + 6 is 6 + 6 + 2). Multiplication is multiple addition, so I encouraged Christina to go back to a fact she knew and use her addition strategies (like to get 8x7 go to 8x6 = 48 and then add + 10 - 2). Once you have solidly learned addition and multiplication, then subtraction and division can be figured out by reference to the former (17-8 turned into 8 + what = 17).

After I assessed Christina's developmental level in spelling, drawing on guidelines in Bear's et al. (1996) *Words Their Way*, we brainstormed rules and practice words that would build a solid foundation for future spelling growth. Christina would have rebelled against endless, boring drills of math strategies and spelling features, but she was quite motivated to practice on games she created, varying the rules to keep us on our toes.

Today, a year and a half later, Christina is a far more confident learner. She has grown in her reading, writing, spelling and math skills, although she still tends to go into a shorthand version of spelling in writing "on the run." She has her own Alpha Smart portable computer and has the option of doing her classroom assignments and homework on it. The computer helps her focus on expressing her thoughts, bypassing her handwriting struggles. Gail, her art mentor, is working with her on calligraphy, bringing Christina's artistic talent into handwriting, enhancing her confidence and pride in this area. While not as fluent a reader as a classmate she works with, Christina amazes her teacher with her depth of understanding inference, characterization, and theme in the books they read. She writes more easily, but still needs that spark of inspiration to create a story with strong voice and energy.

One day recently, while Christina and I sat together on the mailboat that services her island, I noticed how absorbed she was in reading a babysitting handbook for an elective course she was taking. I smiled because I had been wondering how her independent reading was developing. At one point, she looked up at me and said, "Sometimes I really love riding on the boat because I get to read a lot and relax."

In discussing my work with Christina, I have described aspects of facilitation employed by many Whole-Language teachers: the honoring of developmental level, the offering of choice-making in all aspects of learning experiences, and the offering of many opportunities for creative initiative. But beyond these wonderful tenets, I applied a lens through which I "saw" Christina as a learner who needed to be true to her passionate interests and who energized her learning through creative expression. I understood that her obstacle to learning had been her inability to connect to curriculums that felt developmentally intimidating and personally irrelevant. And most importantly, I truly valued Christina's struggle to be loyal to her internal agendas and her refusal to engage with what felt like "bogus" work.

The lens that honors a child's compelling inner agendas requires a radically different philosophy of education from the acculturalization theory underlying traditional teaching (that education is about training future citizens to "fit" into the culture). Maxine Greene (1988), a professor of philosophy and education at Teachers College, Columbia University, warned in a *Language Arts* article:

> There is a growing tendency to describe children as "resources" rather than persons, with all the implications of "use value" and even "exchange value." Proposed improvements in their education are argued in the name of the nation's economic competitiveness, not for the sake of the growth of persons viewed as centers of choice, agents of their own becoming.

Creatively gifted children often wilt within the acculturalization model of education with its thrust toward "fitting in" and "measuring up." When rigidly interpreted, today's prescriptive learning results and standards can further squeeze out the "growth of persons, agents of their own becoming."

How would it be, I wonder, to articulate a learning result of "The learner will feel deep resonances with self-selected stories," or "The learner will grow in making choices sourced from his or her inner knowing."

Creatively gifted learners can develop an intense struggle around fighting the prescriptive learning agendas that can feel so disempowering to them. As a teacher/facilitator, I honor the angst that has often caused them to shut down or rebel, while at the same time, I encourage their deeply felt learning agendas. In *The Child's Discovery of Himself* existentialist therapist, Clark Moustakas(1972), says,

> The therapist is sensitive to the self of the child, to the healthy and sick components of behavior, to the means that suddenly emerge and enable a particular child to stop fighting against his own unique selfhood, to stop battling himself and the world, and to begin to actualize his own special potentialities. (p.3)

I believed in Christina, in her strengths, her talents, her interests, and her passions. I honored her need to be true to her compelling internal agendas. More than the choices I gave her or the games we created together, I feel that this lens of "seeing" and honoring *Christina* was the catalyst for her empowerment.

Most of my work as a "teacher/healer" is with private students who come to my home. Many of these students, like Christina, initially think of themselves as failures in traditional school settings. When their authentic learning agendas are unleashed, their maverick forays illustrate an evolution of learning that is creative, deeply personal, and intuitively wise. To feel successful, they need to feel personally honored and respected for what they are striving to bring forth from their passionate visions.

When parents call me and ask if I will tutor their child who has fallen behind in literacy or math, I ask, "Does your child have any passionate interests? Is your child often distracted on the one hand, but hyperfocused, at times, on the other hand? Is your child especially sensitive? Does your child like to express him/herself creatively in drawing, building (like Legos) or imaginative play? Does your child have strong interpersonal skills?" Somewhat surprised, the parents begin to bring to light the positive strengths of their child—they begin seeing them through a different lens. We then develop a "cover agenda" for my work with their child—the area of instruction needed for reading, writing or math. I gather materials for a first session based on the parents' report of their child's interests and my own intuitive sense of that child. We have our first session and my work of revaluing begins.

The Reenchantment of Learning

Learning that is inspired, passionate, juicy, and fascinating is self-directed and self-determined; it is a wonder to behold. I am continually amazed as I begin working with children who have become shut down or resistive in their school learning (particularly those with behavior characteristics of AD(H) D: off task, distracted, disorganized, nudgy etc.), how they blossom into excitement when I encourage their personal interests and passions. In the blink of an eye, they can shift from underfocus to hyperfocus when their personal agendas are tapped.

I often find out about my students' passions by asking them what they love to do at home on their own time. In the PBS video production, "The Creative Spirit," the commentator reports,

> The more we learn about creativity, the clearer it becomes that it is a child's early fascination with a *particular* activity that paves the way for a creative life. This spontaneous interest leads a child to the sustained efforts and hands-on experiences that build mastery—whether at the piano, painting, or building Lego towers.

Roger, a fourth grader, was obsessed with Pokemons. We integrated our reading work of learning blends, diagraphs and short vowel sounds through Pokemon names. He had previously resisted every effort to scaffold his literacy development which had become stuck at an early first grade level.

Karen, a fifth grader, came to me recently for a reading assessment. Her mother described her as an extremely active child who rarely sits still. Karen kept telling her mother that she couldn't "hear" what she read. During our session, while Karen exhibited competent decoding skills in her reading, she did not use appropriate intonation and often ignored punctuation cues for appropriate phrasing. The one exception was a *Garfield* book I had included in my reading choices on an intuitive hunch. Karen adored *Garfield* by Jim Davis, *Calvin and Hobbs* by Bill Waterson and other comics. Her reading of *Garfield* was focused with effective intonation and lively dramatic expression. Karen's experience of delight and focus in the reading of *Garfield* helped to unlock her confidence in reading; it helped her to recognize what it feels like to "hear" and enjoy what she has read. We then looked for other stories which could similarly engage her delight.

Brian, a second grade student in an outer island one room school, was passionate about pirates. In his mind's eye the ships out in the harbor were not regular sailing vessels but pirate ships. His teacher, Cathy Kozaryn (see Cathy's story), herself a creatively gifted learner, honored his obsessive interest in pirates. She joyfully witnessed him overcome the disablement of his skills-in-isolation early reading instruction, as he practiced a beloved pirate story over and over until he figured out how reading worked. As he reenvisioned reading through his enjoyment of that book, he grew naturally in reading competency.

Christina (case study of the introduction) literally "fell in love" with characters in the books we read. She also felt a strong affinity for the underlying themes of these books. She connected to, I believe, that deep level of mystery related to our human questing to understand who we are. In an article, "Reclaiming Mystery" in a *Sounds True* catalog, Rachel Naomi Remen, M.D., a psycho-oncologist, writes,

> The experience of Mystery strengthens and changes us, and awakens us. When a culture loses its Mystery, it loses its soul. Our culture doesn't value that power, and rarely recognizes it. We have traded Mystery for mastery and have become a culture of control. By ignoring and even rejecting Mystery, our culture has disconnected us from our strength. Perhaps this culture-wide search for mastery is the shadow of science. But science is only one way of looking at life. Life is larger than science. Things happen that science can't explain. These things aren't replicable or measurable. These things are touching, moving, inspiring, powerful, and profoundly Mysterious. Science will always define life as too small. When we define life as too small, we define ourselves as too small as well. Reclaiming our Mystery allows us to reclaim a sense of aliveness and wonder. Perhaps we need to know a little less and wonder a little more.

My son Matt, during his homeschooled third grade year, spent every spare moment developing his drawing skills. He was completely self-driven as he pulled down picture books from our shelves to study line, expression, perspective, and shading. He intently watched "how to draw and paint" shows on public T.V. One day he said to me, "When drawing works, I feel nice and sharp and get that tingling feeling." That's the elegance of learning hooked up to the internal agenda. I love stirring the passionate chord in my learners that sparks them into joyous engagement. And I trust that all learners have inner passions which can lift them up into heights of wonderment and joy. Inspired learning sources our authentic growth as "agents of our own becoming."

The Cosmic Curriculum: A Treasure Hunt

During my years teaching in the teacher education program at the College of the Atlantic, Bill, a middle-school science teacher took my course "Reading and Writing in the Elementary Classroom" for continuing education credits. I love his following reflection from his essay, "The Discovery Method of Learning:"

> I remember my first field trip to Rocky Point, Sonoro, New Mexico. As a young graduate student at the University of Arizona, I was faithfully following behind our major professor—and his graduate teaching assistant—with a group of fellow budding-ichthyologists, heading towards the famous tidal pools exposed by the equally famous (and enormous) high and low tides of the Gulf of California. We were in search of fish specimens to swell the ranks of their alcohol-floating relatives back in Tucson, Arizona.

> I particularly remember a remark made by the graduate teaching assistant to our major professor as we trooped along. The professor was explaining how he would verbally expound on the various species of fish that would succumb to his retonone poisoning and float to the surface of the tidal pools. The assistant replied that he should not tell us the names of all the fishes that we would collect but save one or two as "Christmas presents," for us (the lowly students?) to discover for ourselves. My thought at the time was, "Why not save all the fishes as 'Christmas presents?"

I love the initial exploration phase of planning a unit of study for my students. As I gather books and resources, I feel like I'm on a treasure hunt, marveling at how all these disparate resources might fit together under particular magnetic themes. Learners, in general, and creatively gifted learners most certainly, love treasure hunts and the opportunity to gather a variety of resources—if a topic feels compelling to them. Rather than having all of the resources presented to them, they thrive on discovering their own "Christmas presents."

Each of us, I believe, has strong affinities for learnings which resonate with our inner agendas. Creatively gifted learners feel these affinities acutely. They become passionate (sometimes obsessively so) in their exploration of topics and ideas which interest them, exploring them on a level and to a degree beyond typical grade expectations.

> Anita painted houses for days and days in nursery school—big houses, little houses, fat houses, thin houses. The observant teacher, thinking that perhaps adults had overpraised Anita's first representational house (fixating her to houses?), said quietly, "Anita, you've painted many, many fine houses. Wouldn't you like to try something different?" "But, Miss B.," said Anita, "I haven't finished with houses yet." (Berger and Cushman, 1970)

I call these strong affinities our "cosmic curriculum."

I remember the first time I took off on my own treasure hunt within academia. I was in my forties, pursuing a masters in literacy at the University of Maine. More than twenty years before, my first teaching job was at a nursery school. Preschool teaching really appealed to me, because I could focus on child development and support children's physical, emotional, intellectual and imaginative growth through creative forums like dramatic play, music, movement, and free choice of activities. I often wondered what kind of curriculum in elementary school could support as strong a child-centered approach.

Searching for an answer to my question became even more compelling in ensuing years, as I took time off from my teaching career to raise my three sons and sought to support their creative learning needs. I've described my eldest son Michael's divergent learning orientation and his initial struggle with learning to read in a skills-in-isolation, artificial language reading series and subsequent success as a reader when he became passionate about *Mad Magazine*. In third grade, Michael shared his despair one day over failing a language arts test on referencing. He told me, "I've been doing terribly in math and now I'm failing language arts." His teacher, however, told me a few days later that she realized that Michael had actually *cross-referenced* on the test, a skill she never expected a third grader to know. She suggested that I do some research on gifted children. In fifth grade, Michael had a severe anxiety attack at school following a very frustrating math class. As I comforted him at home, he asked me, "Am I mentally retarded?" He just couldn't understand why he had so much trouble doing school work. I took Michael to a perceptive counselor, Bob Keteyian (see Bob K's story) who along with giving Michael wonderful support for his creative orientation, helped me to understand the nature of creatively gifted learners.

Meanwhile my youngest son Matt was exhibiting many of the sensitivities and divergent learning needs as his older brother. As I was beginning my masters in literacy, he was having an intense struggle with a traditional kindergarten program. His teacher felt that he might have a small motor disability, because he took so long to write his name at the beginning of his work sheets. Meanwhile he was winning art prizes from *Cricket* magazine for his creative drawings. My suspicion was that Matt took a long time to write his name on worksheets, because, unconsciously, he was avoiding doing work that felt confusing and personally irrelevant. We had Matt tested by Bob Keteyian, our creatively gifted resource specialist, and he shared a number of helpful insights like:

> Matthew has a good attention span for activities that interest him, and gets very absorbed in his creations. Since he is also a very verbal child, he gives a lot of information about the process he is going through in thinking about things. He has a very well developed sense of cause and effect relationships and uses metaphors extremely well for a five-year-old child.

> Matthew is very aware of his internal creative stirrings and gets a lot of satisfaction from exploring and expressing these things. Further, he needs to express himself creatively in order to continue learning and integrating new information and skills.

Related to both Michael's and then Matt's debilitating experiences with traditional learning in general and with literacy in particular, I had developed compelling questions about how curriculums could be less prescriptive and more personally empowering. In my masters program in literacy, I was most fortunate to connect immediately with courses which supported my quest; my cosmic curriculum was launched.

My first curriculum course was the Writer's Workshop, a concept developed by Donald Graves (1983) whose initial book about the writing process, *Writing Teachers and Children at Work*," has become a basic text. The hallmarks of the writer's workshop are time, ownership, and response.

Students are given the time to thoroughly develop a piece of writing from rough drafts to revisions and editing. They are given ownership to choose topics which relate to their personal interests. They are given response to what *they* are attempting to bring forth, through conferences with their teacher and their peers. I chose this course because of my son Adam's experience with Writer's Workshop in his fourth grade classroom. I witnessed him become an enthusiastic and versatile writer through the inspired facilitation of his fourth grade teacher. She was one of the first group of teachers in the state of Maine trained by Donald Graves' student, Nancie Atwell, whose book, *In the Middle Writing, Reading and Learning with Adolescents* remains a foundational treatise on the workshop approach in education.

During my course on the writing process, I was told by some fellow students about Whole-Language reading. Three of the forerunners to describe Whole-Language reading and learning are Don Holdaway (*Foundations of Literacy*), Frank Smith (*Reading Without Nonsense*), and Ken Goodman (*What's Whole in Whole Language?*). Whole Language describes the reading process as a personal transaction between reader and text. It places primary emphasis on meaning-based prediction strategies to make sense of print. Whole Language teachers differ from teachers using a prescribed reading program in their individualized facilitation of an orchestration of language and print strategies and in their use of texts with natural, predictable language. I had found the missing piece in my quest for an approach to teaching reading in which the teacher scaffolds each learner's developmental level and honors personal interests, tapping individual strengths.

I fortuitously connected with a marvelous Whole Language professor, Phyl Brazee, who preempted me from basic level requirements enabling me to take her Remedial Reading Class. Phyl then launched me into a series of independent studies on Whole Language learning. She "saw" my passionate interest, my ability to explore it independently, and my ability to integrate it creatively into my teaching.

I dove into my studies with complete abandon, hardly coming up for air, feeling like I had finally come "home." My quest to learn how teaching in the elementary school could support wholeness of emotional, intellectual, and creative growth within the process of acquiring literacy skills had reached satiation. And *I* was being supported in authentic learning for the first time in my schooling!

I soon had an opportunity to put my holistic, developmental theory into practice through teaching in an all day kindergarten for two years. In each of those years I identified a few children as creatively gifted learners. Some of these children were struggling with early literacy and with most group activities. They had passionate, obsessive interests and, despite their difficulties with handwriting and other small motor pencil/paper activities, were talented graphic and construction artists. They thrived on my open learning forums: Free Play, Writers' and Readers' Workshops, and Exploration (hands on math/science lab).

One of my creatively gifted learners, Robbie, a boy repeating kindergarten who had severe speech challenges and often communicated with me through drawing, surprised me one day. We had been doing a math unit on patterns. A traditional approach to teaching patterns would be to introduce a simple AB pattern, like black/red, black/red, and have the children go color squares black/ red, black/red. Instead of this prescriptive approach, I modeled the concept of patterning with a number of examples and sent the children off to explore it for themselves with a variety of materials (colored cubes and beads etc.). I had the children save their patterns for their classmates to identify. A delighted Robbie was the first to stump the class with a pattern based, not on colors, but on shapes (a string of beads with round, square, round, square).

Robbie surprised me again one day, during a math session in which I asked the children to do a button sorting project using two cut down milk carton boxes (this was the only time I ever gave the children a specific assignment). I gave the instructions and sent the children off. Robbie, ignoring my instructions, took his buttons, put them into one of the containers, and then combining the containers made a shaker. He was insisting that *all* the fishes be Christmas presents!

Context Is Everything

In my capacity as special education teacher, I am responsible for developing IEPs (Individualized Education Plans) for my identified students. Traditionally IEPs are made up of objective, measurable goals. As a holistic teacher, I feel that the implementation of objective, measurable goals is dishonoring of any learner. How could I possibly know the personal goal of any child—that which fuels them as "agents of their own becoming." Creatively gifted children (and it is my suspicion that the majority of identified "disabled" students are actually creatively gifted) will fight the sterile, fragmented curriculums that are created from objective, measurable goals.

I do not want to deny, at this point, the importance of teaching skills essential for lifelong learning. And I do include skills in my IEP's, but I teach them as much as possible in a context of learning experiences which honors a learner's emerging interests and passions. My goals and objectives generally represent a "cover" agenda within which I am actually focusing on unlocking and supporting my students' authentic learning.

I begin my work with an assessment of each learner's obstacles to growth. This understanding helps me to organize activities to reorient the learner toward his or her self-improving system. As my learners begin to take personal risks, I organize a learning environment which recognizes and supports their self-directed and finally self-determined reorientation. If my work with students was driven by *predetermined* goals, I would not be encouraging or supporting *their* self-determination. Every interaction I have with my students is measured by how it enhances or diminishes my honoring of their personal learning agendas. This measurement, not the successful completion of artificial goals and objectives, is my ultimate accountability.

During my two years of classroom teaching in an all day kindergarten, I was able, through the forums of Free Play, Writer's and Reader's Workshops and Math and Science Exploration, to provide a supportive context for individual exploration. Although my creatively gifted learners struggled at times with group activities, they thrived within these open forums. David, is an example.

David adored Free Play. He and his friend spent a great deal of time creating constructions from Legos and art supplies. Although he struggled with concepts of print in reading and writing, David loved drawing fairy tale stories about dragons during Writer's Workshop. At the end of the year, David and his family moved out of state. In October of the following school year, I received a letter from his mother. She asked me for suggestions regarding her son's struggle with school, saying that she believed my comments would be coming from a different viewpoint than his first grade teacher's. She wrote that his teacher was struggling to find *anything* good about David, saying that he didn't like organized games and couldn't sit still for a story (while at home, his mom said, he listened to chapter books for a half hour or so). The teacher seemed to hint that he had a learning disability or was a slow learner, because directions at the top of a workbook page confused him and reading was a mystery to him. David's mother said that kindergarten had been a wonderful year for him which she attributed to my teaching methods and attitude toward him. She ended her letter with a request for another copy of a handout I had given her, "The Creatively Gifted Personality," which she had appreciated for the moment and then thrown out, thinking that she wouldn't need to refer to it again.

Context *does* make an essential difference for enhancing or disparaging learning, and for the creatively gifted learner it can make the essential difference between learning empowerment or learning disablement. David needed to be seen through a lens which recognized his creative learning orientation. He would, I believe, have developed competently in reading through a Whole Language reading program which could have supported his language strengths and extensive background knowledge—scaffolding his print recognition skills within this rich context. David needed to learn through the honoring of his intense interests, with ample opportunity for creative expression. He needed to understand why group situations were intimidating for him and needed to be given support for feeling less exposed within them. David's mother didn't fully realize the enormous difference the learning context made for her creatively gifted son until he was placed in a traditional setting.

During my year teaching special education English classes at Mount Desert Island High School, I received an astounding lesson on the difference the learning context can make for the empowerment or diminishment of a learner's authenticity. One of my freshman students, Charles, really puzzled me. Charles had been brain-injured at birth. He was identified learning disabled in all academic areas.

Coming from a professional family, Charles put tremendous effort into being "the perfect student." He did every assigned task promptly and would continually ask me if he was "caught up." As a Whole-Language teacher, however, I was encouraging him to develop his own learning agendas. I was inviting him to self-select independent reading that was interesting to him, and I was encouraging him to bring forth his voice in writing.

Charles' response to reading and writing was colorless. In his book reviews he would write thoughts like, "The book was interesting because of the details in the story," without sharing any particulars. While Charles decoded texts successfully, he seemed unable to go beyond literal cause and effect thinking to interconnect ideas or utilize inference. His writing had no personal voice and consisted mostly of dry accounts of daily tasks. He never included any expression of his feelings or interests. Charles also held a code of rigid morality. Once, when we were discussing how Matt, the main character in *The Sign of the Beaver* by E. G. Speare, trapped animals to survive the winter on his own, Charles responded that it was wrong to kill animals. He seemed unable to consider the context of the particular circumstances in which hunting was a necessity for survival.

I could not believe, however, despite Charles' diagnosis of brain damage, that he was truly as literal as he seemed. One day I witnessed a glimpse of a very different Charles. We had meandered into a discussion of regional accents. I mentioned that residents of my native city of Pittsburgh had a strong accent, illustrated by Mr. Rogers on his television show, *Mr. Roger's Neighborhood,* which was produced in Pittsburgh. Charles spontaneously got up and did an impersonation of Mr. Rogers (whom he knew well from having watched his shows). We were amazed and quite entertained by his performance. He then proceeded to do other impersonations. It appeared that Charles had a right-brained, interpersonal gift that had previously been dormant.

Charles began tapping his talent throughout our class and this transformed him as a learner. Through skits, in which he impersonated Mr. Rogers, Charles explored a number of deep concerns he had—like fears of being labeled retarded and confusion about his future ability to live independently. Both Charles' writing and his reading became more connected with his personal interests and life experiences and, as a result, he became less rigidly literal. Charles had always been tactile defensive, flinching whenever a fellow student physically interacted with him. One day, while playing Mr. Rogers, Charles allowed himself to be tickled by this student, rolling around on the floor in glee. Fascinated at this transformation I thought, "So much for a purely neurological basis for tactile defensiveness." Context seemed to make all the difference!

Charles' role playing, gave him a safe container to explore and express his true feelings, loosening the filtering of his perceptions and responses through his carefully created "good student" persona. Interestingly, he had been able to create this very persona because of his intra/interpersonal giftedness. I began to wonder, how much do we, as educators, encourage the creation of false personas through reinforcement of compliant behavior?

My assistant teacher hypothesized that Charles chose Mr. Rogers as his main impersonation because of Fred Rogers' famous statement, "I like you just the way you are." Through expressing his fears and concerns in a context which honored his authenticity, Charles grew in accepting his deeper nature.

Esteeming the Self vs. Measuring Up

As I discussed previously, my son Matt struggled with a traditional kindergarten curriculum. His teacher was a warm, loving woman who freely gave hugs and verbal praise for the children's efforts and accomplishments. But Matt struggled nonetheless. While he coveted those hugs, he felt paralyzed over doing the required worksheets to merit them. Under the preconception that the teacher's expectations required perfectionism, Matt would not risk being wrong. Although he resisted the worksheets at school, he peppered me with questions about print at home. From Bob Keteyian's kindergarten assessment of Matt:

> Though Matthew was eager to attend school and obviously has the ability to understand and learn new things easily, he was worried about meeting his teacher's expectations. Matthew is also very curious about people and works hard to understand them. He has very high standards for himself and others and is very sensitive to anything he perceives as criticism. He usually senses what will be difficult for him and exerts caution getting involved. Paradoxically, he is also determined to master those same things.

We took Matt out of public school kindergarten and sent him to a nurturing Montessori School, followed the next year by a progressive alternative school. Although his teachers at the alternative school allowed Matt his own timetable of literacy development, they were not trained in Whole Language teaching and did not know how to provide literacy experiences which would scaffold his risk-taking. He told me one day that he would not learn to read until he grew up and knew all of the words! I realized that his definition of the reading process was one of "word identification," with no recognition of the huge scaffolding of language prediction. He was not going to risk being wrong.

The following year we had the good fortune of finding a Whole Language first grade in a nearby town (calling the year at the alternative school a year of "time out"). His teacher helped Matt overcome his learning resistance through giving him ample room for self-exploration within a literacy curriculum which emphasized meaning rather than discreet skills work. His teacher modeled the reading process through the reading of engaging Big Books (on an easel for the whole class to see), tracking the print with a pointer stick. Following the reading, the children were given an opportunity to identify those print features which matched their developmental level. All print skills were thus shared within a meaningful context rather than in isolation, and the children were invited rather than coerced to learn. His teacher also encouraged Matt to integrate his enormous creativity into his learning. In her classroom, he became a joyful reader and writer. He was able to honor his inner integrity as his teacher honored his self-determination and need for creative initiative.

He no longer experienced the conflict of *measuring up* to specific standards vs. honoring his need to learn on his own terms.

In his *Language Arts* article "Do Teachers Communicate with Their Students as if They Were Dogs?" Lowell Madden (1988) warns:

> By . . . using the language of praise with such statements as "You did a great job!" or "You are an excellent student!" the desired behavior of the student is "engineered." Although the use of praise is well intentioned, it is also judgmental and manipulative. Teachers also use the language of praise to affect their students' self-perceptions. Beane and Lipka (1984) state that self-perception has two dimensions. One is self-concept which is defined as the way a person views himself or herself; the other is self-esteem which is the degree to which one values or is satisfied with the self-concept. When their behavior pleases their teachers, they are rewarded with statements of praise and they view themselves as having worth; if they displease them, their worth becomes questionable." (142)

Madden asserts in the face of this:

> (Students are) unique individuals who have the right to self-determination and the joy of personal worth and dignity based on the undisputed value of their personhood. (p.144)

Madden also says that it is not only the less academically capable students who might suffer under an external evaluation system, but paradoxically those who succeed:

> Their feelings about themselves become contingent on teachers' judgments of their performances. They become dependent on these judgments rather than on their own feelings of satisfaction of personal growth and contribution. Unfortunately these students become adults who continuously look for approval from significant others in their lives. (p. 143)

For creatively gifted learners who are *driven* to be true to their internal integrity, maintaining healthy self-esteem can be quite a challenge. In her book *The Cloister Walk,* Kathleen Norris(1996) describes the following experience:

> I have . . . met visual artists who as children were so intent on playing with the shapes of numbers and letters that they fell behind in both English and math, to the despair of their teachers, who recognized that these were intelligent children. Yet visual intelligence . . . can be a handicap in this culture. Years ago, when I was a kindergarten aide at a Quaker school, one little girl demonstrated a capacity for attention unusual at the age of five. Every afternoon, she would paint huge blocks of color onto newsprint, working for nearly an hour. Then she would ask me to hang the painting to dry so that she could work on it again the next day. The teacher and I were fascinated but soon found that we had to protect her from the other children, who, once they noticed that her paintings didn't "look like anything," made fun of them. The girl, remarkably was undeterred, already adept at exile. (pp. 58-59)

The fierce determination on the part of that young child to be true to her inner vision seemed more important to her than acceptance from her peers. While her ego self might well have felt sad and bruised, her inner Self was alive and flourishing, and she chose the latter no matter what the cost. When creatively gifted learners succeed in accepting and expressing their Self-esteem, even if they are relegated to exile, they offer an empowered vision for all people to transcend to inner-direction and self-determination. Our culture would be transformed if all individuals were encouraged to be true to their inner guidance.

Don Miguel Ruiz (1997), a former surgeon, who today teaches and writes about ancient Toltec Wisdom, speaks to the impetus in our Western culture for developing a false self based on the need for approval. In his book, *The Four Agreements* he says:

> We pretend to be what we are not because we are afraid of being rejected. The fear of being rejected becomes the fear of not being good enough. Eventually we become something that we are not. We become a copy of Mamma's beliefs, Daddy's beliefs, society's beliefs, and religion's beliefs. (p.7)

Ruiz calls this the process of domestication.

> During the process of domestication we form an image of what perfection is in order to try and be good enough. (But) Not being perfect, we reject ourselves. And the level of self-rejection depends upon how effective the adults were in breaking our integrity. (pp, 17-18)

Continuing, Ruiz states,

> Everyone talks about freedom. All around the world different people, different races, different countries are fighting for freedom. But what is freedom? In America we speak of living in a free country. But are we really free? Are we free to be who we are? The answer is no, we are not free. True freedom has to do with the human spirit—it is the freedom to be who we really are. (p. 93)

Teachers who value their learners' intrinsic self-worth can fuel the flourishing of their full personhood, dispelling the conflict over honoring inner integrity vs. "measuring up."

On Perfectionism and Being True to the Blank Page

In Bob Ketetian's kindergarten report on my son Matt he wrote:

> Matthew is very concerned about pleasing his teacher with his performance. He expresses a lot of worry about getting positive feedback and perceives school as "hard" for him. The work, of course, is not difficult for him; however, he seems to be confusing his difficulty in complying with the structure and expectations with the schoolwork itself. He appears to be compelled to be precise at school, which is anxiety producing for him.

Most of my creatively gifted learners have exhibited tremendous anxiety over meeting their teachers' expectations. In the face of prescriptive standards, they become frozen from risk-taking. In the process, their own creative learning agendas and capacities go underground—at least in school; on their own time, at home, they might be building, painting, or reading up a storm.

Within their area of passion, the creatively gifted learner may be compelled to be—what artist and writer Ashley Bryant calls—"true to the blank page." Ashley described the meaning of this phrase to me in an interview I had with him at his home in Islesford, ME. When Ashley sits in front of a blank canvas, he senses an agenda from within to which he must be true. This is a different kind of perfectionism than Matt's anxious need to be precise related to his teacher's expectations. While anxious at school, Matt, on his own terms, was also driven to be true to his artistic visions.

I have marveled at the commitment of my maverick learners to be true to their inner visions despite, at times, enormous struggle. Jordan was a frustrated writer when he came to me in fourth grade. Because he found handwriting extremely awkward and tedious, he avoided written work in all forms. To encourage his confidence in written expression, I invited him to write on my computer. He still struggled. Jordan's parents had him tested, and his scores revealed a significant discrepancy between his gifted verbal IQ and his performance. He was coded with a learning disability in writing. I noticed that Jordan thought a lot about spelling, and I conjectured that his need to produce perfect spelling might be impeding his risk-taking. However, over time, he revealed a willingness to create spelling "on the run" as well as a wonderful curiosity about how certain words were spelled.

One day, as I was continuing to puzzle over Jordan's writing intimidation, he said, "I want to say . . . and I don't know how to say it!" We discussed his thoughts, and all of a sudden he wrote out a sentence and said, "I did it! I got my thought out." He had expressed his ideas with just the right words "true to his blank page," his inner vision. Hiding behind his frustration and reticence was his gifted sense of exquisite word choice longing for expression. He explored his linguistic prowess in an amusing book, "The Perfect Guide to Make a Dog (mainly me) Happy." One of the dog's "ten commandments" is:

> There is to be a bag attached to my flee collar that has *premium* dog biscuits. I will be needing it filled enough on a routine basis so I can easily reach in and (with my extremely cute snout) take one when the slightest rumble from my nicely rounded stomach occurs.

With growing confidence in his ability to find just the right word, Jordan discussed on the occasion he wrote the above section, "I need something less vibrant than hunger." Jordan began to love writing. At his PET the following year his teacher asked, "So what happened to his writing disability?"

When I homeschooled my son Matt for a year and a half, in third and fourth grade, I wanted to support his passion for artistic exploration. During this period Matt drew constantly, practicing a particular motif over and over until he got his idea "just right." He was hooked up to an internal perfectionism. One day, related to his artistic endeavors, he discussed the difference between seeking outside approval and self-approval as being similar to the difference between warm-blooded and cold-blooded animals. "Cold-blooded," he said, "depends on outside conditions whereas warm-blooded stays the same no matter what happens on the outside."

Being true to the blank page demands one's total integrity, but the rewards are enormous. In his book, *Wisdom of the Ages A Modern Master Brings Eternal Truths into Everyday Life*, Wayne Dyer, quoted Patanjali, ancient author of *The Yoga Sutras:*

> When you are inspired by some great purpose, some extraordinary project, all of your thoughts break their bonds; Your mind transcends limitations, your consciousness expands in every direction, and you find yourself in a new, great and wonderful world. Dormant forces, faculties and talents become alive, and you discover yourself to be a greater person by far than you ever dreamed yourself to be. (p.17)

In an interview with Michael Toms on the radio program, *New Dimensions,* Wayne Dyer gives an apt description of Ashley Bryan's term, "being true to the blank page" in a quotation from Michelangelo. It is said that when Michelangelo was asked, "How could you have created such a perfect specimen of sculpture from one piece of marble?" he replied, "David was already in the marble. I just chipped away the excess." Wayne Dyer followed this famous quotation with his belief:

> There's a David inside each and every one of us. The greater danger
> is not that our hopes are too high and we fail to reach them, it's
> that they are too low and we do.

Our creatively gifted learners can bring forth the brilliance of their inspiring inner vision when we support their determined attempts to be true to the demanding but magnificent challenges of their own blank pages.

Holding the Tension of the Opposites:
Walking the Fine Line

Stefan came to me for a reading evaluation in the summer before his fourth grade year at a private Waldorf inspired school. His parents shared that Stefan was becoming increasingly aware of being outdistanced in literacy by many of his classmates and was really upset over his virtual inability to read. The Waldorf philosophy of his school encouraged a natural development of literacy, and his teacher had not yet considered an intervention program, holding a "wait and see" stance. Stefan, however, really wanted to learn to read.

During our initial session, Stefan spoke softly and reluctantly. Using early predictable books, I assessed that he had no idea how to consciously engage his language prediction to process print information; he narrowed in on an ineffective attempt to sound out words he didn't recognize. He also shut down almost immediately when he couldn't get a word. With some coaching on using prediction, within the scaffolding of engaging predictable books, Stefan was more successful, and I was able to find a comfortable developmental reading level for him at a mid-first grade level. It was clear to me that Stefan's language abilities were outstanding, and I looked forward to witnessing his reading growth as he began to employ these in the reading process.

Stefan's mother had described him as an unusually sensitive child who loved to draw and had an intense interest in animals. Stefan's high sensitivity, artistic ability and intense interests coupled with his left-brained auditory-sequencing weakness, led me to believe that he was creatively gifted. As a part of my initial assessment, I asked Stefan to draw a picture and write about it. He drew a fisherman reeling in a huge fish (as big as the man) from a small pond. He chose to write on my computer. A condensed version of what he wrote is:

> bbbbbbiiiiiiigggggggfffffffffiiiiiiiiiiissssssssshhhhhhhhhhhhiiiiiiiinnnnn aaaaaaalllllllyeyeyeyeddddddddllllllllppppppppppppppoooooooooonnn nnnnddddddddhhhhhhhhhyyyyyyoooooooooouuuuuuuuuuuuuiiiiiiiis sssssssggggggggttttttttttttttttiiiiiiiiiiiiiiiiinnnnnnnnnnnnnnnggggggggggg ggcccccccccccccooooooooaaaaaaaaaaaaattttttttttttttt (Big fish in a little pond. Who is getting caught?)

His picture (and subsequent art he did with me) showed wonderfully expressive line, exquisite color sense and overall integrity of composition.

He chose an extremely creative way to risk-take writing with me that first session with his repeating letters. I felt like he was conveying, "I'll write, but I'll invent my own way." His message also expresses his lively humor.

Stefan continued to be a reluctant risk-taker in reading for a long time. Much like working with someone wanting to learn to swim who was terrified of the water, session after session with him, I walked a fine line, honoring his reluctance *and* inviting him into safer, more buoyant waters—the waters of engaging predictable books which naturally encouraged him to bring his language sense into reading, the waters of books which matched his ability level, stretching him just slightly, encouraging him to risk a little bit at a time. If I had focused (in frustration) on Stefan's reluctance, I believe I would have lost him; I certainly would have dishonored the difficulties of the demands he struggled with—not just those related to the ghosts of his early failures, but also those related to his perfectionistic need to be true to his own blank pages (his beautifully crafted artistic pieces).

To encourage Stefan's risk-taking in the face of his long-standing intimidation, I encouraged his artistic expression and creative initiative. Stefan, like Christina, thrived on choices in every aspect of our work together. He chose which book we would read, what and how he would write, the design of hands-on projects in conjunction with our work, and the implementation of our skills practice games. During one session when we were playing a short vowel game in which we would identify the word we landed on and then brainstorm another word with that same vowel sound, Stefan decided he would make his next word begin with a "b" because he had two previous words written, "set" and "gum" and SGB were the initials of his name. This is the kind of creative expression that really heightened Stefan's learning engagement and encouraged his risk-taking.

Stefan's passionate interests and creative expression played a critical role in his eventual literacy empowerment. He had a strong love of animals and a particular obsessive interest in chickens. He convinced his parents to acquire some and was devoted to them. The fact that his school had chickens, quite endeared him to it. A literacy tutor, who was hired to work with Stefan at his school, suggested that he read Farley Mowatt's humorous book, *Owls in the Family*. I joined in sharing the oral reading of this book with Stefan. Although the reading level was beyond where he had been working, Stefan was so captivated by the humor and the human/creature bond of Billy and his owls that he sailed forward.

Stefan struggled for many months within the tensions of the opposites— the opposing forces of his fear of risk-taking and his strong desire to engage meaningfully with literacy. Walking that fine line with him—honoring his resistance while still stretching him, inviting in his inner passions and strengths—was enormously challenging and extremely rewarding. I needed to be acutely present to Stefan's process. I needed to remain steadfast to the faith I had in his true learning ability as I navigated through both his frustration and my own (triggered by his strong resistance). I needed to travel that rough road with him, holding space for the breakthroughs. Although I took into account Stefan's developmental strengths and needs, I was driven neither by curriculum goals nor by deficit labels. I created enticing waters for exploration—learning experiences which had the capacity to activate the passions that Stefan longed to explore and express. I sustained the faith that, "We all have an expert on board."

One year, after we stopped working together, I had an opportunity to check in with Stefan's mother about his reading progress. She said that he was now spending self-initiated time reading books of his own choosing: survival stories, rescue stories, informational books on birds and fish, scouting books, and books on historical events. He recently picked out a book, while waiting for his mother at Borders, on the events around 9/11. His mother observed him stretched out on the floor, completely absorbed while people walked over and around him. One evening his mother asked him about his school summer reading list as he was glued to a book on wilderness survival. She pointed out to him that he was a lot more interested in that book than any on his summer reading list. He replied, "That's the way I work."

In *The Child's Discovery of Himself,* Clark Moustakis (1972) writes of his experiences as an existential child therapist.

> The focus is on the immediate process of human engagement and commitment where the integrity of the persons and the flow of life between them is the primary ingredient, rather than any theory or concept or preconceived plan. (p. ix)

And

> The therapist never surrenders his conviction that the child has capacities and resources for healthy self-emergence . . . The therapist never loses sight of the fact that the child is seeking his own way, however fragmentary or futile or destructive it may appear, to find an authentic existence, to find a life of meaning and value, and to express the truth as he sees it. (p.5)

Facilitating a learner in the process of the struggle between resistance and the desire to emerge requires tremendous patience. A learner acting out the struggle through a sometimes paranoid level of resistance, needs limits, but face-saving space within these limits to move out of reactivity. Recently I was playing a multiplication math game with Jeff, a brilliant, creatively gifted youngster. Math is a strength for him, and we are working together in this arena to buoy him up related to struggles he is experiencing at school. Even in Jeff's area of strength, however, he is sometimes reluctant to risk making a mistake. He has a strong need for his own felt sense of a process before being willing to share his exploration with a teacher. At the same time he seeks challenges to engage his tremendous mind appetite.

In this particular session, Jeff began to act out his struggle through moving playing pieces randomly all over the board. I gently put them back, without engaging a power struggle, and opened up space for him to invent some new rules for our game, giving him power through choice-making. Jeff happily created some new rules (no doubt feeling they gave him some advantages) and the game continued peacefully.

Along with patience and calmness, I also employ playfulness and special effects to create an inspiring and safe learning context. Theron, a private student of mine and a highly divergent learner, was reluctant to illustrate a book he had published with me. He saw his older brother as a talented artist, and I sensed he was reluctant to risk his own drawing. While honoring his concern (especially since I feel that I, too, am hopeless at drawing), I also felt that Theron might, with encouragement, feel some success; I refused to let him off the hook. Fortunately my artistic son Matt was home from college on his winter break, and I asked him to do an illustrating session with Theron. As I left them together, heading off to do my own work, I saw them huddled in at the dining room table with a stopwatch, sheets of paper, markers and pencils. I heard Matt saying, "What is your first picture about?" Then, "You have two minutes to draw it." When I arrived back an hour later, Theron was sitting there with piles of illustrations, looking awfully pleased. Matt explained that he gave Theron a time limit for each picture to unleash his risk-taking. Following each drawing, they would examine it together and decide what to keep and what to discard or improve etc. When Theron came for his next session with me, he sat down and confidently illustrated each page, drawing on the scaffolding of his session with Matt.

Christina is more inspired to attend to punctuation using a special purple pen for periods, commas, question marks etc. Many of my creatively gifted learners feel energized and inspired writing stories to my CD of action and science fiction movie hits. Jason breezily practices his spelling skills on a skate boarding game he created with the opportunity to move ahead by landing on "ride the rail." When I am feeling the need to nudge my sometimes reluctant, creatively gifted learners towards growth, playfulness and special effects can work miracles, side stepping potential power struggles.

When I begin walking the fine line with my learners, I feel like we're skating around the periphery of a pond together avoiding potentially thin ice in the middle. As my learners overcome their longstanding intimidation and access their inner learning abilities and passions, I feel like we are skating freely over a vast expanse of solid ice. These rewards far outweigh the energy demands of our initial struggle as my learners move from reactivity and avoidance to self-determination. Then the pulse of authenticity continues to energize and inspire our work.

Mirroring: Creating the Container for Empowerment

> I think that the true definition of a miracle
> is really a shift in perception.
>   —Angeles Arrien

Over and over again I have experienced the empowering effects of honoring each learner's integrity. In her tape series, "Sitting By the Well," (from *Sounds True*) Jungian analyst, Marion Woodman asserts:

> A person who is growing up needs mirroring. We have to be able
> to see who we are through the eyes of another who loves us.

In *The Educated Man: Studies in the History of Educational Thought* (Nash, P., Kazamaias, A., Perkinson, H., 1965), Morris Friedman's description of the existentialist philosopher Martin Buber's "I-Thou" theory describes the mirroring of true empowerment:

> Genuine dialogue, like genuine fulfillment of relation involves
> acceptance of otherness. Influencing the other is not injecting
> one's own 'rightness' into him but is using one's influence to let
> what is recognized as right, just and true take seed and grow in the
> substance of the other and in the form suited to his individuation.
> (Friedman, 1965) (p. 378)

Friedman describes the nature of Buber's "I-Thou" relationship to be one of directness, mutuality and presence. The "I" relates to the "thou" in his uniqueness, for himself, and not in terms of his relation to other things. In an "I-It" relationship, Friedman says, the other is my object, not my partner. He is observed and used and is established in relation to a general category, not an independent quality. In the "I-Thou" relationship, emotion, reason, intuition and sensation are all included in the wholeness of the person responding to whom he meets. (p.363)

Many of my learners have been seen through a deficit lens. Assessments diagnose what they can't do rather than tapping what they are trying to bring forth. If a parent or teacher looks at the learner through a deficit label, they are mirroring deficiency. Disagreeing with this deficit perception, I believe that the creatively gifted learners' challenges serve the purpose of skewing them towards their incredible strengths: their ability to learn passionately through their deeply sourced intuitive and creative sensitivities. By challenging the deficit perception, I hold the space for my learners' authenticity to come forth—mirroring my faith in its existence. When their passions have gone underground, in the face of long standing intimidation and sensed failure, they need a period of revaluing to reemerge.

I am intrigued by Marion Woodman's concept of the "container," the energetic as well as the physical context in which one works with a learner, a client etc. In discussing her concept of the empowering "container" (in an interview with Michael Toms on the radio program, *New Dimensions),* she says,

> A container that loves the child for what it is, not what the agenda of the parent or teacher is—but who is this little creature and what are *his* desires and *his* gifts? Who is this little soul . . . (who) wants to live his own life. (2001)

In *A Child's Discovery of Himself* (Moustakis, 1972), child therapist, Eugene D. Alexander, describes his collaboration with the teacher of a highly sensitive child misdiagnosed as mentally retarded:

> We were concerned when other children manipulated him. We were at times bothered by his passive, non interfering philosophy of life, but we had infinite faith in his potential. We both believed in his individuality, in his being, in the importance of choice, in freedom, in Jerry's becoming. We beamed at his unique

and creative expressions. We shared the thrilling moments we experienced with him in his successes. We strengthened each other's values and convictions; we grew in awareness and sensitivity by exploring our intimate experiences with this unusually silent and perceptive boy . . . Jerry continues to grow and emerge as a self in this thirst for new experiences, in his discovery of the wonders of life. His sensitive teacher waits and takes each step of the journey with him. When Jerry is ready, he shows her the way to open up new vistas for him. She follows the path and, at the same time, introduces him to new resources and opportunities. (pp. 125-126)

The teacher and therapist of this child supported each other in their belief in Jerry's self-emergence. They mirrored this belief to the child and created the container which nurtured his blossoming.

Honoring Their Sensitivities vs. Toughening Them Up

I have written earlier in this chapter about my son Matt's struggles with a traditional kindergarten program. I remember discussing his acute sensitivities with a gifted and talented teacher at his school. Her response was, "Can't you toughen him up?" I discussed her remark with his counselor. He believed that Matt's extraordinary sensitivities were the conduit to his rich inner life and the sourcing of his creative expression. Rather than "toughen him up," he recommended helping Matt learn to manage the demands of his sensitivities without becoming overwhelmed by them. Matt's journey of learning to work effectively with his sensitivities is an integral part of his learner story in the section, "Heartsongs: the Struggles and Triumphs of Creatively Gifted Learners."

Bonnie Cramond (1995), in her article, "The Coincidence of Attention Deficit Hyperactivity Disorder and Creativity," writes,

The stories of creative individuals with what are considered difficult temperaments are so abundant that the characteristic has become a stereotype. According to Dabrowski (Piechowski &Colangelo, 1984), the emotional volatility that is a key to this perception would be expected in a creative person because of the heightened sensitivity and reactivity to emotions.

Individuals who exhibit unconventional behavior, as many creative people do (Sternberg, 1988) may be seen as lacking in social skills. Getzels and Csikszentmihalyi (1976) described the personalities of the artists that they studied as aloof and nonconforming to conventional standards of behavior.

Kerr (1985) proposed that some antisocial behavior that creative people exhibit may be a defense against others' reactions to their differentness. (p. 8)

When I am working with a highly sensitive, creatively gifted learner, I'm tuning into a particular radio frequency, monitoring facilitation that creates static and facilitation that broadcasts clearly. As we grow in trust I experience, not a greater toughness in my learner, but a stronger resiliency and flexibility. I honor that many of my creatively gifted learners are blessed/cursed with a hyper-vigilant awareness of themselves. This kind of sensitivity can be a catalyst to enormous personal growth but can also be an impediment to risk-taking.

Because I understand the demands of this level of self-awareness, I honor my learners' gifts *and* use a light touch (often humor) to dispel their heaviness—helping learners move forward in the face of sometimes paralyzing perfectionism. And sometimes I just bide my time, supporting what Joyce Salvage and Phyllis E. Brazee describe as "Risk Taking, Bit by Bit," (1991) patiently waiting for the moment when a learner's elegant but often exhausting sensitivities give birth to a creative vision. Then we're off and running with a creative project, drawing from the same sensitivities that formerly spawned self-defense.

Thou Shalt Not Rush: About Spirit Space

A student in my exceptionalities class at the College of the Atlantic, gave me the beautiful term "spirit space." She wrote this term in a journal entry about a low literacy level high school student she worked with who was diagnosed with ADHD. She was initially told by the special education teachers working with him that this student would need frequent work breaks to stay on task. She was to be sure to schedule these at regular intervals.

My student launched this high schooler into a research project after she discovered his passion about fire fighting. It just so happened that she had worked for a spell at the London Fire Department when she lived in England. She helped her student organize small pieces of writing under pictures of fire fighting which they had pasted into a scrapbook. She also wrote to the London Fire Department asking for artifacts to give to her student at a completion celebration.

In conferencing with his teachers, my student said that they were amazed by the amount of writing he was willing to do on this project. When they asked if she had been giving him his scheduled breaks, she had to admit that they seem to have forgotten about them! She wrote in her journal that what he needed was "spirit space" to explore his passions, rather than breaks from tedious work. Years later, my student told me that her former student had fulfilled his dream of becoming employed in his community fire fighting force.

"Spirit space" is a term that describes the time to be with one's deeply sourced passions from within. Rather than a break from work which is not personally connective, "spirit space" gives time to reflect, to gestate ideas, and to let go of mentalizing in order to transcend to intuitive depths of understanding. In the "Spirituality in Education" Conference sponsored by the Naropa Institute (1997), John Gatto (author of *Dumbing Us Down* and *The Exhausted School* and New York State teacher of the year in 1991 and three times New York City teacher of the year) states:

> Our present system of schooling alienates us so sharply from our inner genius that most of us are barred from being able ever to hear our calling.

> The best lives are full of contemplation, full of solitude, full of self-examination, full of private, personal attempts to engage the metaphysical mystery of existence. There must be a reason that we are called human beings and not human doings. I think the reason is to commemorate the way we can make the best of our limited time by alternating effort with reflection . . .

> Whenever I see a kid daydreaming in school, I'm careful never to shock the reverie out of existence. Buddha is reputed to have said, "Do nothing. Time is too precious to waste."

Creatively gifted learners thrive on intuitive processing. They gain insight through connecting to their internal awareness. Intuition is not dependent upon the process of reasoning although reasoning may be used after the fact to describe an insight. As we grow in understanding of multiple intelligences, we need to look also at multiple ways of knowing, especially intuitive processing from which much innovation and true genius springs. In an interview with Michael Toms on the radio program *New Dimensions* (2002), Eckhart Tolle, author of *The Power of Now* described true intelligence:

> We equate intelligence with the ability to formulate thought, to analyze through thought, to store up more information and then to be able to repeat it or to compare. So intelligence the way we see it is a very narrow thing. It can be measured by IQ tests, but it is a very narrow definition of intelligence. It's simply how active your mind is.
>
> And our school system is based on that. You get good marks if the teacher asks a question and the children will put up their hand first, "Here I know the answer, I know, I've got it." And then there are some children who don't put up their hand, because their mind doesn't immediately kick in. In fact in some children naturally there is a greater ability to stay in the realm of "no thought" for a while before thought comes.
>
> So some children are considered slow. The question sinks in first into a depth that is beyond thought and there is no answer yet coming when the question is asked. Because of our narrow definition of intelligence, those children who have greater depth and perhaps greater intelligence that is deeper than simple thought formulation . . . are often called stupid. And even people who later became extremely creative, they were not very good at school. Einstein wasn't good at school. I'm sure he wasn't quick enough. There was too much depth. And what depth means is to dwell in the state of "no thought."
>
> . . . all creative people, people through whom something radically new arose . . . They've all told us that their creative insights, their deeper creative impulses came at a moment of stillness when the mind subsided. At that moment when the realization came through out of a vaster intelligence, they were not trying to find an answer. Perhaps before they were. The mind was active and then it stopped,

having access to a vaster consciousness within ourselves that is not separate from the mind but of which the mind is only a tiny aspect. And to be impoverished is not to know that dimension in oneself.

In Rumi's poem about the lame goat, cited in my introduction, he says, "There are many different kinds of knowing. The lame goat's kind is a branch which traces back to the roots of presence. Learn from the lame goat and lead the herd home." I believe that Tolle is describing the "lame goat's" kind of knowing sourced from a place deep within. The "lame goats" are those learners often labeled "learning disabled" and/or AD(H)D. These learners also are sometimes diagnosed with processing disorders because of their inability to respond quickly to left-brained sequential test tasks. I suspect that the so called weakness of a "processing disorder" may sometimes point to the strength of a deeper kind of processing, one which thrives on "spirit space."

I think of the term "spirit space" over time as well, not just at particular intervals. Jerry, a homeschooling highschooler, came to me to work on his writing. While he is an avid reader, he had avoided writing of any kind. His mother was becoming quite concerned about his reluctance to risk-take in this area of his schooling. Jerry and I developed sessions around reading and writing. Since reading is a huge strength for him, this gave him an opportunity to shine. He chose Susan Cooper's *Silver on the Tree*, from the series *The Dark Is Rising*, a genre of fantasy fiction he thoroughly enjoyed. He was more familiar with this series than I was, and he filled me in on the background I needed to understand it. He also had developed a skill of pronouncing the Welsh proper names, and he taught me these as well. Clearly Jerry *was* a risk-taker in reading.

Interspersed with our reading discussions, Jerry would tell me humorous stories—some he learned from others and some he made up about his own life experiences. He had a wonderfully satirical take on life and made connections between a variety of divergent sources. Clearly, he is a creatively gifted learner.

Jerry began writing, using my word processor. His spelling was somewhat primitive, but understandable, and I wondered how much courage it took for him to risk revealing it. He plodded forward, however, writing short satirical vignettes which he eventually published and illustrated in a small book. His witty illustrations supported his satirical writing; I believe that he is a natural cartoonist. Supported in his creative orientation, over time Jerry found his voice in writing.

Off Whose Task: To Focus or Not to Focus

Wherever I go in the United States these days, I hear about
something called the crisis of discipline, how children are
unmotivated, how they resist learning.
That is nonsense, of course. Children resist teaching, as they
should, but nobody resists learning.
John Taylor Gattin, "Spirituality in Education"

Whenever I am told that a learner is "off task," I want to know more about the nature of those tasks. Are the tasks personally relevant, interesting and developmentally suited to the learner or are they 'bogus' agendas, work isolated from personal meaning? In my experience, creatively gifted learners will almost always be "off task" with the latter to a greater or lesser degree. They find it extremely difficult to connect to personally irrelevant learning. Also, highly creative learners sometimes reveal what Rutter (1989) describes as diverted attention rather than what appears to be inattention. He says,

> Because it is difficult to differentiate between inattention and diverted attention, it may be informative to discover whether the daydreaming child is not attending or is attending to alternative stimuli, plans, or ideas that are focused. (quoted on page xvi of "The coincidence of Attention Deficit Hyperactivity Disorder and Creativity")

As they reveal bogus agendas through their resistance to tasks, highly creative learners also reveal authentic learning through their passionate connection to tasks of personal resonance. E. Paul Torrance (1970), in his book, *Encouraging Creativity in the Classroom,* says,

> (A) . . . common creative need and one that many people have difficulty understanding is the need to give oneself completely to a task and to become fully absorbed in it. The creative child frequently becomes so preoccupied with his ideas and problems that he is inattentive to whatever is going on around him. Such individuals are frequently absentminded. (p. 19)

Highly creative learners *demand* authenticity in their learning, often displaying the distracted behavior of AD(H)D or learning disabilities when confronted with regimented, prescriptive teaching.

Timothy, was a seventh grader in a tiny outer island school when he taught me how extreme variations of attentionality can be. Timothy, who was diagnosed with multiple learning disabilities in conjunction with strong emotional issues, was more often than not "off task" except for artwork and construction projects which intensely interested him. His teacher, MaryAnn (see "Meeting the Standards through Inspiration and Fun" in section 3) and I racked our brains to find books that would interest him and encourage his risk-taking in reading. However, he made slow and irregular progress and was "gifted" at distracting himself with any object at hand.

Finally MaryAnn found the magic book for him, *Hatchet*, by Gary Paulson. Timothy had grown up on a small, fairly isolated island off the coast of Maine and was attuned to the natural world. He had "smart" hands, as well, and loved creating constructions of all sorts. Brian's (the main character in *Hatchet*) attempts to survive in the Canadian wilderness were intriguing to him. On one of my weekly visits we were reading *Hatchet* together when an adult friend of his stopped in to talk with his teacher after fixing the tire on her truck. Sitting in close proximity to our table, the friend began discussing with Timothy's brother the prospect of building a boat together that summer. I thought, "Oh no, this reading session is doomed," but I was greatly surprised to witness Timothy paying focused attention to both the boat discussion *and* to his reading!

Understanding the intense need of creatively gifted learners for riveting agendas can help a teacher move beyond the apparent but misleading distracted student behaviors. With faith in the learner's ability to connect when truly inspired, a teacher can support not just steady progress, but often leaps in learning prowess. A creatively gifted learner resisting any kind of risk-taking within an inch of his or her life may all of a sudden beg for huge challenges and soar.

Christina (my case study at the beginning of this chapter) has been one of my best teachers of unexpected progress. For example, word study was an aspect of learning that was difficult for Christina and one she put minimum effort into. While creating spelling games together was fun, Christina showed little interest in spelling features and patterns. In sixth grade, she moved into the older group (her small school of thirteen students is divided into two groups), and asked me, for the first time, for *hard* words. Identifying with the" olders," she wanted to "claim her seat" by tackling some challenging spelling. She studied seriously for the first time.

I pulled multisyllabic spelling words from the book we were reading, Farley Mowatt's *The Dog Who Wouldn't Be*. The vocabulary in this book is very high—I had to look up some of the words—and as vocabulary study is part of her class program, Christina delighted in sharing the meaning of some challenging vocabulary with her classmates. I discovered, happily, that since many of the multisyllabic words in the book contained syllables with word patterns we had studied, I could make these "difficult" words quite achievable through review. We also studied the meaning origins of words, looking at the root word for clues, learning about Greek and Latin roots and discussing what language certain words originated from and how that affected the spelling.

As Christina's confidence in spelling multisyllabic words, syllable by syllable, strengthened, her skill in structural analysis (examining the parts of a multisyllabic word) in reading soared. Farley Mowatt's, *The Dog Who Wouldn't Be*, became a proving ground for Christina in terms of reading and spelling growth—a book in many respects beyond her grade level, but so engaging in its richness of characters and delicious humor that she embraced it fully.

Another factor in highly creative learners' ability to focus is their need to multitask. Multitasking, a fairly recent educational term, refers to doing more than one activity at a time. Multitasking can enhance sensory input and heighten focus, particularly, I believe, in those learners often seen as distractible. A majority of my learners thrive on doing tactile projects as they work on our lessons. Left-brained attention to detail is taxing to creative, intuitive learners, and they need opportunities for expression in handicrafts or sometimes just random tinkering to maintain their energy and focus.

I am in the process of learning more about identifying and helping learners with their arousal levels which can be too high or too low for balanced engagement. A favorite activity of my students is natural bees wax which comes in lovely assorted colors (I have also recently used Sculpey which is less expensive and more readily available). Bees wax requires sturdy manipulation to soften it for sculpting—a great example of the kind of "heavy work" recommended for either raising or lowering a learner's arousal level. Bees wax works well for both creative projects (my learners at Christina's school created a whole container of little foods which we use for playing pieces in our games) and just plain noodling time.

Many learners need large motor outlets as well. Gretchen, a high energy, creatively gifted learner identified as learning disabled in spelling, loved learning through games. I was greatly amused one day when she added onto some of the game spaces: do a dance, sing a song, jump. What a creative way to accommodate her needs as a "motor" learner!

In the best of all possible worlds, all students would be able to acquire skills through experiences which totally matched their developmental level and personal interests. Creatively gifted students, especially, need personalized experiences to thrive and soar. Realistically, however, even in strongly holistic classrooms, optimal learning situations cannot be created 100% of the time. Over the years, I have learned some strategies to help my learners through the less than optimal times, and I have encouraged them to build their own energy reservoir to draw from.

I call one of my reservoir strategies, *Garfield* relief. After a less preferred activity with my special education students, such as practicing their spelling list, we read a few pages from a *Garfield* book; they remind me if I forget. Creative humor energizes them (and, of course, my students are also getting some fine extra practice with reading!).

My ultimate goal for my creatively gifted learners is for them to recognize and value their learning needs. My son Matt demonstrated this achievement when he shared his discouragement over his college sophomore year fall schedule. He had chosen five courses that he thought were going to be personally interesting and creative. It turned out that none of the five inspired him, and he could feel his energy plummeting.

However, Matt realized exactly why this was so, and knew that he could slog on through successfully with the anticipation of a better selection next term (the light at the end of the tunnel). I have often counseled high school creatively gifted learners to be sure to include at least a couple of courses in their schedule that allow for creative expression—filling up their reservoir to be drawn upon for more taxing work.

From the Inside Out: The Power of the Organizing Vision

In Sixth Grade my son Matt was given the assignment of an expository composition. I don't remember what he wrote about, but I clearly remember his process. After he completed his clear and well organized piece, he asked me for help to do the required outline—help with the format: numbering, lettering and margins etc. He seemed to completely miss the irony that, for him, the outline was irrelevant since he had completed his piece without it. Getting the outline "right" was an assigned task he attended to separately.

Over the years of my teaching I have witnessed a majority of my creatively gifted learners experience great difficulty with assigned organizational formats. Prescribed formats seem artificial to them, making no sense related to the authentic organizing vision which truly lights and guides their path. If forced to use a particular format, they can feel helpless; it's like they can't get there from here. Matt wrote his paper true to his organizing vision. He researched a topic which intrigued him and and energized a naturally organized piece. Given a prescriptive organizing device, a creatively gifted learner, in great confusion, might focus on the mechanics of the form versus how it could be helpful. Tapping a compelling personal agenda is what inspires a helpful format. Within their organizing vision my learners may benefit from a choice of organizational devices *if* they are compatible with the nature of their quest. They need to learn about organization from the inside out, as their felt need arises.

When we look through a different lens at what the creatively gifted learner is striving to be true to versus what they are resisting, we can increase our understanding of authentic learning. For our creative mavericks, their learning (and indeed all learning) is most authentic when sourced from the inside out.

PART II

Heartsongs: Stories of the Struggles and Triumphs of Creatively Gifted Learners

The following stories share the learning experiences of twelve creatively gifted adults. In their struggle to manifest their passions, these individuals reveal both the obstacles to and the facilitators of their empowerment. In order to bring forth their gifts, through honoring their intuitive knowledge and their inner agendas, they needed to risk being different within the school's culture of norms and standards.

Script directors talk about a "throughline," a theme that moves from the beginning to the end of an entire script, even though many auxiliary events and subthemes may occur along the way. In my interviews with these learners, I kept following their throughline in my questioning—the thread of their struggle to honor their authenticity.

We all have a throughline—abilities we are here to develop and passions we are being asked to be true to. How do schools encourage our "cosmic" agendas and how do they inhibit them? The following stories give us clues.

> When the child moves forward into the adult and has understood its beauty, its wholeness, its trueness, it can enter out into the playing fields of life with more strength, more confidence, and greater wisdom.
>
> Channeled message

The following stories, from the heart, offer us a vision to bring this into reality.

Peter's story feels close to home for me in two respects. Firstly, he is my younger brother and secondly, his varying attentional issues remind me of so many of my creatively gifted learners. In interviewing my brother, I gained a deeper appreciation for both the struggles and the fine achievements he has experienced.

Peter is gifted in visual-spatial abilities. He has "smart" hands. Early signs of his gift are evident in his absorption with inventing things out of "whatever there was that moved and turned." Early signs of his struggles can be seen in his inability to focus on sheet work. When faced with homework, he circled around it, unable to sit still. When building an electronic kit, however, he sat for hours, not resting until his project was finished.

Peter's journey through elementary school and most of high school was fraught with frustration and despair. His visual-spatial acuity translated only in the few courses which gave him the opportunity to manipulate and create. As an electrical engineering student in college, he flourished in lab courses and struggled in theoretical sciences and liberal arts subjects. Finally, after he finished schooling, he achieved success in jobs which tapped his unique gift. In Peter's ideal school, all students would find a place to shine.

> Stand firm in your refusal to remain conscious
> during algebra. In real life, I assure you,
> there is no such thing as algebra.
> —Fran Lebowitz

Peter's Story

Whatever There Was That Moved and Turned

The earliest memory I have of school is the very first homework assignment I ever got, first or second grade. It was a worksheet of about thirty problems (probably adding and subtracting), easy problems. I brought it home thinking, "Gee, this is my first homework," and I sat down and did a few of them, but I couldn't sit for very long. I finished that first homework by doing some here, and then I would take it over there, and by the time I had those problems done, I was desperate; I just couldn't sit and do those problems, and I don't remember much of anything from there up through the rest of elementary school. It was so frustrating. The problems were easy, that was not an issue, but sitting down and doing those problems felt impossible.

However, from a really young age, I sat for hours experimenting with stuff and building with Tinker Toys. I remember that my mom had some kind of dish that had a metal lid with a knob in the middle. I would wind string around that knob and would spin it. Because it was metal, it would spin for a while. And I made elevators with it by tying an empty box to it with some string. Whatever there was that moved or turned, I could always make into things like that.

I also experimented with music. When I was in second grade, I got an accordion. I would even play chords on the accordion with one hand and play the piano with the other hand. I played Silent Night at the high school's Christmas assembly. I basically figured out how to play it just by listening to it. I didn't learn to read music however. My parents tried to get me to take piano lessons, and I lasted a couple of weeks and said, "I don't think so—leave me alone."

I Can't Sit

I don't know at what stage I stopped doing homework. It was an option for me to not do it. My body gets this reaction to this day—it's so much easier to not do something than to do something even fairly simple. And there has always been a restless factor—I just can't sit. If you were to watch me during a day at work you would see me work for awhile and then get up and walk a loop inside the building. However, I also have this insane desire to get something done. What's the easiest way to get homework done—decide not to do it. Decision's made, homework's out of the way, let's move on.

Now if I was working on a Heath Kit (an electronic kit that gives you a bag of parts and instructions to build a radio, hi fi, etc.), I would sit and work hours and hours way into the night until my mother came and dragged me to bed. I didn't need food, I didn't need to get up and move around. When I was twenty-two, I ruptured my spine around Christmas time. One of the things I couldn't do without great pain was sit. Well, that year I got a Heath Kit short wave radio. I sat under intense pain, and I built the Heath Kit short wave radio. The pain didn't mean anything to me.

Being Smart Meant Getting a Good Report Card

By fifth grade my grades were starting to get pretty bad and that upset my mom a lot which, of course, upset me. My father stood in the background thinking, "Maybe he'll get this and maybe he won't, but it's up to him." And I would even try to defend a "D" if I worked hard to get that—"Listen, I worked hard to get this "D."

I remember a Show and Tell in fifth grade when I brought in a high voltage power supply with a big capacitor and two metal posts. I wrapped a thin piece of wire around the two metal posts, pushed a button and the wire exploded. This got a great reception! I never told the teacher that if you touched the two metal posts it would probably kill you. My father figured that as long as I knew that, it was okay.

As for subjects that were particularly difficult, long division was the worst. It drove me nuts. In high school I did better in some higher math courses than others. I had great trouble with algebra, but from the first day I walked into geometry, I understood it—because in geometry you see a line and an angle and a circle and right away, "Oh this is equal to this and these lines are parallel." In algebra you can't see.

I had a great deal of difficulty with trigonometry. However, I had a nurturing teacher who would say, "Boy, you've really worked hard. I can see it (even though my grade might be C or D), so here's your B, because I know that you really worked *hard* at understanding this." That was a whole different experience, getting rewarded for working hard, not just getting eight out of ten right on a test.

In general, through tenth grade I felt really discouraged—the bad grades, the inability to sit, writing what I thought would be an interesting paper in history and getting slammed, having teachers tell me I was no good. The fact that I could build these really incredible things at home did not make me feel smart. Being smart meant getting a good report card.

Well That Was Something!

Then in junior year, a couple of things happened. One was a question on a test in economics class. I looked at it and couldn't recall anything I'd read about it, but the answer seemed intuitively obvious and I wrote it down. That turned out to have been the right answer. That confirmed for me that I could think of something valuable on my own. And I remember the teacher said, when he passed the test back, "Only two people in the class got this question right. Peter, what was the right answer?" Feeling on the spot, I paused, and my teacher said, "You'd better come up with it, or I'm going to take it away from you." Fortunately I was able to recreate my thinking!

The other significant thing was that I got on the honor roll. I'm not sure how that happened. I was in my homeroom and my teacher did something she had never done before. She said, "I have the honor roll list," and she read it out, including my name. And everyone said, "Peter Williams!" Well, that was something! And, of course, in years past my dad had offered me all kinds of fancy electronics for getting on the honor roll—everything but a new car and a boat. Well, this year my reward was a pound of sodium—which we had a lot of fun with creating explosions, but . . . I think you can offer anyone anything, and it will have very little effect. Offering me fancy toys did nothing for the fact that I couldn't sit.

It's Just Like Tinker Toys

I did well enough in high school, that my father, a professor of electrical engineering at Carnegie Mellon University, thought that I might survive there. It was his decision—he had the power to get his children accepted.

My first year was horrible; I hated all of my courses. In chemistry—although I did well in chemistry in high school—I had a terrible time understanding it. I had these horrible hour lectures every week that were boring, and I couldn't care less. I had English Literature which I actually did better in than chemistry, physics (which is a good example of something you can't see—you can't draw what goes on in physics), and a course in psychology (which some people thought was an easy course, but it didn't seem easy to me). But no electrical engineering. It was quite discouraging.

In my sophomore year, I had a second year of physics, some introductory electrical engineering courses, and some liberal arts. The electrical engineering courses were relatively easy, because I knew all of the answers—I had done all of the experiments at home in my bedroom. I was beginning to feel like I could succeed.

Throughout my years at Carnegie Mellon there were two kinds of electrical engineering courses. The one kind of EE course, like field theory, was math-intensive (calculus, abstract math, figuring out fields on L shaped objects) and not at all intuitive. I just barely survived those courses (again they were not something you could see). Then there were the hands-on labs where the math wasn't all that complex. It was, "How do I put together little pieces of resistors and capacitors to make circuits?" Those I did very well on. I'd be living in the gutter today if I had to rely on how well I learned some of the non-lab courses. I still don't know, to this day, how I got through four years of college with the non-lab EE and liberal arts courses. Really, overall, college was hell for me.

I function well using intuition which means that I have learned a certain set of basic tools, and it's no problem for me to put these tools together to build something. I need to create my own systems. I need Tinker Toys. That's what I do today as a computer programmer. I know the various pieces that make up all programs, and I can put them together. I only had one actual programming course in college, and it was so long ago that really none of that applies anymore. I'm not, unlike most of the people around me who are younger, a classically trained programmer. But the pieces are simple, and it is completely obvious to me how to put them together fairly quickly. I can organize horrendously complex programs fairly quickly. It's just like Tinker Toys.

I Really Started To Feel Smart

I did very well in my first job at Digital Equipment which involved designing computer logic. There was no fancy math involved. It was literally building blocks—you could hold them in your hands in those days, putting them together, wiring them up, making computers and computer-like things. I did very, very well at that. A lot of my colleagues knew a lot of things that I didn't know, but it didn't mean that they could put things together in the right way and make them work. They had been fed more facts in college, but had less of the, "Here's how you think your way through problems."

For many years, on my various jobs, I had no difficulty with my ability to stay focused, because I was building something that I knew I would be able to play with later—I wasn't building a little thing and handing it off to somebody else and never seeing it again. I went from a pencil drawing to a machine that did something. It was very, very satisfying.

I really started to feel smart as soon as I started working after college, and I noticed that I could get things done really well. Often people came to me with questions, not the other way around. Most of my schooling, which was memorizing things and doing things I couldn't see in front of me, didn't fit me. There may be legitimate things they teach at school that I just couldn't get, and no matter who taught it or how it was taught, I just couldn't get it.

Like Meatball Surgery

My current work is involved with creating software and maintaining software that other people have written. I troubleshoot and solve problems with software that was written over the last twenty years by people who are gone and didn't write down how it worked. I try to get into their minds and find out what's wrong, what their software is supposed to do, and how to fix it. And often there is a customer screaming bloody murder, so I don't have a lot of time. A lot of my work is crisis-based. It's like in the movie, MASH, meatball surgery—just getting through this crisis. I usually don't have time to look at a piece of software and say, "Boy, I really could have organized and written this better."

There's a penalty for me working this way. When I get a problem, I go in, like with a microscope, to just that problem area. I don't do well with learning all about the whole system, so each crisis call means going in anew—and I can't answer questions on the spot, because I don't know the whole system. That can put me into a panic. I need time to research, an hour or two to come up with the answer. They might ask over the phone, "Remember the thing you did three weeks ago?" Well, I've done twenty-eight things in the last three weeks. No, I don't remember.

I think that's a penalty you pay for being creative rather than a good learner in the classical sense. I think if I really tried and actually somehow succeeded in learning the whole program, that three weeks later I would have forgotten it. Sometimes it's embarrassing when someone walks into my office and says, "Pete, remember that thing you did for me three weeks ago?" "No." Or I go back to the guy and ask,"Now how does this thing work again?" And I know I've asked him that two or three times before. I am starting to write down the things I am likely to forget—notes and notes and notes. And I can always call on that creativity. If I have to invent something twice, O.K. I can do it. I can still go in and fix any problem there is in a whole program. I can still come up with answers to problems that people have long ago given up on, but it doesn't mean that I haven't used up a year of my life for every month that I've been dealing with that problem.

The pieces that I get that aren't crisis-oriented are definitely less stressful, and there are some bits that I do literally from scratch, which are more enjoyable for me. Other people write programs differently than I would, and I think in a lot of cases they're terribly written. People come out with these high falootin degrees in programing, and what they create is just crap. Mine are different: very, very well organized.

I Love to Explain What I Know

I do enjoy the role of being an expert—that is knowing more than the group around me; and I am happy to spend time explaining to others in great detail how something works. That does come up fairly often. Back in the seventies, we had a secretary named Betty. She didn't know computers, but part of her job involved word processing. She worked for me and my co-worker. I would spend the time to write down her procedures exactly: Take the disk out, do this and this and this, and I included a column which said, "This is why you're doing it." My co-worker just said, "She needs to know computers. I not going to waste any time with her." It just seemed like the right thing for me to do—to spend the time that was necessary to explain things to her. I love to explain what I know. When I fix something, I like to say, "Come into my office and I'll explain what I did." That's very satisfying for me.

In the Real World They Don't Give Tests

My ideal school would be a school which creates a sense of ownership for all of the kids, even for the ones who aren't doing well. Each student would feel an important part of the school. The teachers would help all of the students to feel pride and ownership. My wife, Sue, who teaches math and science in a sixth grade, does this very well. In a recent situation she was supporting the choral teacher. There was one girl who was a behavior problem. It was Christmas time and Sue said to this girl who was Jewish, "Would you like to read this Hanukkah piece, and we'll add it to the program?" All of a sudden the problem student now had ownership, she now had pride, and her problem behavior disappeared.

So how do you get somebody who's lost like me to take pride and ownership? The few teachers that I had who enjoyed talking to me really made a difference in how I felt about myself. Related to my homework issue, what could they have done to make even simple homework not agonizing to me? Perhaps fewer problems, I don't know. Fortunately, today computers can help poor handwriters create papers they can be really proud of, instead of the messy blotches they would create otherwise. You can never have pride in those messy papers no matter how good the thought processes are.

Another question is, since I've been very successful, what is schooling really all about? When somebody comes up to me and tells me, "Oh no, my kid is flunking," I say, "Well, that's a concern, but the same thing happened to me, and I now make $100,000 a year as a computer programmer. Be careful about how much you panic." When you get out in the real world, you don't take tests.

Carolyn is an interpersonally gifted learner with a strong affinity for music. In her elementary schooling, she struggled against the prescriptions of lackluster curriculums. In high school, she felt labeled as a mediocre student and lost any incentive for success until inspired by two teachers, one who created exciting classroom forums and one who believed in her ability and got her extra help. In college, Carolyn's learning soared in courses which invited her interpersonal understanding and passionate interests. Post college, Carolyn again struggled in work that did not inspire her creative expression until she once again stepped out of the box and chose her heart.

> If a man does not keep pace with his
> companions, perhaps it is because
> he hears a different drummer. Let him
> step to the music he hears, however
> measured or far away.
>
> —Henry David Thoreau

Carolyn's Story

I Was So Proud

I really liked kindergarten. My favorite day was when the teacher made a game based on a captain's hat that I brought in for Show and Tell. She set up a whole boat system, and I got to rip the tickets and seat the passengers. Then I got to be the captain, because I had the hat.

I always liked art and music. I think I liked art because I got good grades—as long as you *tried* you got a good grade. My drawings were terrible, but I would spend hours on them, making fancy rainbows all over—so I always did well. We walked down to a separate area of the school for art, and I felt comfortable there. There was cool stuff on the walls, and I really liked my art teacher. I really loved music also; I was a good singer and was in choirs all through school. I was in two musicals: Marta in *The Sound of Music* and a chorus member in *Fiddler on the Roof.* Outside of school, I was always singing.

I Just Couldn't Do It

As I moved up in the grades, I became really unhappy in school. In third grade, for the first time, I remember having a really hard time with reading. The reading program we had was: read the story, answer the questions, go on to the next story. I was the last one to finish the questions, and I always got them wrong. At this time, I first starting getting into trouble. I was taken off to a side table and made to write, "I will not talk in class," a hundred times.

My handwriting was slow and really awful, so I was taken out for special help in second and third grade. They thought I might be left handed, and they actually tried to make me write with my left hand for a month or so—and it was worse. So they switched me back to my right hand saying, "One of your hands has to work." But they didn't like the handwriting of either of my hands.

I really disliked being taken out of class; it was a big deal. I'm sure they were trying to do it discreetly, but I felt like they were saying, "Okay, Carolyn, you have to go to your special class because your handwriting is so awful!" And then I would get up and walk through the silent classroom with everyone staring at me. In the special class, I worked on cursive. If they had just said, "We're going to teach you how to sign your name and everything else you can do in print," that would have been fine, but I remember crying and crying and crying because I couldn't get cursive. My cursive writing was so messy, nobody could read it, including myself. Teachers were frustrated, and I was distraught, because I thought that I was going to have to write in cursive for the rest of my life, and I just couldn't do it.

Overall in elementary school, I remember doing well on a few assignments, but in general, not doing very well. In sixth grade I started really falling behind in social studies, because I couldn't take notes very fast. I felt that I needed to write down everything, and I was always the last one to finish. The whole class would have to wait for me, and I remember being singled out for that.

Why Did I Do So Well On This?

I can remember choosing an experiment for the science fair in sixth grade. When I came home and showed it to my dad he said, "The book's wrong." So what I ended up doing was proving that my school's encyclopedia was incorrect. I remember being really excited by that, because I was able to prove it. The experiment is the one where you have a candle in a basin of water, and you put a jar over it and the candle goes out. The encyclopedia said it was because the oxygen got used up—that's not true. Actually, the candle heats the air inside so much that the air expands and suffocates the candle. To prove it, my dad got a high voltage generator and found a way that we could respark the candle and relight it without lifting the jar up. Therefore, if we could make the candle light up again, obviously there's oxygen left inside. I wrote the experiment up on the computer, typing the six stages of the scientific method.

This was the first time I felt excited about science. I think that the quarter before, I had actually flunked that science class. I think that I failed because once you start getting some bad grades, it's so easy to just not care anymore—it becomes not that big of a deal.

I remember in geography that we had to draw a map of Africa. I was trying to hand draw it and write in the names, and that wasn't working. So my dad put a map of Africa up on the computer screen, and I drew the outline of the continent and all the countries just by pointing with my finger and telling my hand on the mouse to move the same way. Then I was able to type in the names of all the countries, and it turned out really nicely—I actually got an A on it. It was one of my first A's, and I asked, "Wow! Why did I do so well on this?" My teacher said, "Because I could read the words finally." I learned that if I wanted other people to understand what I was doing, I couldn't hand write it; It had to be on the computer.

Why Am I Here?

In high school I got into band, and that was really cool because I was succeeding at something really fun, and it created a new social network for me. In seventh grade we had moved to California from Massachusetts, and that was really tough because I wasn't accepted socially. I was so scared about not making friends, that I retreated and withdrew. All I wanted was to fit in, so it was nice to finally find my social group. But I didn't enjoy school except for band. I would look forward to band once a day. It would be band and then lunch and then, "Ugh, two more hours, and I get to go home."

I almost never read all of the assigned books in high school—I read maybe a chapter or two if it was boring, and I wouldn't go on. Maya Angelou's I *Know Why the Caged Bird Sings* was the first book I completed. But *The Great Gatsby* and *The Scarlet Letter*—Whew! I definitely did *not* read *Great Expectations*. We had quizzes on assigned reading in that book every day, and I bullshitted every single test. I liked Judy Blume's, *Are You There, God? It's Me, Margaret.* It was about a young girl, just like me, getting her first period and contemplating God. That was a deep book—the first book I actually read twice.

The year that I was reading *I Know Why the Caged Bird Sings,* a mother of a student in my grade tried to get that book banned because it had a rape scene. I remember thinking, "That was wrong." After she had been defeated by the school board, I saw her at a band fund raiser and started debating with her; I enjoyed egging her on. What sparked my interest in this book was the controversy around it.

I remember reading history books in elementary and high school and having great difficulty retaining what I had just read. I was not able to summarize information or pull a fact out and keep it. In order to retain any information, I had to take notes after each paragraph or draw a picture. I was exceptionally good, however, at memorizing tunes and lyrics to songs. To this day, my mom is astounded about how I can recite a scene from a musical and sing everyone's part.

In high school, I became increasingly discouraged. I felt like my teachers just looked at my name and put a "C" on my work and passed it back, because they knew I wouldn't complain—they thought I was fine with C's. I got labeled as a "C student," and even if I really tried and reworked an essay a bunch of times, I would still get a "C."

I actually did an experiment for about a month in my junior year. I didn't bring any books with me to school—I brought a coloring book and a box of crayons. I went to every class, opened up my coloring book, opened up my crayons and colored. When the class was over, I would close up my coloring book, close up my crayons and walk to the next class. And that's all I did for a month. When a test came my way, I filled it out and gave it back and *nothing changed.* It didn't make a difference if I sat there and took notes or not—my grades didn't go up or *down.* The teachers didn't seem to care that I was coloring. Students around me started thinking it was cool and by the end of the third week, five or six people around me all had coloring books. I thought, "What a joke! They don't care that I'm not paying attention, they don't care that I'm not learning. Why am I here?"

One day I went into my mom's sixth grade classroom to visit, and she said, "Boys and girls this is my daughter." A student raised his hand and said, "Are you the "good one" or the "drummer?" My sister, a good student, played the trumpet, and I played drums. My mom will never live that one down!

It Felt Cool To Do Really Well

A class I really did like was Mr. Ladd's World History in my junior year. He was one of those teachers that comes along once in a million years. He showed movies about the Civil War and then talked about the Civil War. He split us up into Democrats and Republicans, and we had political debates (we wouldn't know whether we were a Democrat or a Republican until that day, so we had to research both sides). We had a fake presidential campaign. We created a Senate and a House of Representatives and got points for getting our bill passed. For current events, we had a RAP (read and response) notebook. We clipped current news articles out of the newspaper, and then wrote about them. We learned the abbreviations for the states through a bingo game—Mr. Ladd would say "Massachusetts," and we would mark off MA. I remember debating about abortion and writing speeches about pro choice. These were all extremely creative ways of learning, participatory learning at its best. My classmates and I all were really jazzed about the class, and our mutual enthusiasm created mutual respect.

It was during this class that I experienced success in a writing project. We were assigned a major thesis paper about a family relation from a former time period. Through writing about something that happened in that person's lifetime, we had the opportunity to personalize history. I selected my grandfather, Everard Mott Williams, and wrote about how his expertise in radar led to his contribution to the D Day Invasion of World War II. The reason that there were only half the number of enemy troops on the Normandy Beach was because my grandfather's radar jamming devices intercepted their radar signals and messed them up—they thought we were going somewhere else.

I did a lot of research. My grandmother sent me newspaper reports, and I looked up World War II information and actually found my grandfather's name referenced in a few encyclopedias and other sources. And I learned about radar. However, when I came to the writing part, I had difficulty organizing all of my information into an outline. My dad helped by asking, "What are the different things you're going to talk about?" We listed the six things. Then my dad helped me create an index card system in which I wrote a piece of information with its reference on each card and numbered it related to one of the six categories. Did it answer, "How did World War II and radar relate?" Did it answer, "What did my grandfather do with radar?" Did it answer, "What is radar?" etc. Then I sorted my index cards by number and wrote each section, making sentences out of the bits of information. I remember a light bulb going off—wow, I was finally able to take all this information, separate it out and organize it. It turned out to be an awesome paper; I got 197 out of 200. It felt cool to do really well!

I remember my senior year I had a chemistry teacher I really enjoyed talking with. While we were doing a lab, she would call me up in front of the classroom and ask, "How are things going and how is band?" When I started doing poorly on some of her tests, instead of saying, "Oh, I guess she's not going to do well in this class," she pulled me aside after school and said, "I think you need a tutor." I got a chemistry tutor, and my teacher let me retake the tests—I couldn't get an A, but I could get a B (you lose one letter grade when you retake it). I started doing really well once I had the one-on-one attention. Everyone said that was a really hard class, and I was doing really well. My teacher had a lot of faith in me and didn't give up on me, and I remember her so gratefully for that.

I Was Doing It!

During my high school senior year I felt a spark of, "Hey you might be a lot smarter than you thought you were." I did not, however, feel solidly competent about myself as a student until 1997 at the end of my first semester at Sonoma State. Probably for about the hundredth time my dad said, "You know, you're really smart," and for the first time I believed him. I went to a junior college for two years prior to that, and I did okay in some classes, not so good in others—I just didn't have a whole lot of interest.

At Sonoma State, I felt like I had a chance to start over. I also felt socially isolated, so I threw myself into my studies. That first semester I got a 3.7, and I was blown away! And I had really hard classes. In one of my classes, "Theories and Methods of Psychology," we had a ten page paper once a week requiring incredible amounts of researching, writing and rewriting. I was doing it, and I stepped back at the end of the semester and said, "Wow, look what I did!" I ended up getting an A- in that class.

I don't know what changed so dramatically, but I finally started seeing myself as a good student. I took a women's study class with a terrific teacher who made learning really fun. We individually researched information and presented it to the class in groups. I found that I retained the information in the books I was reading because the information was embedded in stories that brought forth women's issues that I really cared about. I discovered that I have a passion for women's history and for learning about women's rights.

I Was Choosing the Classes I Wanted to Take

For a class on media censorship, I researched stories for an annual yearbook of the top twenty-five underreported news stories—"News That Didn't Make the News." We were able to choose our stories, so I chose ones about women and gays—the causes I believed in. My intense interest in the project inspired me to do very well in that class.

I worked hard in college to get the good grades. To read a text book, I took a full page of notes for every three pages. I typed my notes up later at home in outline form. I think that outlines helped me a lot, because they put organization into my thoughts. I was so good at taking notes that I got a reputation, and the disabilities center paid me to take notes for students with learning disabilities. That was a trip! If only they knew . . .

It felt really good to do well, to get A's, to be respected by my teachers, and to have people come to me to ask questions. School wasn't boring anymore because I had chosen my major, sociology, which included women's studies. In junior college, I took all general education classes. Now, finally, I was choosing the classes I wanted to take. I *wanted* to learn about sociology and gender, and I *wanted* to learn about racism, classism and sexism, and how racism, sexism and classism all interconnect. That's when I started blossoming.

I Decided to Follow My Heart

After college, I worked for a while in non profit agencies: Face to Face, an organization which gave support to AIDS patients, followed by a rape crisis center, where I trained the volunteers who worked on the hot lines. At the crisis center I was given carte blanche to share information however I wished, and I really enjoyed the challenge of teaching the subject matter in a way that connected to the varied abilities and interests of the volunteers. This challenge inspired the budding teacher inside of me.

I left the crisis center due to depression (triggered by my intense involvement with our clients) and began a stint of customer service work in a credit union, then State Farm Insurance followed by a private health insurance broker. While I won several awards for my public relations work at the credit union, I got into trouble for laughing and talking too loud (every ex-boss told me to become a standup comedian). In all three jobs I rebelled against being put into a box in terms of protocol and paperwork—I simply wasn't meant for cubicle life. During my exit interview at State Farm Insurance my boss said, "I don't know if this is appropriate to mention, but I've never seen anyone light up the way you do around children and relate to them so well. You should consider a career with children." I had really enjoyed playing with the children who came in with their parents while they did their business.

And so I followed my heart and began taking child development courses (I needed 12 units to qualify for jobs in this field). After being unemployed for a number of months, I began to work at a center for infants and preschoolers called Gymboree. At the center I facilitate play sessions between parents and their children. Although the program is scripted, I find ways to bring in my own inspiration and adaptations. I am so fed by interactions with the kids and am enthralled with witnessing their growth over time. The curriculum involves a lot of singing, rhythm and movement—a great match for me. I have been recognized by both parents and my employers for my exuberant spirit.

As I continue to take child development courses, I look forward to a career in teaching preschool or kindergarten. As much as I enjoy my work at Gymboree, I long to create my own program. One of my sessions at work is a sign language class for infants, and I can see how much of the curriculum does not match their developmental level. For now, however, I am content to be doing work that stirs my passion and feeds my soul.

You Do Have Oars

After I graduated from college, I was feeling scared about my transition into the outer world. At that time my friends Jan, whom I worked with at Face to Face, and Mary Stella, a visual intuitive, invited me to a Summer Solstice celebration. At the celebration Mary Stella did a personal reading on me during which she saw a picture:

> I was in the middle of a vast but calm ocean. It had no edges; it
> went on in every direction that you could see. I was in a rowboat
> looking around and feeling lost.

Mary Stella told me, "You don't know it, but you do have oars. You actually have everything you need within you."

That reading has become a metaphor for me reminding me that I do have everything I need within myself. I have me, which is the power, the oars which are the mechanical, and I have the ocean on which I can go anywhere. And as I have opened up to my heart's true choosing, I have developed greater confidence in being the captain of my own boat, using my oars, and enjoying the journey.

David's story shares the poignant journey of a gifted dancer striving for self-validation in a culture which values head work over kinesthetic expression. Also, as a highly creative learner, David experienced a great deal of frustration with prescriptive, skills-in-isolation learning. He needed to feel the inspiration of his own learning agendas and "discover the steps on his own." A highly sensitive person, David thrived only in small groups in which he was "seen" for who he was. From only a few isolated opportunities to explore movement as an integral part of his learning, David came to claim his dancing as his modus operandi for being in the world. Today he shares, with students of all ages, his vision of how creative movement can inspire empowering learning explorations. David provides opportunities for others that would have meant so much to him on his educational journey.

> Don't ask what the world needs. Rather
> ask what makes you come alive; then go
> and do it. Because what the world needs
> is people who have come alive.
>
> —Howard Thurmon

David's Story

I Was Discovering the Steps on My Own

I have very few vivid memories of my elementary school experiences. One clear memory I do have is in fifth grade with Mrs. Harvey. It was an interesting time for me. I remember being very extroverted that year, which was unusual for me. Mrs. Harvey was a calm, cool, collected teacher, and whatever she did in her room allowed me to be myself a little more. She did a lot of project-based learning. I particularly remember a frontier project that involved building a log cabin in the classroom with a few other students. I remember how excited I was when I found an old refrigerator box on my walk to school one morning. That became the main part of our cabin. We had to do research, because the project involved doing a living history presentation while touring kids through the cabin. I remember being really engaged in both the building of the cabin and the research, because I had a definite goal in mind, and I was discovering the steps on my own. That's what gets my energy going. It was not like somebody walking me through *their* steps.

Another neat thing that Mrs. Harvey did was a class talent show. I had a great time with it, and I actually choreographed a dance! I talked a friend into doing a movement piece to some music. Back then, I wouldn't have known what to call it, but we used our bodies, basically to music, and it was dancing!

I remember getting bogged down with most of what happened in school, because I could never really see the bigger picture. We were just given what's right in front of our face, and that usually wasn't particularly interesting. The teacher may have had in mind where that was going (you will need this math at some point later on, or you're going to need to know a sentence structure), but I never had the energy or the interest for the isolated pieces.

I Was Always Tinkering With Something

While I wasn't failing in school, I wasn't a stellar student like my older brother, who was a bookworm and went to an academic magnet high school. There was my brother and then there was David, me, and the familiar phrase I often heard was, "Well David's good with his hands." Typically, the minute I got home from school, I was out the door taking my bicycle apart, painting it, taking the lawn mower apart, taking the radio apart—doing some type of project. I was always tinkering with something. I also liked to be in the kitchen a lot with my mom or my grandmom; I'd always want to bake the birthday cake or help with the Thanksgiving dinner. I can remember being told that I might become a chef when I grew up.

However, I always felt inadequate about being able to do boyish stuff. I don't know where that came from—perhaps because I had no father in my home. I had a friend who lived down the street who was a little more rough and tumble than I. The cooking definitely didn't fly with my friend, and I got jived about that. In the neighborhood, I was considered more effeminate and was an easy target to pick on. I think that I was easy to tease, because I was so sensitive; I still am.

I Just Can't Do It; This Is Too Hard

We would always be tested every year with the California Achievement Tests. I had a lot of anxiety about them, sweaty palms etc. I would always do the best on reading comprehension stuff; I was quick to get the gist of what was going on. I remember, however, living in fear of spelling tests all through elementary school. To this day, I have difficulty spelling, but I'm freer not to worry about it because of word processing and spell checkers.

We didn't do much writing in elementary school—I'm amazed with how little we did. In the upper elementary grades, the writing was always reports— you go to the encyclopedia, and you can't copy, but you can creatively repeat what they just said. I remember getting my older brother to help me write sometimes. I asked for his help with my college application essay, because I wasn't quite sure how to do it.

Although, on my own, I enjoyed art, I actually felt in fear of art classes in the upper grades of elementary school. The teacher would almost have me in tears if I was a quarter of an inch off on a picture. I often felt, "I just can't do this; this is too hard."

Hey, That's My Idea!

I went to a huge high school of around four thousand students. I'm sad to say and think that I had very, very few, if any, friends in high school; I just kind of drifted in my own world and got lost in the crowd. High school wasn't a complete loss, however, because I took drafting for two terms and woodshop right after that. I found out that I could meld the two classes by designing my own projects in woodshop using what I learned in drafting. I didn't follow the templates that were already there. One of the things that I made in woodshop was a wooden guitar stand. The teacher was so impressed with the design that he made it into a permanent template for other students to use.

When I went to Penn State right after I graduated from high school, I really wasn't clear about what I was doing there. I started out as a horticulture major, because I had built and maintained a garden while in high school and had done some landscaping around our house. The initial courses that I took for my major were hard science classes with large groups of students enrolled. Although they were not as practical, I found myself liking the elective arts and humanities courses much more. I remember one dance class that I took as a physical education credit. I just loved it, but I was too insecure to switch to become a dance major. The dance teacher in that class did a lot of improvisation. We were working in groups, and I had a suggestion for this one movement. Later, the teacher used that movement in a piece she choreographed for our culminating concert. I remember thinking, "Hey that's my idea!" I was the spark for it. Although I did feel somewhat validated by that, I wish she would have come up to me before she used it and said, "Oh I really like what you did."

I feel a sadness that I never had a mentor up to that period. I really needed that, because as I got older in elementary school, I was teased a lot, felt inadequate, and had low self-esteem. I feel like I could have covered more ground sooner in my dance (which now has become my life's passion), if I could have had some support that way.

I Needed To See Myself Valued in a Group

I ended up leaving Penn State because of an emotional crisis. My family didn't understand why I was dropping out of college after a year and a half, so moving back home was really difficult. Although I was suffering from anxiety and panic attacks, I knew that there was a reason for them. I had always grown up with a protective stance toward the feeling part of myself and knew that I wanted to understand that better.

For a couple of years I worked with therapies that used modalities that were feeling based. I was very wary about any cognitive approaches that could result in denying feelings, like desensitization techniques to break anxiety cycles. That might work on a symptomatic level, but that didn't ring true for me. I really felt that there was something important about my feelings that I needed to explore and let out. I was involved in a couple of therapy groups, and those were transforming for me, because I was able to see myself valued as an individual in a group. The group could see David—"Wow David, we're glad you're here. You contribute this great energy. You're really important."

I started taking some part-time weekend and night courses which were mostly visual and performances art classes with small groups of eight or ten people. Everyone had an opportunity to share ideas in class. Except for the group projects in fifth grade, that was a completely rare and new experience for me, and I realized that this was how I needed to learn. So when I did a search for colleges to continue my undergraduate degree, one of my main criteria was student/teacher ratio. That's how I ended up choosing College of the Atlantic, a small alternative college in Bar Harbor, Maine. I knew that I needed to be able to see myself valued in a group. To sit in a huge lecture hall with four hundred people with a professor down there at the bottom with a huge screen, taking notes and then going off into my own little world and doing the readings was really difficult for me.

The Whole World Was Contained in that Circle

A number of positive learning opportunities opened up for me at COA. My writing moved along there, because of the sheer volume of papers required in conjunction with the freedom I had to develop my own formats. The teachers put the responsibility on me to decide what I wanted for an outcome. In the process of developing and expressing my ideas, I cracked open some writing reference books to learn more about the fundamentals. Learning skills in the service of my goals is the most effective way for me to learn them.

One of my early high points at COA was during an education class. Our teacher, Peter, ran it as a seminar. We were divided up into interest groups and each group ran the class for two weeks. One particular moment touched me deeply, and I still remember it vividly. My group, the "Arts and Education" group, did the culminating class. We had created eight stations to travel through with different art modalities connected to a theme. At the end we had a sharing component involving group movement and vocalization. At one point, we were in a big arm-in-arm circle chanting. All of a sudden I felt so connected to everything, not just the people in the room; it was like the ceiling opened up, and the whole world was contained in that circle!

I Relished that Intimate Sharing of an Inner Experience

While I was at COA, I participated in a number of dance and movement classes in the local community. I remembered how much I had enjoyed my dance class at Penn State. Actually from the age of about seven or eight I always found myself moving to music. When given the opportunity, I would express myself that way.

I took improvisational movement, modern dance and African dance. I felt really sparked by that, and I also felt a part of the larger community. Two of my teachers, Joan and Don, sometimes put on concerts. A few of us participated with them doing improvisational dance. Out of these informal concerts grew a core group of us, who practiced and performed together; we became known as "The Motion Collective."

At first "The Motion Collective" did a couple of concerts a year, mostly improvisational in nature. But recently, over the past several years, we have been invited to perform all over the state of Maine doing about six concerts a year. I remember the first dance that I choreographed. It was an experience similar to the fifth grade frontier cabin project in that it gave me an opportunity to take an idea and bring it to life. The big thrill for me has been when members of the audience come up to me after a concert and share their experience of our work, and I find that it was akin to what I was attempting to express—especially when the piece is more of an abstract concept. For example one piece I choreographed was about a larger order in nature. The movements were piece-oriented but when put together I attempted to convey an overall flow, an unfolding. A woman came up to me after the concert and told me that the piece reminded her of seeing a time lapse film of flowers going from bud to bloom. I relished that intimate sharing of an inner experience.

I Noted Hearing the First Calls of the Spring Peepers

The type of teaching that I'm drawn to now reflects that intimacy of connection and co-creation that I have experienced in my dance group. This year I co-taught a class on creative movement for adults. We worked in groups and used writing, art, and other modalities along with movement. It was very much about play, but there was also work in the play. I have learned a lot about how to facilitate a group to feel comfortable. Typically I would have a plan for the full hour-and-a-half class, but this would often grow and evolve depending on where the students took it. One night I was really flowing with the group's energy. The group transformed into children dancing on a playground. No one was inhibited. We were all moving in the same vein, inspired by the music. I remember driving home that night, hearing the first calls of the spring peepers—a "spring is almost here" kind of feeling.

It's Really About Who We Are and Who We Are Becoming

I still sometimes struggle with the question of what I want to be when I grow up. After college, I became certified as a teacher and taught in schools for a few years. When I was an elementary school teacher, I tried to bring creative spirit to every subject, but it was a lot of work. I applaud teachers that are successful at that, but I got bogged down in the details of classroom teaching and never did it long enough to learn to do it well.

I now have a part-time job which gives me flexibility and a steady income, allowing me to explore dance opportunities on my own time. I've been pleasantly surprised that over the past two years, increasingly, a percentage of my annual income has come from work related to dance.

Recently, while I was involved with a major choreographing project for an opera, I was devoting so much time to it daily, that this question about my future just dropped away. I was doing and being at the same time; it was total engagement. I'm now at the ripe old age of thirty-five, and most dancers are younger—but that doesn't matter. I want to be dancing as long as I'm breathing.

Unfortunately in this culture, dance is not looked on as a serious art form; it's seen more as a social function. But the older I get, I'm becoming convinced that to be a dancer is just as valid an occupation as a postal worker, a scientist, or a therapist. And that, yes, dancers are intelligent and articulate and that they can grow in that intellect. It's not just about your body, because some of the best dancers I've met are some of the most amazing, intelligent and creative people that I've seen on this planet.

Also on a play level, there's a joy that I get in dancing. I'm one of those dancers that will dance anything. I also go to social dances, and I often have people come up to me at these dances and tell me, "I want you to know how much fun it is for me to watch you dance." After I deal with how hard it is for me to let something like that in, I realize how I'm giving to other people by being myself in that way.

We build these structures around us, like our economics and our jobs, to keep us contained or afloat to survive, but it's really about, in the larger meaning of life, who we are and who we are becoming. Unless I'm moving from that elemental space, I'm not open to change and growth. It's so closely related to dance. If I really let myself into the movement fully in the moment, it opens up all kinds of possibilities. Full engagement means opening up to unknown outcomes, living my whole life as a dance.

The Crux of It All Is that Each of Us Has a Unique Gift

Just recently, The Maine Alliance for Arts Education asked me to give a professional development workshop for teachers, "Integrating Movement and Dance Across Your Curriculum." One of the participants came in, seemingly in a rush, saying she was going to have to leave early. I could feel that she was nervous about being there.

I started the workshop with some movement activities through which everyone got to learn a bit about each others' background. We imaged a map on the floor and I told them, "Go to your place of maternal origin." Then, "Give me an image or a short story that was told to you about this relative when you were growing up." One woman said, "I remember my great grandmother sitting on her bed in the morning with her hair down, and it was so long it went down to her knees, and she would brush it like this." From this gesture, she generated a movement and others did, as well, from their stories. Then we put these movements together into a short dance. Remarkably, when I turned on background music, the performance that happened in that moment couldn't have worked out better if we had worked on choreographing it for months. The simplest gesture in their hand became elegant, because it came from an authentic place, a place within their own lives. They truly embodied the movements, because they were coming from the inside out. This is a sharp contrast to a focus on technique, unfortunately the way much art is being taught in our schools. Exploration from the outside in does not tend to elicit the authentic hookup of the inner experience.

After this initial activity, the teacher who was at first in such a hurry to leave went out and made a phone call and stayed for the rest of the workshop. At the end of our time, as I was wrapping everything up, this woman stepped in and said, "Before we go I want each of us to go around and say something that touched us personally in this workshop." As she began to facilitate the group in this personal sharing time, I thought, "God this is great; this is what it's all about!"

One of the last exercises I did in this workshop was about how you can make a dance about anything. You can take a topic like "Endangered Species" and offer an option to do a dance for a final project. It's just as valid a process as writing a paper. I broke down how the scientific process in an experiment, the writing process, and the creative process of making a dance follow almost exactly the same steps and sequences. Once you get familiar with the vocabulary of movement, you can realize that movement is a very valid way of being in and experiencing the world.

My hope is that these teachers will bring these modalities to the children in their classrooms, especially those children inclined towards movement as I was. When I spontaneously choreographed that dance piece in fifth grade, I didn't even know to call what I did dance. Given some exposure and support for dance expression, children will be able to see that dance can be a richly expressive modality for learning.

The crux of it all is that each of us has a unique gift, a talent that we may not even recognize as special. If we could be encouraged to pursue that, this could so enhance our learning. We could pick up the skills we needed in service of that. And most importantly, we would feel a validation of our own inner learning strengths.

I now know enough about myself to validate that I need to be that way in the world, learning and communicating through my body in dance.

Emily's story portrays a learner who insisted on following her sense of personal purpose at all costs. While she loved learning on her own terms, Emily's refusal to do required school work set her apart from the main classroom program and her peers, leading to her placement in middle school in a class for behaviorally disturbed children. Emily experienced some bright lights in high school and more in college as she was given greater flexibility to manifest her considerable learning strengths. In her Teacher Education Program in college, while Emily continued to give only minimum attention to written work, she did extensive, outstanding volunteer work in schools. Coming full circle to become the teacher she would have benefited from, Emily reveals that high level learning involves the self-directed pursuit of one's passion.

> I hate school. They make you do
> work for no apparent reason.
>
> —Andrew Allen
> A creatively gifted nine-year-old

Emily's Story

This Is a Safe Place

One of my earliest school memories is trying to explain to someone that I really liked learning, but I really didn't like school. From first grade on, I was sent to the resource room because I wasn't doing any work in my class. Both resource room and classroom teachers saw me as an intelligent, capable learner, and my classroom teachers were clear that I was understanding everything, but they couldn't get me to do any assigned work.

My experience of the resource room generally was, "This is a safe place. There are not many people, and I'm not getting picked on." The resource room teachers did not make me do the classroom work. Along with literacy skills work, we read books together and then watched movies related to the books. We chose personal reading books and activities based on our reading (I was reading way beyond my grade level—for example, I was reading Tolkein's *The Lord of the Rings* in third grade). The other students in the resource room were there for special assistance, and they paired me up with them to help their skills.

I Never Understood the Point of the Work

In fourth grade my teacher decided that I should be friends with a girl named Diana; she put us together and said, "Be friends now," and it worked. In fifth grade the two of us worked out a cooperative system for getting our work done. Diana's language skills were underdeveloped as Portuguese, not English, was her primary language. I helped her do the homework, and she would write down a copy for each of us.

Doing work just for myself didn't seem to be useful. I never understood the point of the work, and nobody was able to explain the point satisfactorily enough so that I was willing to do it. And so if there is no point in it, then why bother. I could see that for Diana there was a purpose in doing it. If we sat down and did it together, she would learn something. So I got my work done that year through Diana. I don't know how we got away with it, because Diana had nice handwriting and I didn't, so the teacher had to know that it wasn't my work.

Learning Was Important to Me

I did so little work in sixth grade that at the end of the year they considered holding me back. However, my fifth grade testing showed most of my skills on grade level and beyond: I tested at an eleventh grade reading level; after I finally memorized my multiplication tables, my math was right up there; my understanding of things was very clear and my vocabulary was superior. I didn't often write, however, and it was clear that writing was something I could not do well. What I did write was short and concise. Throughout school I thought that I was smart. Learning was important to me. If they would have left me alone and let me learn, I would have been happy.

The consensus was to send me on to seventh grade but to put me in the self-contained special education classroom for behaviorally disturbed children. At first it was very strange—the kids in my group played a lot of pranks. Our teacher left after two days. We were told that he had taken another job. After a string of short-term substitutes, we got a teacher who stayed. Things stabilized fast after she got there. She was able to allow all of us to be who we were.

We did some mainstreaming. I attended Spanish and science classes the first year. I did well in Spanish and fine in the second semester of science after doing poorly the first semester with a teacher I didn't like. In eighth grade they wanted to mainstream me in math. My mother asked that I go into the upper level pre-algebra class, however the administration wanted me to go into the regular eighth grade math class, because I had not been mainstreamed in math in seventh grade—even though I had already gone through most of the eighth grade text book at my own pace. The regular eighth grade math class was O.K., but boring. I already knew it all, but I liked the teacher, and that always made a big difference related to how much I was willing to do, willing to show them.

In high school they didn't have the disturbed class. They had a special program called the Interdepartmental Studies Program, but were wary about letting special education kids into it, because the demands were a lot higher. But it was written into my IEP (Individualized Education Program) that I be in the Interdepartmental Studies Program because it seemed liked the best place for me. The program had classes that were interdepartmental in nature. Examples are: a science/PE class that did hikes and nature walks and a humanities/Western civilization class in which all of the reading we were doing for humanities paralleled the time period we were studying in Western civilization. Students called teachers by their first names. Everyone was equal, sharing in the learning. All of a sudden, I wasn't the scapegoat, because I had a peer group that respected me. They were nice, and they were there to learn. I remember liking ninth grade mostly because of the ISP program. I still didn't do any homework or writing, but I contributed enough to pass.

Things Weren't Going Quite So Well

Tenth grade came and I don't know what shifted, but things weren't going quite so well. I had been doing poorly in an ISP writing class, because I wasn't writing. So I was transferred to a tenth grade English class which consisted of, "Here's your blue book of vocabulary words and here's your grammar text book." The first day that I was in there, I went through the vocabulary book, and I circled the only five words that I didn't know. I went to the teacher afterwards and I said, "I know all but these words, and I will look them up now if you want." I was told that I had to go along with the rest of the class. I have no recollection of whether I passed that class or not.

I was assigned a therapist at my high school because of my attitude. She told my mother that everything would be okay if I would just wear mini-skirts and earrings—if I would just try to fit in. I had a nightmare that, still to this day, I remember vividly. I woke up in the morning on the day I was to see my therapist. She came and picked me up, but she wouldn't let me go. She kidnapped me for the entire day. At the end of the day, I was back home. It was one of those very vivid dreams that made me question whether or not it might really have happened.

It Was Fun!

About half way through the year, I had a friend who attended a small private alternative school around the corner from my high school. The school had about forty students and was aimed at kids who would otherwise drop out. I started hanging out with them after my school got out (their school day was longer). Just before Christmas time, I started skipping high school to hang out there all day. I had already met all of the teachers and blended in well with the other students. After the second week of doing this, the headmaster came to me and said, "You know. I'm sure that somebody has noticed or will notice shortly that you're not in school, and people might start to worry about you. We would really like to have you as a student here, but maybe we should go through official channels." That school and my school wanted me to transfer, but my mother said, "No. She's not going to give up and quit halfway through the year. We'll look at schools for next fall, but she's going to have to finish what she started this year." So I had to stay at my public high school during the school day.

Meanwhile, I got to be part of the alternative school's after-school theater program which was just fabulous. I helped them out with a play they had written about Picasso. They built a set with multidimensional things from the painting "Guernica." I helped them with the set, and I helped students learn their lines. I sat with the teacher and gave critique, and it was fun! The next semester we wrote a play based on Paul Klee's paintings, and I acted in that even though I had not matriculated.

Just Do the Challenge Problems

My mother and I investigated alternative schools for my junior year. We found the Cambridge school, which really clicked for me, because when I talked with some of the students and the faculty, I felt that they respected the students as learners and allowed them to be who they were. And not many mini-skirts were worn except by some of the boys. It was democratic in nature. The students, the faculty, the staff and some of the townspeople all had equal vote in the school meetings. For me the school really worked. The faculty was there because they wanted to be with the kids. I became deeply connected to a number of them and that made a big difference in my investment in my learning.

At the Cambridge school, I also, for the first time, developed really good friendships with a peer group within my school. In elementary school, while I related well to children older and younger than myself, I had great difficulty relating to my peers; I was teased a lot and hated that. In eighth grade I developed my first good friendships with a peer group outside of school through an MIT program which offered unusual classes like ESP. The program was attended by a bunch of misfits like myself who didn't fit into standard programs and really wanted to learn. I first met some of the kids I hung out with at the alternative high school there. But until the Cambridge school, I did not have a sustained, satisfying peer group within my school.

Academically, I don't think that I did any more work than I had been doing before, but I was allowed to express what I understood in different ways. My algebra II teacher, Maxine, let me sleep in class if she was going over material for the second or third time, because she knew I had gotten it the first time. She would nudge me if she was starting something new. Her ego wasn't running her—she didn't need me to be paying attention for her sake. When we went on to trigonometry, another student and I were allowed to go out into the hall and do as much of the work as we could, coming back in if we needed help. When Maxine realized I wasn't turning any homework in, she said, "Just do the challenge problems." In contrast, in my tenth grade biology class at my former high school, I was driving my teacher nuts, because I was scoring higher than anyone else on the tests, but I wasn't turning in any homework. Homework represented a third of the grade. He couldn't change his grading scheme for one student, but he didn't want me to fail . . .

I did have to write some papers at the Cambridge school. I took Short Story and I wrote a couple of short stories. They were *very* short—one was less than a full page of lined paper. When I tried to write on paper, I could not get the ideas down as fast as I thought of them, and then they went away. Also, on paper, I couldn't just backspace and rewrite it. And I had this constant editor thing going on. If I was thinking about a story, and I tried to write it down, by the time I got to the third word my brain already edited it out saying, "Nope, that's no good."

I started using the computer at the Cambridge school for some things like German homework. I did the German homework because I was responsible for getting my friend, Matt, to do the homework. He was equally clever and didn't have a problem with any of the concepts, but we found it more fun to do assignments together. So I made him sit down, and when we were supposed to write a couple of paragraphs in German, we would together write a three page story with dialogue, back and forth—an extension of a conversation we were having fun with anyway. We were able to play off each other and get it done. And I think that being able to do it on the computer helped—that hadn't been an option for me before.

At the Cambridge school, if you were knowledgeable in an area and showed responsibility, you could be a guild master in that area. I became a guild master for the computer lab. I had a key and anytime I wanted, I could open it up and have other students come in; I was responsible for what went on in there.

If Only She Would Do Some Work

The college that I went to, College of the Atlantic (COA), was similar to the Cambridge school in many respects. My evaluations from COA were much the same as those from the Cambridge school. Most of them said, "Emily really excels in this area; she could go further in this area if only she would do some work. I would gladly give Emily an A in this course, but she didn't hand any assignments in, so I can only give her a C."

I majored in elementary education. I had a practicum with one of my instructors in a K-2 classroom in a small island school where she taught special education one day a week. After that course was over, I continued to volunteer there for the next term and then followed my instructor to the school where she taught kindergarten for two years. I volunteered in the kindergarten and a fifth grade where I eventually did my student teaching. My COA teacher felt that I had developed unusual expertise in teaching remedial readers, and I worked with a group of troubled readers as a part of my student teaching experience. That worked out really well for me and the kids.

Oh Good, You're Wearing Running Shoes

After college, I moved to Oregon and began teaching in a private school. Eventually, I moved into special education, beginning as a substitute teacher at the Farm Home School, a public school that served children who were in a residential treatment facility for emotionally disturbed children. I made good impressions as a sub and was hired as an assistant teacher. The first thing that my co-teacher said to me was, "Oh good, you're wearing running shoes." Four of the kids from the program had run away the night before, and they knew that could happen again at any moment. I spent the morning in her classroom, and in the afternoon I worked with an amazing teacher who taught horticulture. He gave these kids (who were in some cases violent and in all cases severely emotionally disturbed) pruning shears and took them on walks to the slough—he had absolutely no concerns. One boy, who had been there for three or four years, had been able to connect with this man so well that he opened up for the first time in his life and began working through his emotional issues. Watching this teacher with these kids was a tremendous experience.

Eventually, I was given a permanent position at the school. My strength lay in my ability to connect with the kids by allowing them to be who they were and giving them freedom to move past that. I also honored their interests. I worked with an older boy one-on-one, at first. He couldn't be with the other kids because of his behavioral issues (they were actually afraid to have him alone with one or two adults because he had been violent—I never saw that). I thought he was pretty neat. He had a really strong interest in tornadoes, so we made use of that and did a whole curriculum unit on tornadoes.

The Editor Works Less Well After Midnight

I started taking graduate courses at Western, at first to get a special education certificate and then my masters in special education. My first class was called, "Programming for the Seriously Emotionally Disturbed." Since I had already been working at the Farm Home School for a couple of years, I felt that I had a good grounding in the subject. The teacher pulled me aside after the first class during which we had shared our previous experience. She asked me, "Are you sure you want to take this class? I'm not sure we have anything to offer you?" In fact, there was a lot of knowledge that I already had, but the class helped me to put all of the pieces I had learned into place and gave me some extra tools. And I really liked the teacher; she was wonderful.

In my graduate work, I was surprised to discover that for the first time I was actually able to write. At first, I believe I was motivated by my need to do the work toward qualifying for my credential. If my purpose was to get the credits, then I *had* to produce the work that was required (if I simply want to learn something for myself, then it doesn't matter to me what I produce for the teacher). But that class also turned out to be meaningful learning for me, and I don't know if I would have been able to do the required writing if it had felt less purposeful.

Also, I wrote a lot of my papers starting about one o'clock the night before they were due, and the editor works less well after midnight. And I eventually got better at starting earlier. There were a couple of pieces that I started a few days before they were due, although I always finished them the night before; I always wrote only a first draft.

I decided to go on for my masters. I did well—A's in most of my classes—and at first, that was really shocking. I connected well with the teachers in my program, and I knew what I was doing. I did the written work, because it was important toward meeting my goal, *and* because I was allowed to make the work purposeful. In that first course, the teacher set up the work be meaningful. She would present a scenario about a group of kids and say, "Talk about how you would handle this situation or talk about a real situation that you have had." Based on that model, I asked to continue tapping my personal experiences in my other courses. In the two courses that I received B's, the teachers did not allow me to do that.

Full Circle

My job now is teaching in a self-contained middle school classroom for severely emotionally disturbed children. It is full circle for me, because it is a class similar to my middle school class. During the first week of in-service before I met the kids, all of the teachers told me, "Good luck!" I was told all kinds of horror stories about the last year, about how awful the kids were—chairs being thrown, kids running away etc. I heard that the children had had a string of substitute teachers. This was similar to the beginning of my own middle school experience—those children had gone through exactly what I had gone through.

But I came in and met these kids, and they were wonderful. Clearly part of the difference for them was the atmosphere they experienced the very first day. There was a level of comfort and stability that I brought into the classroom just by walking in. I wasn't afraid of them; I welcomed who they were. I have a class of six children who are happy and are finding success. I begin the class with a morning group where we set goals—everyone sets a daily goal and a weekly goal. We talk about any concerns or excitements that have happened at home; everyone gets their turn in the spotlight. I give a timed multiplication test just for fun, because some kids set this as a goal and the others like the routine. Most of them never knew their multiplication tables before, but now almost all of them are through the basic ones. So now they feel better about knowing their multiplication tables. I felt really weird when I first started doing that, because it seemed wrong to be spending time memorizing multiplication tables, but it was something that they wanted to do, and it can be useful if you can just do it. Then I read to the kids, and we also read together. I ask them to write responses after I read, and sometimes I ask them to draw a response. I also have them respond to each other in their reading journals. Sometimes I ask the children to write questions about the reading, and I choose some of these for a chapter test.

We do story problems in math. I focus on, "What is this asking us?" I use ideas from the Real Math text. Everybody has a workbook for computation. Two of the kids are working at some really basic levels of number concepts, some of the kids are working on fractions, and one student is working on algebra.

We write about everything. There is a boy who writes like I used to write—he's desperately afraid it's wrong. At Halloween time he wrote a great story about killer candy corn. At first, his story was two sentences long. So we asked him, "if somebody read this book, what would they want to know?" Together we wrote down a series of questions, and he answered them, expanding his story. One writing activity that really took off was a class newspaper of stories including interviews the kids did with various people in the school, even the principal. One of the boys did an advice column—all of the other kids wrote him questions which he answered.

I've had lots of comments at my school about how wonderful I am, how amazing I am. But I want to say, "Hey, I'm not doing anything out of the ordinary." When I first started working at the Farm Home School, I drew on my own experiences of school, giving the kids what I had needed. I have continued to teach this way. For all of the children who are struggling as I struggled, I wish for them to have teachers who can see them for who they are and can see past what they want the kids to produce to what the kids want to produce, finding other ways to see that they are meeting specific requirements.

Addendum

A number of years after this interview, I had a phone update with Emily. She has moved to a small, remote Eskimo village in Alaska where she is in her fourth year of teaching (formerly special education and currently literacy) in a K-12 school. She continues to love her work. She also told me that she had won a first prize and an honorable mention for short stories she submitted to a quarterly internet writing contest, Writers Weekly. The contest is capped at five hundred entries. After a prompt is posted, participants have twenty-four hours to submit their stories (we laughed about how the editor works less well within a short time limit). Emily is also writing a series of essays about her life in the village and her teaching, which she intends to publish someday in a book.

Bob K's story describes an intriguing profile of an interpersonally gifted learner. From a very early age Bob showed remarkable leadership skills sourced from his intuitive understanding of others' needs and strengths. His story shares his poignant struggle to validate his particular kind of intelligence despite his difficulty with traditional academics, a struggle many highly intuitive individuals have in a culture that lauds rational, logical thinking. I believe that recognition of his interpersonal orientation in his schooling would have relieved much of Bob's anguish and lifted his learning to a joyful plane. Today, a part of Bob's counseling practice is devoted to validating those, who like himself, have unusual, nontraditional abilities.

> We will discover the nature of our particular
> genius when we stop trying to conform to our
> own or to other people's models, learn to be
> ourselves, and allow our natural channel to open.
> —Shakti Gawan

Bob K.'s Story

I Was the One Orchestrating the March

My earliest learning memory was of kindergarten. I remember being with a group of kids and stringing large, multi-colored beads making a thing you could put across your chest like a belt, like those things a crossing guard wears. Then we marched around, and I was the one orchestrating the march.

My next memory, which connects to that, is a story my mother told me about her experience at a parent-teacher conference when I was in the third grade. We kids were out on the playground at the time. The teacher told my mother, "Look out on the playground. Within five minutes all of the other kids will be looking to Bob for direction, and he will give direction in a way they will all take and be happy with. They will all be accounted for and everything will be fine." My mother told me that's what happened over the next five minutes. It all got organized and everybody was happy doing whatever they were doing. I also remember that year a classmate that I took under my wing who did not have a father. He was always acting up, and I could see the things he needed to do in order to stay out of trouble. I helped him stay out of trouble all that year. I looked after him and included him in our play. I guess that is where, for me, the greatest satisfaction was in school.

One experience that really stands out was being captain of the safety patrol in sixth grade. That job included organizing all the corner-crossing posts, sitting down with the lieutenants and figuring out where the posts should be and who ideally should be on each of the posts. I loved that kind of responsibility; it sustained me more than anything else. I took into account who these different kids were and what they were like, where the busy corners were and who could handle those, and where they lived in relation to those corners. I put all those pieces together to make it work. I had the lieutenants check in on the kids at certain intervals enabling us to discuss that kind of thing. It was a group process in which we paid attention to what people were about. It felt like we were "reading" people.

I would end up in those kinds of positions all the time in school. That's where I would shine; that's where the teachers appreciated me, although occasionally I ran into a teacher who didn't like me. My fourth grade teacher, I think, didn't like my having so much authority, power, control, and influence. That teacher wanted to put me in my place and looked at me with a certain eye I found very disturbing which made me sick to my stomach. I can still feel just how toxic that felt to me. I had, however, only two or three teachers my whole kindergarten through high school life who treated me that way.

It Was Like a Kick in the Chest

I got good grades, all A's and B's, but I felt like I was struggling; I felt like I should have been doing better than I was doing. I remember the first time I got a C in a science course in the seventh grade. That was the year we changed to a junior high. I was reassured that it can happen when you go to a new, bigger school. However, I was so mortified and humiliated by getting that C that I really scrambled to make sure that didn't happen again. I felt like I was smart on the one hand, but on the other hand, I felt like I was not smart. I felt that the really smart kids seemed more comfortable than I was and didn't have the struggle I was going through internally.

I received the same confirmation that I was a B, B+ student instead of an A student from my guidance counselor in high school, who called me in and said, "You're an overachiever." I was mortified. I remember that it felt like a kick in the chest, physically. I asked him what he meant by that. He said, "Well, you get good grades, but you obviously have to work really hard to get them." I said, "I don't work hard to get those grades. Maybe I do a half-hour to one hour of homework a night. I mostly get my work done between classes." He said, "Well, of course you're saying that you don't work really hard, but you obviously have to study a lot to get the grades that you get." I denied this again. I was really furious inside, but I would never show that. It was a huge blow to me to have the confirmation that, while I was certainly above average, I was not smart. Also with the tracking they did at the time, I was never in the accelerated classes. I was always in the good classes, but never with my friends who were in the accelerated classes. While I felt like I could do those classes on the one hand, I also felt intimidated. For example, I did everything I could to avoid taking physics, because I thought physics was the hardest kind of math-science course to take.

Looking back, I feel that I was hungry for something. I think that I needed more depth in my life, but had no way of understanding that at the time. I wanted to be seen and recognized for who I was and who I could become, but at that time grades were the ultimate stamp of recognition.

As I made plans about college, I signed up for the SAT exam. I went to the exam and I feigned illness, put my head down on the desk and had to leave. I never took the SAT again, because I had decided that the ACT was easier than the SAT. I don't know if it was or not back then, but that's what I had decided. I took the ACT, because I knew that was the one I had to have to get into Western Michigan University, where I felt most comfortable going. Although I really wanted to go to the University of Michigan or Michigan State University, I didn't apply to them because I didn't think I was smart enough to do well in those places.

I attended Western Michigan continuing to earn a grade-point average of about 3.3. It was the same pattern all the way through, not believing that I could really consider doing courses at a higher level. And I would never consider any professions which I thought required high intelligence. At the time I knew that the smart people went into law and medicine, and I believed that there was no way I could do the volume of reading and memorization required for either graduate program. They were out of the ballpark.

Yet I Still Have a Yearning

I do remember two experiences in junior high and secondary school that were in some measure better for me. The first, in junior high school, was when my social studies teacher set up a newspaper project for learning American history. I was the editor, which meant I got to organize the newspaper. I figured out what articles should be written and who would be best for writing them. I would then give out the assignments and organize the process for putting the paper together. That project, along with another experience I had in high school, was probably the best educational experience I've had in school.

The second experience was when I was the point guard on the basketball team. I got to decide, with every defensive, where we were going to set up on the floor, whether it would be a full or half court press, or a trapping defense once they came down and got into their set. I was in charge of that, and I gave the signals for that. I ran the offense, as well. I would start out with the ball and decide what set we were going to run.

As I remember these experiences, I feel a deep sense of loss as well, because I never had the proper mentoring in those roles that really allowed me to see what was possible and to truly value my abilities. I needed that. Yes, those teachers recognized I was capable, but basically what they said was, "Do it," and left me to my own devices. That is fine to some extent. However, in terms of teaching and taking people where they need to go, you need to recognize what they're about and help them find experiences to support further growth—then, mentor them, teach them, and help them get to a higher level of operation.

I didn't get that kind of mentoring then, in college, at graduate school, or really at any time in my life. I've gone into whatever new territory I could on my own and have done the best I could with it. I can get philosophical about that and say, "That's part of the story of your life and what it's about. That's not what you need; it's what you think you need. Even though there is that sense of loss, there are lots of losses and you have a good life; do what you can with it." Yet, I still have a yearning. I still feel it emotionally right in my chest—a real yearning for a mentor. I've always gotten recognition, but I think that's different from the kind of validation that I've needed on a deeper level to open certain doors.

It Was Always in the Wrong Order

One subject that I had a great deal of difficulty with throughout my education was writing. I really wanted to write well. I would get excited about doing something in an English class, and then my paper would come back really marked up—awkward sentence etc. It didn't make any sense to me, because I felt I had expressed myself well. Everything was there, but it was always in the wrong order. I never knew what to do about it and ended up feeling really badly about my writing skills. It kept me from initiating any kind of writing at all, other than some poetry. Poetry connects with a whole different part of my brain. It doesn't have to be in logical sequence.

Ten years ago I had testing for learning disabilities, and one of my documented disabilities was sequencing. The basic upshot for me with writing is that while all the ideas are there, they are never going to be in an order that makes any real sense. Somebody's got to look that over and put it in the right order for me. So that is what I do now, and it has taken me ten years to accept that it's okay. *And* I am much more fluent verbally than I am in writing. I recognize that my linguistic abilities are not primarily with the written word, but more so verbal, because I am much more inter-personally driven in my style.

Part of my sequencing problem also manifested in my slow processing of reading. When I took freshman English in high school, I had to read eight novels and take a multiple choice test on them. I knew I could not read eight novels in one semester, so I would read the first and last chapters. Then I would meet with two friends who were smart, good readers and listen to them talk about the books, asking a few questions. I'd go and take the test and get a B on it without having read those eight books.

And that is a real clue to my learning style, which is again much more inter-personally driven. That is how I learn things. In my counseling practice, I have been able to talk with a variety of people, and I have learned about so many things that a lot of people learn about in novels or informational literature. I get that from talking with people.

Connected to my interpersonal orientation, I did do some unusual writing about eight years ago. I wrote a series of twenty-seven short pieces based on my memories of being an Armenian American boy. I called them *My Armenian Stories*. I began by telling the story about going to the shoe store to buy shoes. I called it, "The Shoe Man." I wrote it in the voice and vision of a little Armenian American boy. To me these stories are very funny. I don't know if they would be funny to anybody else, but I can pick up one of those stories today and laugh hysterically, even though I've read it so many times. It was part of a process of pulling something together about my ethnic identity, integrating my life better, and making sense of my growing up. It was fun for me to do that. And the difference with that writing was the interpersonal process, telling stories.

An impediment to my writing has also been my conception that I thought you were supposed to have a goal, to know where you were starting and where you were going, and to understand what the steps were to make sure that goal happened. What I discovered in the process of writing the Armenian stories was that if I tried to do that, I couldn't. Instead, I wrote the alleged goal, the gist of the story, down as the first sentence and went into the unknown from wide open spaces, saying whatever I wanted to say, rather than writing coherent, sequential steps. And there wasn't any trouble with sequencing when I did that.

In contrast, when I took the test for the learning disabilities and the examiner put down five mixed-up picture cards and asked me to put them in order, I struggled with that. I looked at the five picture cards and, of course, I knew what the story was immediately. It wasn't that complicated, but I couldn't feel confident about the correct sequencing. When I finally completed an order I said, "I don't know, maybe the first one should really be last and the last one should be first." How could I be saying that when I knew what the story was? That represents that whole mess for me of trying to make sense of something from a particular frame of reference.

In My Work, I Go into a Different Zone

The other part of the testing story that is interesting to me is that the pattern that came out of my scores and responses indicated a person who is highly distractible and has an attention deficit/ hyperactivity disorder. The person who did the testing knew me well enough to know that I am a very competent, professional counselor and basically said, bluntly but nicely, "How the hell can you be doing this work with people if you are this distractible, and you have this much trouble with sequencing?" My instantaneous response was that I don't listen to my clients from the point of view of trying to get things in order. That's not the point, and it's a waste of time. Maybe other people do that, and they need to line up certain things sequentially and logically so they can hang other things on it, but that's not how I operate.

For me, my work centers around emotional affect and something interactional that I understand about my clients. In my work, I go into a different zone. I don't mean to imply that I sit here, get into an altered state and do something mystical. I simply become present, available, and open. I think there is a way my mind—my whole self—doesn't expect to be in a logical process, at least a certain kind of logical process. It is a different way of relating that I call intuitive. When connecting intuitively with another individual, I move into a process of authentic guidance that I can trust. In the process of connecting and being present, available, and open, my intuition lights up.

In some way I feel (it's a funny way to put it) like I'm worthless on my own. I need other people. If you wind me up properly and put me in a place where there is someone else who is breathing, I will come alive. I will participate in a way that makes things work. If I'm not connected, then I can easily get bored. I can feel stupid and depressed. It's taken me a long time to understand what that's about. Learning about the theory of multiple intelligences (from Howard Gardner's *Frames of Mind: The Theory of Multiple Intelligences*) and the existence of an "interpersonal intelligence" as a primary language of comprehension and expression, has given me a tool to make sense of and value my own experience—to realize it is trustworthy and helpful.

I have also learned that I need to be involved in multiple ideas because of the circular nature of intuition. They are all related on that circular level. I learn not just through interactions with people but through interactions with ideas, and there is a way I can move amongst these ideas in some circular, spiral fashion, seeing the interconnections between them. There is an optimal level of stimulation for me that allows everything to work with everything feeding off of each other. But I can get overloaded, and if I have too much stimulation, I can't reach the depth I want to achieve.

Last month, for example, I had four or five different projects in which I was participating, such as presentations, educational programs, and workshops. I initially felt I was a little too busy, but, interestingly, I did not panic about them the way I might have some years ago. In the past I told myself, "I have this thing to do, and I have to sit down and make time to do it." That's what I learned in school, that's what they teach you about homework—to sit down and make time to do it—only that doesn't work for me. Last month, as soon as I had the conversation with somebody about what they wanted me to do, I had a flood of ideas which I immediately wrote down in list fashion. Then, I trusted an incubation process for those ideas to ripen. I trusted that I would be able to move from that flight of ideas to pulling it all together. Over the next weeks as other thoughts popped into my mind I jotted them down in the same fashion. I planned time on a Saturday to pull everything together. On that day, when I opened up my folder of ideas, the project was basically done. It was just a matter of moving things around, fleshing a few things out here and there, and then interacting with my wife about it so that I could give it the life it needed. Then, the next week, I polished it off.

There is a whole process before the sitting down time, that is invisible, that is really what is accountable, although not quantifiable in terms of time. Sometimes I can do something like that and spend maybe only a few hours of actual sit-down time to pull it together. But there's been a lot of thought and movement around it over several weeks. Learning to validate that process has taken me a lifetime. I'm only now feeling like I get it. I am not a procrastinator; I'm not stupid; I'm not irresponsible, and I'm *not* undisciplined.

I'm Working Like a Maniac to Read

When counseling my clients, I'm riveted and focused, but in other situations my mind is all over the place. I felt terribly restless at school—I can almost feel myself rocking in the chair. I writhed around trying to do homework, because I found it so difficult to attend to. My mind was just all over the place, and I struggled to read. I had a reading evaluation done around ten years ago, because I thought I didn't read very well and thought that maybe someone could help me.

The upshot of that evaluation was that I read fine. My comprehension was fine, and my rate was fine. I kept saying, "You don't understand what I go through when I read. I'm working like a maniac to read. Yes, I'm finishing this within certain norms, and I can tell you what I've read. However, you don't see what's going on during the process for me. I'm rereading things, and my mind is going all over the place; I'm exhausted. I know I haven't gotten all the details that I am capable of getting here."

There are times, though, when reading feels different for me. It could be a novel, a book on education, a psychology book—it could be anything. It's books I feel a certain personal connection to, that easily and cleanly allow me to follow the thread right through them. If I'm reading something for a reading evaluation, a contrivance for the test, I'm going to have difficulty with it because it's not real to me. Whereas, some people—maybe a lot of people—can read that as purely reading.

It's the Most Grounded Thing I Have Ever Known

I never got much out of my course work in college, but I had a really valuable experience as an Resident Assistant in my dorm. They had an experimental program where the eight RA's met one evening a week with two counselors from the university counseling center. I had never experienced anything like that before. After one of the groups, I made a comment about finding it really interesting. One of the counselors said they were starting an experimental program at the university counseling center, where they were going to accept two undergraduates into the graduate practicum to be a part of weekly meetings and be at the center ten hours a week or so. They would sit in on staff meetings and maybe get to work with a few students under supervision. So, I went in and that became my life. I was there not ten but thirty hours a week, and at age nineteen I worked under supervision with students in the counseling center. I absolutely loved it.

I did connect with a author mentor in this situation, Carl Rogers, who I think isn't fully appreciated in the mental health field—he is seen as just a little too soft. People have misinterpreted his idea of bringing your whole self to the therapeutic encounter, being authentic and truly listening without judgment or evaluation. Every time I become reacquainted with his writing, it brings me right back to center. It's the most grounded thing I have ever known. His ideas are so fundamental to my life and my understanding of things. I spent hours listening to his tapes—with no restlessness—and loved it.

One other author mentor for me has been Clark Moustakas, particularly his book, *Psychotherapy With Children*, which includes transcripts of working with children in play therapy. Moustakas' authenticity and his ability to listen and really hear were so extraordinary. Reading that book was another one of those captivating experiences. I have heard him speak twice in person, and he embodied his philosophy in an extraordinary way. Being in his presence was really special for me.

Following undergraduate school, I taught second grade very briefly. I couldn't stand it more than a semester. It was too painful for me to be in a classroom with kids and see how they were suffering. Also, I don't think I have that kind of ability to teach—that's not where my inter-personal skills are. I recognized that I needed to do something else with kids.

I worked as an assistant teacher in a preschool for handicapped kids for a year, and that felt a lot better. At this school we worked with the whole child. A supportive team of a variety of therapists worked along with the teacher and myself, and I was free to explore the play therapy I was naturally drawn to. For example, I could go off into a corner with a child and use puppets to support a child's dramatization of compelling issues.

He Could Not, However, Take Me Where I Needed to Go

After I moved to Maine, I decided to pursue graduate work, and I got into a graduate program through Antioch in Northampton and Cambridge. Initially I had looked into doctoral programs such as clinical counseling psychology and the so-called "better" MSW programs. I knew that I was not smart enough to do a doctoral program, so I didn't apply to any of those. I applied only to Smith School of Social Work, which, at that time, had the best reputation. In hindsight, thank *God* I didn't get accepted to that program, but at that time their rejection was a huge blow to me. That confirmed I was not smart enough to get in. I did *horribly* on the Miller Analogy Test, which they required.

My later experience with students I worked with from the graduate program at Smith was, that while they had an extraordinary ability to articulate a psychodynamic theory to describe any situation we discussed, their theories offered me no useful information for guiding *genuine* interaction with a client. I realized that these theories, although brilliant, felt one-dimensional and in actuality seemed like a dead end. There was no soul in them, no hint of contact on a human level. I know that I am not capable of that kind of theorizing, and today I am really grateful that I can't do that, because I am not skewed from my intuitive way of operating.

The Antioch program was a real hands-on program. I was in two years of intensive supervision and worked with people who were very experienced clinicians. They taught me *and* let me do what I needed to do. A negative aspect of that experience was that I had to take some required courses which I felt were ridiculous. These courses involved information I could (and already was) reading on my own, and the level of class discussions was not challenging intellectually nor consonant with the rich therapy work I was doing in my practicum.

The supervisors of my clinical experience were rather conservative but not stifling. They respected my radical forays into insight-oriented therapy which involved acting out scenes with my clients. I remember one particular sixteen-year-old child I worked with who had cerebral palsy. He had developed a way to explore his issues (such as abandonment) through acting out T.V. programs. I did not see his behavior as psychotic which might have been a traditional interpretation. I saw his behavior as his attempt to communicate what was really important to him, and I interacted therapeutically with his dramatizations. When I presented my work to my supervisors, I was shaking. But they responded positively, valuing what I had done. As much as they could stretch in that situation, however, they still operated within a box, a paradigm which didn't easily allow for spontaneous and authentic interactions. While I had no real mentors in this group, I was good friends with the director and felt comfortable sharing my work with him. He taught me a great deal about mental health, and I respected him. He could not, however, take me where I needed to go.

At the Antioch program, I needed them to teach me the language. That's why I was there and I knew that at the time. I needed to de-code the language, so I could have credibility and credentials.

I Help People Negotiate Things

Today, I feel I am continually defining and redefining my position. I don't really have a professional title. I have never, ever been able to call myself anything and feel comfortable. I always wince inside when I say I am a mental health counselor or a therapist or a mental health consultant—the titles that could legitimatize me. They offend me. Recently I have felt most internally congruent with referring to myself as a negotiator. That's been very sustaining to me. I help people negotiate things—from negotiating something emotionally within an individual to negotiating interpersonally within the structure of an organization, related to either defining its structure or resolving conflict. My focus is on negotiation across the boards in any type of situation. I'm much more at home with that internal recognition of negotiating than with any of the mental health titles.

Today I realize that I'm interpersonally smart. It's been a circuitous process of recognizing that. After my learning evaluation ten years ago, I suffered for three or four years by focusing on my deficits. I told myself that I couldn't write because I couldn't put anything in the right order, and I always thought I had more details than I actually did. It's not there and I thought I put it there, so I must be stupid. And I was distractible as well. With that attitude, I messed up my life where I had good opportunities, and I became anxious and depressed.

However, over the subsequent five years, I evolved all of that into some sort of coherent whole that I think "the negotiator" embodies more than anything else. I now understand that the structures that tell me what I'm about are structures from a particular point of view that don't express my essence. They are limited in their abilities to conceptualize what an individual is about. Testing is not going to reveal what I'm about. My IQ score is not going to reflect my inter-personal intelligence which is my primary language and how I understand the world.

I will never be a physicist, but I now know that field is not the only mark of intelligence. Someone who is a physicist will have a certain kind of intelligence, a kind of intelligence that I defined in high school as being the absolute. If you took the other courses and did really well, you weren't as smart as someone who took physics and did really well. And there wasn't a course in interpersonal "whatever."

People Have to Feel Accounted For, Recognized, and Really Seen

A dream I have for the future, that tickles me to no end, is to think about what it would be like to participate in negotiating situations on international levels. I can imagine bringing a different frame of reference to them, one that is not so politically driven. One has to be mindful of politics, religion, culture, and economics etc., however there are still some essential qualities about humanity that are not being considered. Nothing will happen until that is understood. People have to feel accounted for; they have to feel recognized and really seen. If they are not, nothing sustaining is going to happen.

That whole process of negotiating in different settings is really interesting for me. It seems to embody more of where I feel at home. When I am clear with myself that I am negotiating, I don't feel uncomfortable in situations that might seem foreign. For example, if I was asked to work with the board of directors of an arts organization, I could be intimidated by having never worked with a non-profit or arts organization before. However, if I say that I'm a negotiator, it doesn't really matter. It's listening, it's understanding, it's connecting, it's getting to the essence of things, and it's helping people be in touch with the fundamentals of the foundation. Once you cement that in with them, then they create the structures they need to accomplish the tasks at hand. I don't have to know how to build a widget, so to speak. Whether someone is coming in for therapy or whether I'm working with someone in another setting, being clear about that process is really what it is all about.

Bob C.'s story is one of remarkable contrasts. The boy who failed miserably at school later became an outstanding educator and leader. The learner who couldn't organize or focus on classwork and who could barely read and write showed gifted achievement in subjects of high interest in college. The child who received scant recognition in his elementary schooling now insures that every student in his class is given an opportunity to succeed. Today, as a student of the world, Bob has not allowed the standardized goals of schooling to impede the enactment of his vision of respect for and understanding of all people.

> Trust that still small voice that says,
> "This might work and I'll try it."
> —Diane Mariechild

Bob C.'s Story

I Was a Student of the World at an Early Age

My first learning memory is when I was only two years old. I was sitting on the floor next to the radio listening to President Franklin Roosevelt's speech after Pearl Harbor was bombed. It is a very vivid memory.

Some other memories that I have in my preschool years during World War II are of air raid practices and going to launchings of destroyers (we lived in Bath, Maine the location of Bath Iron Works, one of the major shipyards in the U.S.). My uncles all fought in World War II, and they would come home on leave in their uniforms. We visited with them at my grandparents' house. At a very young age, I had an interest in world affairs and the ability to understand the information my uncles shared within a worldly context.

I was a great radio listener, and today, as well, a lot of my learning is achieved by listening to the radio. I listen to public radio for news, more so than TV, because I get overstimulated and distracted by the pictures on TV. However, I am comfortable watching TV programs that are documentaries having to do with history, because it's something I'm really interested in. If I have high interest in something, I can focus.

I can remember when I got my first radio at age eight. There was a contest at school to get points for selling magazines. The points could be traded in for a variety of items. What I worked for and won was a little red plastic radio that I could have for my own next to my bed. It had both standard bands and short wave bands, and I was fascinated to see how far away I could pick up a signal. I would listen to world stations, like BBC, on short wave. I was a student of the world at an early age.

School for Me Was a Total Nightmare

On my first day of kindergarten, the teacher introduced us all, and she introduced me as Wilfred Robert Chaplin. I got angry and said, "My name is not Wilfred; it's Robert." My teacher said that Wilfred was my first name on the class list and that was what she was going to call me. I was so upset I started to scream. My father's name was Wilfred, and I didn't like my father; I didn't want to be called by his name. She took me to the principal's office, and they sent me home to calm down. Before I left, I told them that on the next day, when I came back, I wanted to be called Robert. I walked home alone crying all the way. When I went back the next day, I was called Robert from that point on.

I have absolutely no memories of school in grades one, two and three. In the fourth grade I went to a different school, and I do have some memories of that. We had moved from one part of Bath to a housing project. I had a lot of difficulty in school. I wasn't doing very well grade-wise or behavior-wise. On the last day of fourth grade the teacher gave us our report cards. I looked at mine and saw all F's, and I ran down the hall and hid in the boys' bathroom until all of the students and teachers had gone. I couldn't bare facing anyone at school, and then I didn't want to go home and show my parents, so I went and hid in the woods in one of my hideaway places. I was terrified by my parents' physical and verbal abuse.

School for me was a total nightmare. I constantly struggled with the work. The only thing that saved me was my sports ability. In seventh grade, I got to play on the baseball team and the basketball team. But when I got to High School, I experienced such high anxiety about playing on varsity teams in front of people that I would quit before we actually played games.

In my classes, I was always looking out the window or doodling; I was never focused. In seventh grade I was such a handful that the teacher put me out in the hall. Sometimes I was allowed to go down to a little room where I would help out with the collation of the school newspaper and do other menial tasks. So, academically, I didn't accomplish a heck of a lot then. Most of the time that year, I was in the hall or in that little room.

I Was Very Successful

In eighth grade I had a math teacher who was really helpful. She could see that I was struggling, so she helped me after school. With her help, I eventually worked up to an A in math. I was real excited about that. That was the very first teacher that I can remember who had any real interest in me with the exception of my sixth grade teacher—she was the only teacher up to that time who wasn't on my back because I wasn't doing well all the time. Although I didn't do well in sixth grade, I actually did behave myself in that class.

On my own time, outside of school, I was learning a lot. I continued to have an intense interest in the world. I listened to the news every night, and my grasp of political issues came easily to me. When I was in high school, there was a World's Fair in Belgium, and I tried really hard to figure out how to get there. Unfortunately I didn't succeed.

Another part of my life that felt positive was my participation in Boy Scouts. I started out as a Cub Scout; I just loved it. There were always neat things to do, and you got badges and rewards for what you did. It was all hands-on activities geared to a way I learn easily. Our cubmaster, who was a priest, was a kind and gentle man, and so I responded well to him. As I progressed through scouting, I worked with incredible focus and motivation to get one badge after another, and I ended up getting thirty-five merit badges. I also succeeded in earning the prestigious honor of Eagle Scout.

In Boy Scouts, I gained skills in a large variety of activities like canoeing, archery, Morse code (we had to be able to do twenty words a minute), and animal husbandry. I was fortunate to be able to go to a Boy Scout camp, and was able to earn a lot of merit badges there. I was elected by members of the camp troop to the Order of the Arrow, which is a secret order in the Boy Scouts. They were looking for leadership qualities. I was really good at organizing and whenever we had small group activities, I could lead them well. It was a place where they didn't know me as the kid who also got in trouble.

After two summers of Boy Scout camp, I was nominated to go to the National Boy Scout camp in New Jersey for leadership training. There I learned camping and survival skills to teach scouts back home. When I came back from that experience, I became a patrol leader in my scout troop. Patrol leaders are in charge of a smaller group of scouts within the troop itself, usually younger scouts. I also went to a conservation camp which was part of scouting. I became an assistant scout master when I was a senior in high school. In this arena I was right out there as a leader. I felt safe to risk in ways I never could in school environments. In scouting, I showed a talent for organizing; at school I could never organize my work.

I Couldn't Believe It!

During the first two years of high school, I tried to do college prep courses, because I thought I wanted to go to college. But I couldn't pass the courses, because I struggled over reading and writing. In my junior year, I decided to go into industrial arts. I liked doing mechanical things, and I did very well.

My schedule of nine weeks of industrial arts alternated with nine weeks of academics. My language arts teacher noted that no one could read my writing, and she checked out my reading as well. She discovered that I was barely a reader, so she began working with me, and I really respected her for that. She was able to help me improve to the extent that when I became a senior, I decided I wanted to try to go to Maine Maritime Academy. I hadn't taken any college prep courses, so Miss Connelly recommended that I do post graduate work to qualify. I took the post graduate course, and I passed the aptitude test to get into Maine Maritime Academy (training for the Merchant Marines). I have no idea how I did that. When I got the letter that I was accepted, I couldn't believe it. From my early years a major passion of mine was to be on a ship and to eventually become a naval officer (after Maine Maritime I had the option to get a commission in the navy).

I spent one year at the academy, and it was agonizing. I had worked at the Bath Iron Works before I went, so I could do the duty sections, because I already knew a lot about engine rooms. But the academic work was incredibly frustrating for me. Also, students were hazing me because it was military. I had encountered ongoing abuse from my parents, and I couldn't tolerate more. I remember thinking, indignantly, that they could have gotten the same results from me without the hazing. In the light of my sense of ethics about how the world should work, what they were doing just didn't fit. I went into an anxiety tailspin. When I told the head of the school that I was going to leave, he said he wanted me to stay. But at that point I felt so badly inside, I just wanted to escape. I left and went back to Bath.

I Thought I'd Like to Be a Teacher

The following summer, I had an opportunity to work as a cook at Pine Tree Camp, a camp for physically handicapped children. It was an incredibly moving experience for me. When the campers arrived they were in total disarray. The growth gains they made were amazing. One girl came in crawling down the driveway, and when she left at the end of the summer, she walked.

From that experience I realized that I would like to consider being a teacher because I really enjoyed working with children. My YMCA basketball coach in high school, who had befriended, encouraged, and counseled me, said that he had a contact, Max Sennet, at Washington State College in Machias, Maine. Max invited me to have a phone conversation with him. I informed him that I had been a student for a year at the Maritime Academy, and had subsequently worked at Pine Tree Camp. I said that I really liked working with children and that I thought I'd like to be a teacher. Max said, "Well, we're going to start classes in another week, and I expect you to be here." It turned out that he was the president of the college! I had saved some money, and I got a college loan and a job on the campus, so I was able to go.

Little did I know that the faculty of this college was going to be incredibly beneficial to me. At first I thought the place was really hickey, because of its rural location. But I soon discovered that the professors there had, for the most part, retired from prestigious universities, like Columbia, to come to live there in semi-retirement. They were top notch. I started in, and I did pretty well, although the reading and writing were always a problem. But it was a very small college (around 250 students), and I got extra help. They wanted you to make it.

How Did You Do This?

In my freshman year, I took US history with Red Lewis. He was noted for giving these very intricate multiple choice tests, and it was said, "You'll never make it through a Red Lewis test." During class after our first test, Mr. Lewis came up to me and said that he wanted to see me in his office. I thought, "What the heck does he want ; I'm out of here." But he handed me the test, and asked, "How did you do this? You got them all right," and I almost fainted. He said, "No one does this on my tests." I got A' s in all of his courses, including his math courses, because I could understand the way he was teaching. I also had a tremendous background in history from my passionate interest in world affairs over the years. Red Lewis engaged the depth of my understanding, for the first time, academically. I also discovered then that I could think analytically pretty well. However, in literature courses I really had to push myself to get C's. I managed to get a 3.0 average all the four years I was there, but I had to really work at it.

I continued to develop my leadership skills in college. As a freshman I was among six other classmates chosen to be in a service fraternity, Kappa Del Phi. We did public service projects in the community of Machias. When I was a sophomore, I engineered the idea of a winter carnival and set up what was called the Inter-Fraternity Council where the fraternities and sororities and other campus groups all banded together and created this event. Along with winter carnivals, this council also put on shows and other events. I was the prime mover and leader for that. I was also president of my class.

I Attempt to Insure that Every Child in the Room Succeeds

Following my college graduation, I became a K-8 teaching/principal for six years. The input from people I worked with led me to realize I had very good leadership skills, but I received negative feedback from the superintendent about my deficient writing skills. Not wanting to be faced with this problem—which I didn't feel I could overcome—I resigned, and became a sixth grade science teacher in Bar Harbor, Maine. I have continued in that position until the present day, interrupted by two year long sabbatical experiences. In my teaching I feel that I am able to provide the kind of learning environment I would have benefited by, one that could have made such a difference for me.

My interpersonal skills that I use in working with children are very intuitive, beyond any training I have had. I attempt to insure that every child in the room succeeds. I tell the students exactly what they have to study for tests, and tell them that everyone can get 100. I believe that the more gentle you are with the students, the more they are going to respond to you. I also feel that it is important that students don't see you as a threat to their learning or to their personal space; I honor them as a human beings. While not being judgmental about their ability to meet particular expectations, I always encourage them to work another notch up the ladder, to make improvements on their next project. I make it clear to my students that there are areas I do really well in and other areas I don't do well in. And I work with them, giving them support in any area of need. That's how I attempt to insure that each child is going to be successful.

I also support my students' personal initiative on projects. After I set forth the rubric of expectations, I leave it up to the students to put their projects together in a way that works for them. I always invite them to put their individual stamp on their work. One of the students said it better probably than I or anyone. He said that Mr. C. *trusts* that you're going to learn. And that's basically my philosophy; I trust my students to be responsible for their own learning. I'm just a facilitator.

We Were Ahead of the Curve

My first sabbatical experience was in 1972. I was awarded a Ford Foundation Leadership Grant which enabled me to spend a year traveling around the U.S. and Europe studying environmental education. During this fellowship, I served on the committee for planning the first world conference on the human environment which was held in Stockholm, Sweden. This conference was at the cutting edge, pioneering efforts towards protection of whales, zero population, air pollution control, and towards solutions of other kinds of problems that were occurring around the world. I intuited very accurately where the world was going on these issues thirty years ago.

After I returned to teaching, I initiated a program to involve my students experientially in a foreign culture. In instituting the annual sixth-grade Quebec trip, I was way ahead of the curve in proposing this kind of foreign cultural experience. It was a real nifty idea—very unique—and we kept it going for twenty-five years.

My passionate interest in Quebec City (just five hours away from Bar Harbor) began when I had an opportunity to stay with a Canadian family there. I absolutely fell in love with it. Quebec City is representative of a completely different culture. I intuitively recognized that visiting this unique place would be an expanding and enriching experience for my students. The old city section of Quebec City, where we would stay, maintains the flavor of the historical

French-Canadian traditions. I shared my idea with the school board and the
administration, and they said if it was well organized, we could give it a try.

Right from the very first year, the sixth-grade Quebec trip was a huge
success both in terms of a cultural experience and in terms of the development
of long time friendships between our two locales. Also, the program gave
each current sixth grade class an opportunity to bond in a special way, and
it gave different classes, as well as families in the community, an opportunity
to communicate about a common experience.

The Quebec City experience also fit beautifully within our sixth grade
social studies unit on Canada. The children learned about the French-
Canadian culture in classes and then were able to experience it first hand.
The trip was designed to give them snippets of various aspects of the Quebec
culture and included food, museums, churches, and the atmosphere of
the city itself. Sometimes we had an opportunity to learn a little French
beforehand. Although, over the years, there were some complications doing
the trip, we always overcame them with a positive spirit within a strong belief
in the value of the program. And we never had any problem with student
behavior. No matter what kind of negative reputation certain children had
in school, everyone was absolutely fine on the trip. If you trust children, they
know that, and they all knew that this was a privileged opportunity.

People would ask me how I so successfully accomplished all of the facets
of the project, and I told them it was easy. A project that seems so difficult to
someone else is easy to the person who is connected to his or her passion. I
have an intense interest in other cultures, and I feel that we don't pay enough
attention to them. Through experiencing another culture first hand, my
students developed more tolerance, acceptance and appreciation of diversity.

I have also worked with students in an international program, People
to People, which promotes peace and international understanding. People
to People was founded by President Dwight D. Eisenhower in 1956 in the
belief that individual citizens from different cultures meeting together were
the best ambassadors for peace. As a delegation leader, I have been able to help
students gain a better understanding of world cultures and their environments,
encouraging them to realize that they can make a difference.

I Stuck It Out Because I Really Wanted to Do It

As I was teaching, I continued on in my own studies, through a Ford
Foundation fellowship, getting a masters degree in environmental education,
followed by a Certificate of Advanced Study in science education. In 1991

and 1992 I took my second sabbatical from my teaching and attended a year at the University of Maine as a graduate student and a graduate assistant. It was an incredible year, after my initial struggle over the demands of the courses. They induced such anxiety in me that I almost left, but I stuck it out, because I really wanted to do it. I liked being there. I enjoyed the experience of living on campus, especially at fifty years of age. I stayed in the graduate dorm for international students. Every month we had a program done by students from a different country, and they prepared a traditional meal for us from their country—a wonderful and unique experience.

As a graduate assistant I had to teach a course, and I found out I could teach it well. I succeeded in the courses I took, despite my literacy challenges and anxiety syndrome, through sheer tenacity. I wanted to succeed, and also I was very interested in environmental education. I was awarded graduate student of the year for my leadership during my time of studying for my CAS (Certificate of Advanced Study) in science. I organized a resource center for the science department and the College of Education, and I was a leader among the students.

I Am Able to Take in My Abilities and Successes and Build on Them

Looking back on my education history, I can say that it took a long while for me to dispel the idea that I was stupid and a failure. I did become aware in my scouting experiences that I had some good abilities. But in an academic setting, it wasn't until college in Red Lewis' classes and in science classes that I felt I had any ability. Those successes, however, were short lived, because of my major lack of self-esteem—I didn't allow myself to bask in the light of success. I was always so quick to put myself down, telling myself I should have, could have, I might have done this and that . . . Today, however, I am able to take in my abilities and successes and build on them. Along with my successful life experiences, I now have the help of a minute dose of medication which miraculously keeps my anxiety syndrome from paralyzing my decision-making and risk-taking.

I decided to get a PhD in science and have been accepted at the University of Maine. I may and I may not stay in classroom teaching. I now believe in myself and the sky's the limit really. I believe that I can make a difference. And I think that is primarily what individual people should do with their lives—make a difference in something on this planet, either in other people's lives or the environment.

I have a very different concept of retirement. Although I like to go hiking and fishing and I think that could be part of it, I want to continue contributing to society. I would like to be able to realize more of my creative potential.

I think I'm good at moving people forward. I've done it in coaching cross-country running and track and field, programs which I innovated at my school, moving students to national championships. And I continue to organize new programs. I have an outing club at school for all middle school students. I am in the process of organizing a fifth to eighth grade drama club. I was a leader in developing a Big Brothers/Big Sisters mentoring program in conjunction with the local college. In this program college mentors help grade school students build inner strength and a better self-image. Because positive self-esteem is something that had alluded me most of my life, I want to help build that in others. Today I've got this new-found energy, and I believe very strongly that as long as I'm living and breathing, I can make changes.

Addendum

In the spring of 2003, Bob received two prestigious awards for his excellence in teaching. His first award was the Golden Apple Award given by the local Rotary Cub. This award recognizes the top educator for that year from among all teachers on Mount Desert Island. Their criteria reflect the principles of the Rotary Club, including high ethical standards and service to the community. Bob was nominated by his principal who told the local newspaper, "Bob is an outstanding educator. He is a true lifelong learner. He helps kids connect to learning through projects, camp experiences, and technology. His goal is to make sure each student finds an interest they can enjoy." Bob's second award was selection for the 2002 seventh edition of *Who's Who in America's Teachers* (he was selected again in 2005). This award honored him for his contributions made to the education of our nation's youth and for his excellence as a distinguished educator. He was nominated by a high school honors student.

Two more awards followed in 2004 and 2005. In 2004, Bob participated in Space Camp for Educators in Huntsville, Alabama and received the Homer Hickman, Jr. Right Stuff award, recognizing him as the outstanding student of his class. In 2005, Bob received the prestigious Presidential Award for Excellence in Mathematics and Science Teaching. This award is presented each year to one math and one science teacher from each state, alternating K-6 one year and 7-12 another. The award involves a rigorous application procedure and has stiff competition.

I remember discussing Bob's educational history with a student in his class who was also working with me. This boy, too, is highly creative and experienced challenges in reading and writing. When I shared with him some of Mr. C's own learning struggles, he expressed amazement and said, "And just think; now he's the most popular teacher in the whole school!"

Fred's story shares his long and painful quest to feel at home in a learning environment that supported who he was and who he was endeavoring to become. From the earliest days of his schooling, Fred didn't fit in. Connected to an imperative need to be true to himself, he struggled with all aspects of schooling agendas that made no sense to him and asked "the wrong questions." To eventually find his own way into learning, Fred had to push through huge barriers of frustration and anxiety. One can feel the relief when he finds his first mentor in college who understands and validates the complexity of his thinking. The varied strands of Fred's talents finally come together in the medium of digital graphic art, which gives him a powerful vehicle for exploration and expression. Fred's story provides both a map and hope for creatively gifted learners who are struggling to give form to their compelling ideas.

Once you become conscious of the questions active in the moment
you always get some kind of intuitive direction of what to do and
where to go. You get a hunch about the next step. Always. The
only time this will not occur is when you have the wrong question in mind.
You see, the problem in life isn't in receiving answers.
The problem is in identifying your current questions.
Once you get the questions right, the answers always come.
—James Redfield

Fred's Story

So I Didn't Fit In . . .

I was always depressed as a child. I still don't know if that depression was something that just existed of itself, or if it was a reaction to an inability on my part to adjust to my environment. I think it may have been an inability for me to adjust—being so different from people in my family and other people around me.

I remember being annoyed with kindergarten. I was interested in learning to read and learning how to do things, but the way the material was presented in such a rote, boring fashion irritated me, and I felt like I'd be better off learning it on my own.

In elementary school I slacked off; I wouldn't do the work. I guess maybe I thought that if I got behind enough, catching up would actually be interesting. But I never really caught up. It all just turned into a vicious cycle of annoyance.

Everybody, when I was young, kept talking about how smart I was. I didn't know what that meant. "Why do you think I'm smart? I don't do what you want me to do, so why do you think I'm so good at something when I've never had a chance to do it?" After a while, I began to believe them, but I grew to feel that because I was smart, I couldn't live comfortably in their world.

I wasn't into competitive sports. I think that children, particularly boys, instinctively like to play dominance games. I didn't like people trying to assert social dominance over me, and I really wasn't into trying to assert any sort of dominance over anybody else. So I naturally drifted to the bottom of the pecking order, and kids can be quite vicious in maintaining a pecking order. So I didn't fit in. The fact that I was smart didn't benefit me.

The Wrong Question

After kindergarten, in the early grades, I continued to feel that I was being held back by the curriculum. For example, reading groups. Everyone was assigned to a particular reading group, and somehow I got stuck in the middle reading group early on. When we were going into fourth grade, they assigned reading groups again, and they put me in the top reading group. During the first day of class, the teacher held up the book from the last year that the top reading group had used and said, "Who didn't use this book last year?" Like an idiot, I raised my hand. She said, "Everybody who didn't use this book last year needs to go to the middle group." I was furious that my placement had nothing to do with how well I read. At home I was tearing through all the Tom Swift books; I was reading some Tolkein, and I was reading Isaac Asimov.

The reading sessions at school were really, really boring. We read and answered questions. I felt that the questions were too simplistic, because there were things about the text that the questions didn't take into account.

So I started getting more and more paralyzed, because I felt like I couldn't answer the question that was asked. I didn't think it was the right question, although I wasn't a sophisticated enough thinker to adequately challenge the question. They didn't make sense to me, not because they were complex, but because they were simplistic.

No Safe Place

I felt held back in school most of the time. I felt that the teachers had this agenda of how they wanted to push knowledge at the kids, and I felt that (this is more of an instinctive knowledge, I couldn't really verbalize it particularly) if I bought into their model, they were going to dumb me down. So I resisted their agendas. At the same time, I was crafty enough to squeak by. I had some particularly bad marks in fourth grade, but other than that I managed to get by.

From second or third grade on, I was in the school's gifted and talented program. It was a little better than the classroom. It offered a couple extra toys for the kids who might like them—logic games and puzzles. However, we didn't do anything pedagogically innovative. We were asked to do little projects, and I could never pick out something to do, because I felt that I couldn't do something that was up to my standards within their standards. I couldn't straddle that fence, and so generally I would just wind up not doing anything. That left me feeling frustrated, bored, and afraid. I was more comfortable in these classes than otherwise, but it wasn't really a safe place either.

I had two different teachers for that program, Mrs. Kirch and Mrs. Reilly, who were both nice ladies. They were interested in seeing me do well, but they didn't have effective tools to help me. There were some really bright kids in that class who did well, but they seemed very interested in buying into the program and getting good grades. I didn't feel they were particularly smarter than I, I just felt that they were more interested in doing those things than I was. I felt frustrated when they got all the kudos, but I knew, at some level, that I had made the choice not to comply.

My Own Learning

When I was a junior in high school, I did find a course that met me where I was—math analysis. I had not done very well in trigonometry, but this course was actually the theory behind trigonometry. All of a sudden trigonometry made all sorts of sense that it had never made before, because in the trigonometry class we were just going through the effects of the theorems and memorizing how to manipulate their effects. When we got into the actual theory, all that other stuff made so much more sense.

My teacher was an okay lady. My friend Brian and I used to sit on the floor in her classroom and do whatever we wanted. She mostly didn't bother us, because we were pretty quiet, and we tried to do what she asked us to do most of the time. Right before the final exam I had been getting low B's and C's on all the assignments. I don't know if it's just something I realized or something she said to me, but suddenly I realized that I could actually understand this stuff if I wanted to. She handed out a study sheet and I said, "Okay, I'm going to do every single problem on this study sheet." I did, and I got an A on the exam!

What worked in that situation was the fact that I wasn't dependent on anybody else's teaching style. It was just me and the material, and it was mathematics, pretty cut and dried. In math, there is a logical progression, and if you follow all the steps, you can see what the logical progression is. So it was probably one of the first times in my life when I said, "If I really wanted to, I could do this."

The same thing happened to me in calculus the next year. I was hospitalized for depression for a period during that year and afterward, for the last half of the year, I was on a half day program. I would go in for the afternoon classes, and I would have a tutor that would meet with me twice a week. Calculus was one of the morning classes I didn't go to, but I had all the material and the assignments, and I would just sit down and tackle it. I taught myself calculus, and that was the right way for me to learn. At the end of the year my calculus teacher gave us a practice AP calc test. I got a four, and the student who was voted best science student of the year got a 3. I always knew I had ability, and I was finding ways to make it work for me in specific instances, but I wasn't able to generalize my success.

The Censor

Writing felt risky. With calculus you could set aside all the other things that were going on and just concentrate on this one thing. With writing there was no way to set aside everything else in your life and just write about . . . what are you going to write about? Particularly with fiction writing, but expository writing as well. I had this problem with book reports going back to the second grade. A lot of kids were skimming books just to write the book reports, and other than that they didn't read anything. I was reading all the time, and every once in a while, I would have to do a book report on one of the books I was reading anyway. I felt really angry about having to demonstrate that I was reading. We were asked to write a little synopsis to prove that we had read the book, and I couldn't do that. That was the wrong question for me—to be asked to cover all these things that had happened in a two-hundred-page book in three or four paragraphs; I couldn't make my brain do that. I got incredibly upset.

Those book reports set the tone for my relationship with writing. Writing expressively was not a problem for me. I could do that, because I'm handy with words. I had a really large vocabulary and was an okay speller, and I had reasonably good manual dexterity, so actually getting the letters down on the paper wasn't a really big deal. What impeded me was the constant need to censor myself. The censor was saying, "Don't tell them what you really think about their stupid assignment."

That particular censor broke once in my junior year in high school. For AP English, we were supposed to write a research paper. I didn't think that I could do a research paper, because I just never learned how. During all the opportunities I would have had to learn how, I was fighting battles of, "I have to resist the teachers, because they're trying to make me dumb."

So in junior year AP English the teacher said, "We're going to write a research paper, and I'm going to pick the topic for you. You're going to write the paper about some aspect of Huntsville, Alabama, in the 1950's." Well, by that time in my life I knew enough about the world to know that I hated Huntsville, Alabama. And what I knew about the fifties was that it was this incredibly socially repressive time when everybody was supposed to fall into these molds and everything was supposed to be just so. And *Boy Howdy* I was not into that. I couldn't think of a single paper topic that I was more resistant to than Huntsville in the 1950's.

I couldn't do anything. If I spoke up that would break my censor, and I would be openly rebelling saying, "I don't want anything to do with your malarkey." I had been resisting doing that for ten years at that point. I stewed about it for weeks. My father made me go out to the library, and I got some little factoids about the topic. And I found out that there was actually some interesting stuff going on in Huntsville in the 1950's with the importation of German rocket scientists and the starting up of the space industry.

Then the day before the research paper was due, I sat down in front of the computer and said, "All right. I guess I'll just try to write something about this stuff." It was an excruciating experience. Here I was stuck with this yucky assignment, and I had to turn in something the next day.

Beside the computer there was a pair of white cotton gloves which you wear when you're playing handbells (my father and I were in a handbell choir). For some reason I put them on, and I had this feeling that when I had the white gloves on, I couldn't write bullshit; I had to write what I felt. And so I wrote an appropriate length paper that had an introductory topic paragraph followed by exactly what I thought of that stupid assignment. And I turned it in!

The teacher really didn't have much to say about it. She made some comment in class, "Well I looked over your research papers," and she specifically referred to mine as some sort of sarcastic filler. I think that she thought that I thought I was trying to get away with something, that she wasn't going to really read the paper, that she was just going to see that there was text on there. And I thought, "No, that was totally not what I was trying to do."

I had it out with her in a heated discussion right in the classroom. After we had both calmed down a little, she said, "Well, if you were really having that much of a problem with the assignment, why didn't you come talk to me." And I said, "Because I didn't think it would do any good." And she said, "No, we might have been able to work something out." I didn't entirely believe her, but after that, we did have better communication.

It wasn't a very satisfying experience, because I still didn't feel, coming away from it, that I'd really learned anything. I had just demonstrated that if I got mad enough, I would actually react (which I had never done before). I think that led into the breakdown I had my senior year in which I finally demonstrated the frustration I had always been feeling anyway. In a way, my psychiatric hospitalizations during my senior year were a nice break. It was the first time when the environment I was in actually made sense related to how I felt. But it's not like that experience fixed everything for me.

I'm an Oppositional Learner

Following high school, I spent a year at the University of Alabama at Huntsville. I felt miserable and isolated that year. I found it very difficult to do school work there. I failed a twentieth century philosophy course, because, after a number of sessions, I couldn't make myself go to class. The professor stood up in the front of the classroom, handed out assignments and lectured, and we were supposed to agree with him. I actually had some scraps with this guy. He was a very traditional Western logician type, and I wasn't then and still am not. One day he was talking about apriori knowledge and how some things just seem to be true without us having any real world experience of them. His big example of this was the Pythagorean theorem—the square of the two sides of the triangle always equals the square of the hypotenuse if it's a right triangle, no matter what. I raised my hand and I said, "No, that's not actually always true." He said, "Yes it is." I said, "Well no. You have non Euclidian geometry which actually describes quantum physics systems better than Euclidian geometry." He said, "Yes, Okay." And he just glossed over it and moved on.

I have subsequently found out that I am an oppositional learner. I take a piece of information, and I have to critically evaluate it. I learn something by tearing it apart and putting it back together again. If I tear it apart and I see flaws, I need to work out those flaws before I can put it back together again and understand it. This means that once I get something, I *really* get it. But if there are flaws in it, I can't learn it. If I can't get an explanation for that, then the whole thing is tainted. That's why I couldn't learn trigonometry until I had the opportunity to understand the theory behind it. I work from a central schema and derive the effects of that. I can't keep track of the effects of it if I can't fit it into a schema.

I Hung on Like a Bulldog with Jaws of Steel

I went to Bar Harbor, Maine, to live with my aunt and started taking classes at The College of the Atlantic as a community student. COA was a really good learning environment. It was non-threatening in a lot of ways. In high school I learned that if I really pushed on things, I could actually achieve things that other people liked or appreciated. At COA, I found for the first time that if I really pushed on things and stayed with them, regardless of how painful it might be, it was actually possible to for me to produce useful work.

I found my first mentor at COA, John Visvader, a philosophy professor. Visvader was the first person who seemed to understand what I was talking about, and I hung onto to him like a bulldog with jaws of steel. He was also usually a step ahead of me. He knew where I was going, and he could further explicate my ideas. I really got what he was saying, and I felt like he got what I was saying.

I first felt Visvader's validation of me when I talked my way into my first class with him. I had been reading a lot of philosophy on my own. I asked if I could come to his first class, even though it was already full, thinking that maybe someone would drop out. He was giving an overview of the

Greek philosophers and what they were all about. He talked about Zeno and his mentor, and asked another teacher, who happened to be in the room, "Who was Zeno's mentor?" The other teacher didn't know, and I answered, "Parmenides?" He said, "Yes, Parmenides!" I went up to him afterwards and said, "Do you think there's room in your class? May I take your class?" He said, "Anybody who knows who Permenadies is, is in my class."

His classroom was very different from my classes at UAH. It was structured as a seminar. We did the readings and when we came in, he would talk a little bit, and then we would start a discussion. That gave me an opportunity to tear things apart and put them back together. I had been confident in myself as a thinker, but through this class and others at COA, I became confident in my ability to communicate what I was thinking about.

For one of the first times in my life, I was religiously doing all the readings for a class. As I was leaving class one day, Visvader came up to me and said, "You know, you're a really smart guy. You should come talk to me sometime." I was totally taken aback. I thought, "What did I say that made him say this about me?" I remember struggling so hard on a paper for his course. Whenever I felt stymied, though, I would go and talk to him, over and over, getting the support I needed to see it through.

I struggled with every paper that I wrote at COA. I would push myself to the edge of what I could possibly tolerate. They were very painful experiences. Although I made significant progress as a student in many respects, I still felt so mired in everything that had held me back previously. I was finding that there were outlets for some of the things that I thought about, but the outlets were still blocked; I still had to clear them out.

Becoming a Person in My Own Right

Due to lack of funds, I left COA after two years. Through connections from my college advisor, I landed a first entrance level job in Boston working for a government contractor doing documentation support for the Department of Transportation Research Center. I started out as an office boy, essentially. I would walk around and repair malfunctioning copiers, pretty much unskilled labor. I was pretty miserable. School generally only used one tenth of what I was capable of doing, but at least it used that tenth. This job used nothing until I started, without anyone's explicit consent, playing around with computers, trying to make them do interesting things. I was doing this totally on my own, and I managed to learn enough about how the computer graphics systems worked, that they started giving me actual assignments—for example, doing video effects for an instructional tape about highway noise barriers, and creating a CD-ROM for the hazardous materials transportation training course—all because I had been taking this guerrilla action on my own. I gradually developed a sense that if I could find the right string to tug on, then I could tug on it as much as I wanted and maybe something would change in a direction that felt useful to me.

I began to become a person in my own right. In my precollege schooling, I had a core of selfhood that couldn't be expressed in the world; I had to protect it from exterior threats. At COA, I started expressing it in a place that was very sheltered and nurturing. In this job, I acted on my ideas, often in the face of overbearing, dominating staff who so easily could have intimidated me. I tried to be myself in the world, even if the world wasn't looking for that. That was a turning point for me.

I've Got a Canoe

I succeeded in getting the necessary funding to continue my undergraduate work at Emerson College where I'm studying new media and digital information access and design. I am exploring how to take any sort of information—video, sound, and text—and arranging it so that it can be useful, designing it so that it looks appealing. I like to think that when you're looking at a computer screen, you're actually engaging with an environment. I'm learning about building useful, stimulating environments for people to engage with. That appeals to me, because it brings together so many different things that I've already done. I have some understanding of music and how that operates and some understanding of the visual world and what kind of impact that has. I have some understanding of logical structures and how information can be arranged so that it's easy to access.

I've got a canoe. If the Renaissance perspective is a stream of all the different things that you *could* be working on, I have a canoe to navigate that stream. And I can jump streams. I'm able to do that with my writing, because I'm writing about art and I'm writing about other designed environments, and I can relate those back to science. If I can make a strong enough case, and if I follow the format of the writing assignment I've been given (which I'm starting to learn how to do), then nobody can stop me from making those connections.

What stopped me before was people not wanting to see those kinds of connections in conjunction with my inability to build a convincing argument.

That was the problem in high school with those stupid little research papers. You were basically supposed to tell the teacher something that he or she ought to already know. If you were working on a new and novel thesis, then you were probably doing the assignment wrong.

At Home

I've been able to find teachers at Emerson that I can connect to safely with my agendas. That's very exciting to me. I recently went to a conference about Duchamp, which interpreted him in the light of information that he only made available after his death. Duchamp was an early twentieth century modern artist who was innovative in how to use the term "art" and what roles we ascribe to the artistic process. He was also interested in a lot of very scientific theories. I, too, have a real love for combining art and science. At this conference a group of scientists compared Duchamp with Henri Poincare, an important and influential French mathematician. I felt perfectly at home; I was eating this stuff up.

I have written two papers on Duchamp, and am in the process of doing a CD-ROM project on him in an independent study. I have had a lot of support for my CD-ROM project from a number of teachers, and I've now learned which questions to ask. Design is a decision-making process. What's different now is I'm starting to move under my own power. At College of the Atlantic, I used to make decisions, and then completely stress out about them, stewing over whether they were right or wrong. I was pushing myself so hard. Now I am pushing myself to get useful momentum, which is not that old kind of exhaustion. I make a decision and know that I have to live with that, because I already know what the next decision I'm going to have to make is, and I need to begin working on that.

It's kind of like skiing. The whole point behind skiing is not just going downhill, it's turning and keeping yourself from going downhill too fast and crashing because you can't control your speed. You can learn how to turn, but you're not really getting it until you can start chaining your turns together. You make turns in series, multiple turns in a row and then you're skiing.

At Emerson, I've been able to learn not just how to make the decisions, but how to chain the decisions together, so that it becomes a work flow. It's not like before, struggling to solve one problem and feeling just as lost when I come to the next one. I'm starting to have a vision of where I want to go.

I've always had the tools to get there in one sense, but now I'm learning how to get in a process and stay in it until I reach some milestone. In my Huntsville schooling, while I could clearly see the process that my teachers thought I should go through, and knew that wasn't the way for me to go, I had no alternative path. I was totally flailing around, trying to reinvent the wheel with every single problem that I came up against.

Also, now I'm working on projects that I think are important and interesting. I recognize that I have good ideas that people will support, and that I can describe my ideas clearly enough to get other people interested in them. This energizes me. Previously, I was so stressed out by the act of working that I was really directed towards the end products. I just really wanted to finish, so that I wouldn't be miserable anymore. So I never really learned how to make or chain those turns.

Also, at Emerson, I have finally found a craft that I am comfortable with. Working within digital design has helped me actualize my true learning potential. It's kind of genetic; I get how digital information works, and I get how computers want to deal with things. I found this out by accident. Just through wanting to make things work, I actually acquired a vast array of technical knowledge and problem solving skills with computers. I later found out that this was valuable in the market place. That in conjunction with accessing my creative interests is a powerful combination. The two feed on each other. I have finally found an empowering vehicle to both explore and to translate my ideas.

Cathy's story shares the profile of an artistic and interpersonally gifted learner who needed comfortable relationships with her teachers and strong personal interest to actively engage in her learning. She spent much of her elementary and jr. high years detached from classroom agendas. Cathy struggled with organization of school work while at the same time she developed satisfying organization of her personal projects. Piqued by an interest in philosophy of education in college, she found herself committing to a teacher certification program—a strange paradox for someone who felt so frustrated with most of her own schooling. As the oyster transforms the grit of sand into a pearl, Cathy utilized her insights into the frustration of her own schooling to create a vision of joyful learning. Today she is a highly relational teacher who delights in supporting her learners' interests.

The most dreadful idea in the world for me
is that there is a preordained way to live
and that we all must live that way.
I would rather die than live by a preconceived pattern.
It would be life in death.

—Judith Duerk

Cathy's Story

School Work, in General, Was Painful for Me

In third grade, I remember being afraid of the teacher. I was really shy. I was even too afraid to raise my hand to ask if I could use the bathroom during the day. But that was the first year I got to write a book, and it must have been one of the first times I got to choose what I was writing about. I wrote about Snoopy (I think I had a little stuffed Snoopy dog at home). I loved that book because its shape was of a Snoopyish dog.

I remember enjoying the writing of that book, but I also remembered wondering as I was writing if a sentence had to end at the end of the line. I'm sure I didn't write very freely, and I definitely got hung up on spelling. I think, back then, I probably tried to use words that I knew how to spell, or I wrote messy so it was unclear what the letters were.

A new private school opened up in my town and my mom, seeing the stress I was under, switched me to it for fourth grade. It was a really nice school where we got to do art every day, and the teachers were relational (they asked about things that were important to me), so I was less intimidated. That made a big difference for me as a learner, because I wasn't afraid of them. However, schoolwork, in general, was painful for me. I didn't like to look assignments over after they were done, and I never did a careful job. I read it once and then answered the questions. I remember, however, frequently being surprised at how many answers I got wrong on any given piece of work I handed in.

My ongoing difficulty with spelling definitely influenced the amount of writing that I did. I remember that in jr. high either I would write something really short (if I could get away with it), or I spent a lot of time with the dictionary making sure words were right. I took even more time than I needed to, because even on words that I spelled correctly, I didn't trust my spelling and would look up those words also—I didn't yet have access to word processing and spell checkers. I love spell check today. It really works for me, because I'm now pretty good at noticing the correct spelling from a list.

In elementary and jr. high school, I also had trouble with reading. I didn't remember that I did until my mom reminded me about my difficulty sometime after college. From fourth to sixth grade, I don't remember having a problem reading, but I bet that I wasn't reading at grade level. The school, however, was pretty flexible, and they changed the reading groups around a lot, and the teachers suggested books that I enjoyed reading. I liked reading a lot, but I do remember in school frequently feeling I could do a better job reading something if I could do it at home. When I was reading Nancy Drew at home, it felt comfortable and easy, but school work almost never felt like that. Partly it was because I just loved Nancy Drew and the books at school were both less interesting and at a higher level, but also I felt so much more comfortable at home, relaxed and well fed.

The private school only went to sixth grade so in seventh grade, when I went back to public school, I was in a small reading class of four for part of the year which included special education students. The teacher was really nice, and I was actually bolder than the other students and more willing to take risks in this very small group. While I thought I was doing pretty well, apparently the teacher must have had some concerns, because when my mom saw her a number of years later and told her that I was doing well in college, she said, "She *is*?" She was shocked!

In the regular reading class I had difficulty concentrating related to the possibility of being called on to read. The teacher would often ask me to speak up, and I was surprised when I answered correctly (which I did at least half the time). To this day I have difficulty expressing myself on demand.

If It Weren't for Art, I Wouldn't Go to School

In seventh and eighth grade I had a really nice art teacher. I remember telling my mom several times that if it weren't for art class, I wouldn't go to school. I was really frustrated with my other teachers and classes. I went through a phase where I acted out my frustration with a friend; we got into trouble a lot. I told my mom that I started getting into trouble, because I was tired of everyone thinking that I was just a good kid. That's not entirely true though. I wanted to show my independence and getting into trouble was just an unfortunate consequence of that.

I rebelled against rules at home, and I rebelled at school as well. My friend and I tried to destroy the school a bit—graffiti and gluing the science teacher's door shut. I remember being so angry at school that I just wanted to wreck the place. That was a relatively short phase, less than a year, but it still feels big to me. I'm always thankful that I'm not still thirteen. I am also thankful for the humility this experience has given me, because I can now empathize and honestly understand the frustration and anger of some of the children that I teach.

My friend continued on this track after I stopped, and what helped me pull back from this was feeling uncomfortable about her behavior—for example, she stole things from my home. That betrayal was a real awakening for me. Also our escapades began to feel more pathetic than adventurous. I was thankful that after all the trouble I had caused my mom still loved me. Also what helped me fully move away from this period was a two-week outward-bound course that I took after ninth grade. Through this experience I began to feel great about myself. I carried a heavy backpack for two weeks, made new friends, acquired new skills, and did all this far from home.

Teachers and My Interest in the Subject Made a Big Difference

In high school, I liked four teachers: my art teacher, my psychology teacher, my history teacher, and my English teacher. Psychology class was really easy for me, because I was so interested in the material. Also, I figured out that if you do exactly what the teacher asked, you'd do a better job. It seems ridiculous that I didn't know that before.

Psychology was a lecture class. We took notes, and we watched moderately goofy videos, some of which were actually interesting to me. I remember feeling that if I hadn't been interested in them, I would have been laughing at them like many of the other kids. I remember one video about narcoleptic dogs. It just showed lots of dogs falling asleep all over a lawn, but I was interested in that! That was the first time I remember being successful in a challenging class. I also remember reading a lot of self-help psychology books on my own, trying to figure out my family and myself.

That same semester I started out in a social studies class that was a low track class. It was ridiculously easy and boring. We just read the text book and answered questions from it. So I switched to the college prep history class.

That teacher of the college prep history class was really great. We had some freedom about what we learned; it wasn't regimented. On tests she asked open-ended questions that got us thinking. It was a comfortable place, and I remember working with other students a lot and enjoying it. I never actually read the textbooks in that class except for the little side stories. I did enough, though, because the teacher asked questions that had room for what we wanted to think about, broad questions like, "Choose a conflict or person from this time and write about that." And that was broad enough that there was something from that time that would interest me. I remember working on an assignment from that class on my bedroom floor, being amazed that I was happily doing schoolwork. That class in combination with the psychology class got me thinking about how I learn for the first time. I realized that how I felt about the teachers and my interest in the subject made a big difference.

In ninth grade I had an English class with a teacher that I hated, because it was so rigid. He asked questions in class, and I don't ever remember knowing the answers. But then, when I had him again in eleventh grade, one of the first books we read in the beginning of the year was *The Stranger* by Albert Camus, and I had already read that book at home, because the title had appealed to me. Reading *The Stranger* on my own marked a departure for me from the kind of realistic fiction I had been reading since jr. high like Nancy Drew and then Judy Blume—all about girls around my age. Anyway, my teacher said that he didn't have enough copies of the book for the whole class, and when I offered to bring mine in, that created a nice bond between us that year. When I first read that book to myself, I hadn't really understood it, but I was happy to read it in class, because it gave me an opportunity to understand it and talk about the ideas.

That class was one of the few times I remember volunteering to answer questions. I remember talking about that book with the teacher outside of class which gave me time to think about the ideas when he brought them up in class. Also, it wasn't a very talkative class. The teacher would ask a question and there would be a painfully long pause, and he wouldn't give in. The prime conditions that encouraged me to speak were the opportunity to think about the questions ahead, my interest, those long teacher pauses and, most of all, a feeling of personal connection with the teacher.

I took art all the way through high school. I got to know the art teacher and was pretty comfortable with him. Sometimes he gave us lots of room for creative expression and sometimes his assignments were fairly structured. I didn't really mind that, because I enjoyed the challenge of the restraints he gave within projects. However, my friend Jo (who was and still is a phenomenal artist) really struggled around any constraints—she just wanted to make her own stuff. Looking back, I realize that watching her suffer took away a surprising amount of enjoyment I had in that class.

I Have No Idea How I Could Have Missed That.

Throughout my schooling I was unclear about expectations and had difficulty with organizing my assignments. In sixth grade I started having homework, and I almost never had it to turn in. I remember my teachers going through drastic measures to get me to remember. One teacher wanted me to put a red dot on my nose so that everyone I encountered that evening would ask me why I had a red dot on my nose, and I would say, "That's to remind me to bring my homework to school tomorrow." That would be a week or two after the work was due. I do take full responsibility for forgetting, but also at that time my parents were divorced, and I was alternating spending nights at my mom's and my dad's house, so I found it hard to get the work once I forgot it the initial time.

During this same period, however, there were other things I was frightfully organized with. For example, I had a journal I wrote in everyday. When I was at my mom's house I wrote with a purple pen, and at my dad's house I wrote with a blue pen. If I forgot to write for a day and wrote the next day about yesterday's events, I wrote with the appropriate color pen for that day. I had a whole system I was faithful to. My journal was important to me!

In junior high I played the flute, although not very well. I somehow managed to go through half of the first year without knowing that I was supposed to go to individual flute lessons. I just played in the band during study hall. So half way through the year the band teacher asked why I hadn't been coming, and I said that I didn't know what he was talking about. I have no idea how I could have missed that.

In writing assignments in high school, I didn't do as well if the assignment was big and due some weeks later. I liked it when little parts of it were due all along the way, although I would still work frantically the night before each part was due catching up on a week's worth of work. However, I was so thankful that it was only a week's worth rather than the whole project. I also appreciated getting feedback at the early stages of a project.

I remember doodling a lot in some classes, and the doodling took me off into a dream world which is where I wanted to be.

"Oh, We Had Reading for Human Ecology?"

Although I wasn't strongly motivated to go to college, my mother encouraged me to do so unless I had another plan. I did a computer search which led me to College of the Atlantic and Goddard College. I chose COA in Bar Harbor, Maine because the courses in the catalog sounded interesting (like "Bread, Love and Dreams"), the campus was really pretty, and it was further away from home.

During my first term at COA, I wasn't that excited about my course requirements. But I did the work, partly because my parents were paying for school, and I didn't feel comfortable wasting time, and classes were often interesting. I continued, however, to be unclear about class assignments. Luckily that first year I lived with a lot of first year students who were in my classes. It happened all the time that someone would say for example, "I just finished my reading for "Human Ecology," and I would say, "Oh, we had reading for "Human Ecology?"

I had a difficult time with a biology course, because what we had to read was hard, so I was always forgetting to do the reading. The text was hard for me to read because the information was not familiar, and it was awkward textbook language. In order to improve my ability to read this kind of writing, I had to learn that I couldn't skim read the way that I could with novels, and that I needed to look up a word I didn't know as soon as I felt confused. But it still really makes a difference if the material is interesting to me, and it helps me today to acknowledge when a piece is boring to me while I push through. Last year, while working as a special education aide in a middle school, I felt the reading tests they gave the students were unfair, because if a passage is about baseball, then a kid who plays baseball has a whole different relationship to that piece than a kid who doesn't.

I Realized There Was No Reason for School To Be Painful

After I took a class in philosophy of education, which I enjoyed, I began to piece together other teacher education courses toward certification in elementary education. I did so reluctantly, because I didn't think I would like teaching. I didn't like many teachers and I hadn't liked school, and it seemed like a ridiculous, crazy thing to choose to go back to school as an adult. But the more I learned in education classes, the more I became interested in reflecting on my learning and seeing a way that education could be better. I realized that there was no reason for school to be painful.

During my student teaching in a third grade classroom, I had difficulty with the classical kind of organization: making lesson plans for each day a week ahead and planning a test at the end of some number of days. I especially

had difficulty having things I had planned ready ahead of time. I had lots
of ideas of how I wanted to teach, and I knew how I wanted to begin. I also
knew some things I wanted to do at certain points throughout the unit, but
I didn't know ahead of time how long anything would take. If the students
were really interested in something, it would take more time, and if they're
not interested I would just want to keep moving. To this day, I cannot do
lesson plans like that. It seems torturous and ridiculous.

My first teaching job, which lasted for two years, was on the small island
of Frenchboro off the coast of Maine in a one-room schoolhouse. I had
anywhere from one to five students at a time. When I began teaching on
Frenchboro, I thought that I should be planning all of the units that I would
be doing for the whole year. But just as I had learned in my student teaching,
I found that I couldn't do that. My most comfortable way of teaching is the
workshop model which allows individual students to pursue their own line
of inquiry. I would get some idea to start the beginning of a unit, and then I
would see what direction the kids took it. *Their* interests and focus gave me
the inspiration to plan the next stage.

One very successful unit that I did was on the solar system. I began by
collecting a number of resources and thought up a lot of specific ideas of what
we might to do, but I also knew that I would let the children take it in some
other direction; I knew that if they got interested in space ships, I would leave
room for that, or if they got interested in aliens, I would leave room for that,
and if they got interested in just planets, that would be fine too. When they
brought forth their interests, it wasn't coming from me, it was coming from
them, and I could feel their energy when they were "on." I was so satisfied
with the variety of topics we ended up doing and how they all flowed together
and how, seemingly without effort, the days were varied.

"It's Not a Sailboat. It's a Pirate Ship."

At the Frenchboro school, I had an exceptionally creative student. On
one of the first days of school, Brian burst through the school door early. I
asked him how he was, and he shook his head and said, "Bad." I asked him
why, and he dragged me to the window and pointed to the harbor and said,
"Do you see that big ship out there?" I nodded. He said, "It's not a sailboat.
It's a pirate ship." I nodded again. He looked at me really seriously and he
said, "I had to stay up all night spying on it, and I didn't get a wink of sleep."
He was always full of stories!

Brian was such a fun student for me, because he loved the freedom I offered him in his learning and almost always took it to heart. He did so much better when he had that freedom. When we practiced cursive penmanship, I let him choose what words he wanted to write over and over again, and he thought that was fun. If I gave him some words to practice particular letters, he thought that was torture; he just wanted to write, "James Bond." When he got interested in something, he was *really* interested and present.

When I first came to teach, Brian was in second grade, and he had had struggles with reading the previous year. He had been given lots of phonics instruction, and while he had retained the information, he couldn't utilize it "on the run" in reading. I encouraged Brian to read simple picture books in which the pictures hinted at what the print was saying. I allowed him to read the books he really liked over and over again. His favorite book was *Captain Bumble*, and he read that a million times; he basically had it memorized. He read it daily over a period of months to anyone who would listen to it, and I watched him start to point to the words as he was reading them. He finally made the connection between his memory and the print information. Brian pretty quickly applied his knowledge of the words in this book to other books about pirates (which included some of the same words). He became a great reader. Brian's learning appeared to be uneven. It would look for a while like he wasn't making progress, and then suddenly he would leap ahead. I respected this cycle.

I Love Finding Ways To Make Learning Happen.

Even though the Frenchboro School was really small, there were many organizational challenges for me to deal with: curriculum planning for students in four different grades, all the mail and bills that came to the school to be sorted etc. Some parts of it I did really well with. I got really good at planning ahead for resources that I wanted: art supplies and books for our units—both books that I would buy and ones that I borrowed from libraries. I couldn't do it the night before, because I lived on a tiny island which only had boat transportation three times a week. I felt satisfied about how I was able to organize resources to use again after I taught a unit. I also felt good about my documenting of student work, like keeping copies of writing samples.

I do feel like I will stay in teaching. I would love it more, though, if school buildings weren't so ugly and yucky to be in all day. I would love it more if there was more room for flexibility in so many ways: class sizes, use of time, having appropriate space, and having more support which helps me feel valued. I love watching learning. I love even just thinking about Brian learning to read, how great that was. I love finding ways to make learning happen, to provide whatever needs to be provided to let a kid take off with it. That kind of organizing for learning is very different from planing all the steps ahead.

I'd like to work with kids in a setting where they get to do what they're interested in and what they're good at, and then, from there, have those interests lead back to learning skills they need in service of that. Learning skills isolated from interesting context, drawing only a little bit on students' strengths, is so hard for some kids. I would like to jump off from their strengths.

I see all the time how detrimental the former approach can be. Last year, when I taught as a special education aide in a middle school, I worked with a student who struggled so hard and for whom school was all torture. He got into trouble in school all of the time, yet in regular life, he was fine. He talked to adults and he hung out with his family; he was great. He'll be a terrific adult. If I had had the opportunity to have regular interactions with him all day, I believe that we would have found something that he would have been motivated to write about, and that he would have done a really good job writing it.

You can spend years trying to get a few simple facts across, yet if you presented those same facts when the student was ready for them, it would take minutes. My youngest brother never did well in school. Especially as a young kid, he spent a ridiculous amount of time with his computer, while in school he struggled and struggled. This summer he is a computer technician for a residential school, and he can figure out all of the problems. He's so successful because he was doing all of those things that seemed like such a waste of time to everyone when he was a kid. That's where he got the skills that he's using now.

In my own schooling I would have benefited from having positive connections with teachers who honored me as an individual and encouraged my strengths. I would have benefited from having had a vision of where all the work was going and seeing progress related to that vision—for example, seeing a writing sample from the beginning, middle, and end of the year that showed my progress despite my struggles. It would have helped me to have had fewer spelling words and less homework in general. It would have helped if I had been encouraged to reflect more on my learning. At the end of the day in my private school, we wrote in our journal about our day and sometimes were asked about what we learned. That really helped me to remember something like a multiplication fact. And finally, when I was given any kind of choices about what I wanted to learn, which happened in high school, I felt much more motivated.

My eleventh grade English teacher, with whom I felt a close connection after sharing *The Stranger*, wrote a college recommendation for me. In his letter he wrote,

> "Cathy marches to a different drummer,
> but she is always marching."

In Lesley's story we read about a learner, gifted in musical and interpersonal intelligence but challenged by Dyslexia and Attention Deficit Disorder, for whom learning to read was a trial and doing classwork in general a nightmare. Within Lesley's ADD distractedness, however, lay an ability to hold an awareness of multiple layers of thoughts simultaneously. When Lesley was able to harness this awareness into an ability to multitask, she became a gifted facilitator. Her story reveals the amazing strengths that can reside in and be masked by "disabilities." In bringing these strengths forth, Lesley began to dispel longstanding, internal messages of failure—freeing her creative spirit.

Queer little twists and quirks go into the making of an individual.
To suppress them all and follow clock and calendar and creed
until the individual is lost in the neutral gray of the host is to be
less than true to our inheritance . . . Life, that gorgeous quality of life,
is not accomplished by following another man's rules. It is true we
have the same hungers and same thirsts, but they are for different
things and in different ways and in different seasons . . . Lay down
your own day, follow it to its noon, your own noon, or you will sit in
an outer hall listening to the chimes but never reaching high enough
to strike your own.
—Angelo Patri

Lesley's Story

Which One Do You Choose?

My earliest noteworthy school memory was in kindergarten. I had great difficulty learning my left hand from my right hand. I was told to look at my thumb and first finger on both hands and note that my left hand could make an L. But, because I was dyslexic (diagnosed later), they both looked like L's. I kept saying, "Which one do you choose?"

I remember that my first grade teacher was very nice, however she was puzzled about why I didn't understand the sequence of the months of the year and their placement in the seasons. She probably thought that by first grade I should have known this, and I, of course, just thought: when it snows, then it will be winter; when the daffodils come up, we will then be in spring; when I'm not in school, it will then be summer; when we return to school it will be the fall. This was self-explanatory to me, but I couldn't sequence the months or understand how the months and seasons went together.

When I went to Berklee College of Music, one of my fellow classmates had a band, and put a sign up on which all the letters were backwards. I had no idea for weeks that the poster was unusual. The band did it that way so you would have to take it down and hold it up to a mirror. "Why?" I asked. They said, "Because all of the letters are backwards." I replied, "No wonder it wasn't so stressful for me to read." I am not severely dyslexic, but it feels better on my eyes when the letters are backwards," although a whole page of backwards letters would stress me as well.

I learned to read through memorization. I thought that I was reading. It wasn't until fifth grade that a tester said, "Lesley can't read. Oops, here we are in fifth grade and she can't read. That's a bit of a problem." I was so verbal that I had been able to talk my way in and out of things, and that tripped up a lot of my teachers. From first grade to fifth grade nobody knew that I had absolutely no concept of how to read. I had excellent comprehension of what I heard read, so that had tripped them up as well.

They Didn't Realize I Was Missing Basic Building Blocks for Learning

From an early age, however, I had the ability to "read" people. Socially, in first grade, I picked up quickly that I was not interested in the way girls interacted. Compared to the multiple levels of thoughts and perceptions going through my mind at all times (related to my Attention Deficit Disorder), I found the behavior of the girls to be very immature. I was in conflict over whether or not to meet that level of immaturity, because I did want to fit in. However, I found that playing with the boys was so much easier, because they did not require you to play contrived social games. It wasn't a time when there was a war going on, but I remember we played army every day at recess. I was with the guys playing army, and I was allowed to play the nurse. I remember being slightly offended by that, but I kept thinking that at least I'm able to play with kids I want to play with. And I was very physical and very able—really good at sports.

However, I knew, even back then, that I was compromising to get along. I knew on some level that the kids were missing the mark, not academically, because I couldn't keep up with them in that arena, but in the sphere of personal awareness. Because I could relate to and communicate so well with adults, I think I misled my teachers about my academic needs; they didn't realize that I was missing basic building blocks for learning

My undiagnosed ADD created endless frustration for me as well. My parents and extended family were highly academic. They saw my reluctance to do homework, my inability to remember that I had homework, and my not remembering to do chores as laziness (I was in elementary school in the seventies, before ADD was recognized, so my folks didn't have another way of understanding my behavior). My ADD also manifested in runaway thoughts; I could not get my thoughts to stop. I remember explaining to a college friend of mine (who was writing a paper about me), that my thoughts were like a dripping faucet, because no matter how many times you fix it, you continue to get drips until you get a new faucet. When I was little, I could not control my thoughts at all. I remember thinking that if I could hold my head and bang it against the wall the endless parade of thoughts marching through my head might stop. And all of these streaming thoughts distracted me, leaving me no peace.

Music and Sports Kept Me in School

Playing sports naturally focused and centered me; it was really good for me. By fourth grade I was really strong, and I was the only girl allowed to play baseball with the boys. I craved recess; I couldn't wait to get outside. Also, music was an excellent outlet for me. My mother played the piano, and she had my brother and me sing with her. Because I had such a loud voice, she had me sit across the room. Because I thought this meant she couldn't hear me, I built up a great lung capacity.

At quite a young age, I could sing pretty well. However, to this day, I can't read music; I memorized everything (I later got into Berklee Music School which is fairly impressive for somebody who can't read music). In high school I was in auditioned singing groups. As long as I sat next to Robin Morris (who could actually read music), I was fine. I still thank her dearly for that. I also played the drums—four different drums in the marching band. Music and sports kept me in school.

Within the academic mindset of my teachers, it was hard for me to honor and focus on developing my unique interpersonal strengths. I felt the judgment of, "Obviously you just can't do it, you're just dumb," or "You're just lazy." These judgments, coupled with my challenge of dealing with multilayers of thoughts, fueled additional attentional difficulties.

I always have multilayers of thoughts parading through my head simultaneously, and I often yearn to be able to focus on just one thing at a time. On the other hand, I have the ability, at times, to marshal this multiple awareness into the ability to multitask—to attend to a number of activities in concert. I remember an argument I had with my husband when he was having difficulty managing our baby. I said to him, "Why can't you multitask: change the baby's diaper, figure out what she wants to wear, figure out why she's crying and get some lunch . . . now come on." He just looked at me and said, "O.K, what parts do you want me to do?" I, however, thrive on that kind of challenge.

Personal Connections with Teachers Always Made Such a Difference to Me

So, back to elementary school. I finally got help with reading in fifth grade. My appreciation of this opportunity was less about the reading help than about the chance for downtime out of the classroom. In the classroom I needed to move constantly. I would hear a daily litany of: "Lesley sit down," "Lesley shut your desk."

Personal connections with teachers always made such a difference to me. My sixth grade history teacher was friends with my family, youngish, and I thought he was wonderful. That's what kept me going to class and learning and understanding. In eighth grade I had a history teacher who made history interesting, despite being "old school." He wasn't judgmental and would say to me in a relaxed kind of way, "Look, you're going to get it." So although I didn't have any mentors who recognized my interpersonal intelligence (my ability to intuitively "read" others and communicate on a high level with them), I did have some teachers along the way who dispelled the judgments: "She doesn't get it, she's dumb, she's never going to get it . . . how could she have gotten this far . . . her parents are very bright . . . what's wrong with her?"

Altogether I've attended nine years of college—first Berklee for music and then a school in West Virginia for theater—although I never graduated. Berklee was great at first because my entering class was all studying the same material; we had a common purpose and goal. But then I tested into higher level classes, and I couldn't do them. For example, I tested into the fourth year of ear training (exempting the first three years which teaches students to write down what they're hearing), but I had no idea how to read music, so I failed it. My ability level was never backed up by technical "know how," and I was out of synch with my fellow students with a mixture of lower and higher level classes. I wondered, not for the first time, "Where am I and how did I get into this whole pattern?" I eventually had to go to the chair of the department, and he helped me a lot. We developed a terrific relationship. He was much older than I was, but since I was socially precocious, we were on the same level with each other interpersonally and conversed easily. Our meetings became bright lights in the midst of all of my school difficulties. Once again, it was the interaction that I thrived on versus the academic agenda.

At my theater school in West Virginia I worked with a very talented performance coordinator. I was asked to be a stage manager for a show after I had helped with three other plays. I really had no idea, however, what I was doing until up to the last minute. The play, however, went off really well. My teacher later told the dean of the arts department that I was the best stage manager he had ever had. My interpersonal abilities and my ability to multitask had found a creative medium for expression.

Directing, for Me, Is Like Music

After I left academics, I married and settled into family life on a small island off the coast of Maine. One of the ways my interpersonal abilities translated in this environment was in my strong interest in building communities—from my own family (husband and two small daughters) to a community of those whose interests I shared. In building community I valued helping people to move towards what they needed to move towards, not towards my agenda for them. Because I could perceive others' strengths, I was able to encourage their personal learning and growth. I believe that community is strongest when everyone's interests and needs are being honored and supported, and I thrived on utilizing my intuitive insights to facilitate this.

I continued to feel called to develop my singing talent, as well. I have a music gauge. When I was feeling really challenged in a former marriage, I literally could not sing. When I'm more in tune with life, I can more easily tap into my singing. I have done back-up singing for a local group, sung at church and at weddings—nothing major, but I continue to touch base with it, valuing its importance to my well-being.

I love being the only one on stage when I sing, so I was shocked to realize at theater school that I didn't enjoy acting at all—what really intrigued me was directing. First of all, I like to be in charge, and, secondly, I thrive on multitasking. Directing for me is like conducting an orchestra—all the different parts of a production need to flow together. I have the perfect mind for that, because I can *see* it all going on at once. I can picture the whole thing instead of the small picture of, "O.K. you have to go now and you have to go now etc." It's not rote for me. I could never operate sequentially.

Two years ago I had a marvelous opportunity to put my this interest into practice as assistant director of Acadia Community Theater's production of my favorite play, *The Wizard of Oz*. I identify with the magical part of Dorothy that compels her to persevere through all challenges, never giving up hope, in order to achieve her goal. I have come to believe that, despite knowing there's going to be some tough challenges for me up ahead (I haven't met the monkeys yet, but I know they're coming), I'll always be true to my dreams.

Logistically, managing the evening rehearsals was a tremendous challenge for me and my family. From our island the only transportation to Mount Desert Island (where we practiced at the high school) was a mail boat which ran only during the day. Everything, however, fell into place, one thing after another (including midnight rides on a private boat with a friend returning from her late night job). I felt propelled from start to finish by my passion for the project.

The Oz theater experience was rich with opportunities to utilize my intuitive insights and to practice multitasking. I was aware of what needed to happen now, what was going to have to happen later, who knew what, who didn't know what . . . I had to know who was sick, who was mad at so-and-so, why they didn't get along—all of that was perfect for my brain. Through "reading" the participants' energy each rehearsal, I enhanced the orchestration of effective practice times.

My college drama courses came into play when I coached the stage manager on the particulars of her role. "You have to run the show," I told her. "What do you mean I have to run the show?" she said. "That means that Matt (the director) and I sit back in a chair and say, 'This is lovely, and you run the show.'" So I shared with Michelle all the particulars of running a show: This is how you direct the people, this is where you stand, these are the things you are in charge of . . . I also had taken three lighting classes in college, and I knew the lights were wrong—they weren't focused etc. This experience enabled me to validate what I had learned in theater school.

I Really Needed This Experience

The entire Oz experience felt gratifying to a tenfold degree. It proved to me that I *had* paid attention in college, I had been present. I realized that I had indeed absorbed the information in my classes and could give it back and could see the final product and be genuinely pleased with how it went.

I also felt gratified that I was able to maintain the importance of community during rehearsals, highlighting the performers' strengths as well as making constant adjustments to meet their personal/family needs. I believed that other people's lives were just as important as practice needs—so and so has baseball (I altered the schedule slightly), how many people need to go to this dance? etc. And taking into account the director's needs and my needs as well, I read the psychotic meter. "O.K. who's psychotic tonight?" "I am." "O.K. I'll take practice tomorrow." I sent out an energy sensor each night—who is present, who is not going to be able to come through. That allowed potentially restrictive energy to flow. I learned to work on the spot with what showed up.

Despite the daunting demands my schedule made on my family and myself, we all benefited from my having this creative outlet. When I'm not being creative, I weigh more, I can't sing, and I have a really stressed way of doing my life (a lot of sighing etc.). The logistical stresses literally melted away in the face of the creative benefits. I really needed this experience. I had received so much negative feedback in my life, that I needed this boost to encourage the positive to come forward. Just to have recognized even a little affirmation would have made an enormous difference to my self-confidence, and I had this in spades.

It Might Look Like I'm Just Sitting There, but I've Got It All Managed

During the Oz experience, I also recognized that I needed to continue developing a career outside of my home, and I explored job possibilities with the people I was meeting. I applied to and was offered the job of director of the infant/toddler room at Mount Desert Island High School.

My job is interpersonal on a number of levels and definitely requires multitasking—a good match for my abilities. Last year I had nine babies and toddlers and this year, eight. I also have up to five high school students (doing this for a child development class) every eighty minutes who come in with wonderful, loving energy, but also their own difficulties and problems. There is also the parent tier (currently teachers, no students) who come in to visit and feed their children. So there are three levels that I need to negotiate during the day.

It's surprising to me how organized I am in this job. Among my demon voices of the past resides, "You're so disorganized, you can't get it straight, where's your notebook etc." I had taken in that voice and might as well have worn a T shirt that says, "I am so disorganized." But I have actually learned to become really organized, despite my ADD, on projects of my own creation and execution.

My organization is driven by my understanding of needs. If you walk into my classroom, you won't see a circle time or stations where children should be playing (there is such a variation of ages). But in my mind, I'm happily observing the children self-selecting what they want to do, I'm noticing who needs a bottle, who needs a diaper change, who needs a nap . . . It might look like I'm just sitting there, but I've got it all managed. Again, it's about creating community—responding to my perception of the interests and needs of each individual. I don't preplan a program; I work with what shows up each day.

Sometimes It's Just About Moving

I am continuing to learn how to best utilize my gifts and balance my life. In spite of my past demons that sail in to haunt me upon occasion, I am flourishing in a way I never could have anticipated as a struggling learner in school. When I look back on my schooling, I wish I had heard more often that different isn't bad—"Different is interesting, different is intriguing and what could I learn from you," versus, "How can I make you fit in?" This happened once when one of my high school English teachers handed me back a paper that wasn't marked up in red ink. On it he said, "It's all here; come and see me." He told me that I had not missed the mark, and then proceeded to show me how the paper came together when he moved paragraphs around. He finished with, "What a great story you have here; I really enjoyed it." When I received that kind of positive feedback, I didn't feel like I was being stopped. When I saw the red ink, everything that I had thought about was stopped.

At some point in the future I would like to work with kids who are like me. I would like to say to them the words that I needed to hear. "You need to settle down," would become, "Gee, I wish I had as much energy as you do. How can we work with this?"

My friends who are teachers will sometimes ask me about kids they find challenging. My friend, Sarah, during her first year of teaching, consulted me about one of her students who couldn't sit down. I asked her, "Why does he need to sit down?" I suggested that she give him parameters within which he could travel. She allowed him a space of three desk lengths from the window and back. He was so happy all year. He took his work with him and sometimes did it on the window sill. Sarah told me, "That's all he needed." I said, "Yes, sometimes it's just about moving."

As a visual-spatial, gifted learner with unusual psychic abilities, Sandy did not fit traditional, left-brained oriented academic schooling. While she avidly explored visual arts on her own time, she had no forum for or recognition of her talent at school. As a child she felt spooked by her unusual intuitive awareness because she had a schizophrenic grandmother and thus questioned her own sanity. After earning a degree in nursing, Sandy, through the encouragement of a friend, pursued her dream of studying art. For a while she taught art at her children's private school, giving precious opportunities to children who, like herself, had a strong visual-spatial orientation. Her life today is a weaving of all the strands of talents she has explored on her life path. She combines her psychic gifts with her holistic nursing background as a medical intuitive. She gives sacred time to her painting, and encourages those who seek readings with her to similarly nourish their inner lives.

> Work of sight is done. Now do heart
> work on the pictures within you.
> —Rainer Maria Rilke

Sandy's Story

I Was Shattered

My brother, sister, and I were raised having wonderful confidence about who we were and what we did. My mother used to say, "If you work hard enough at something, you can do it." No matter what it was, if you wanted to do it, you could do it. I was also the oldest child in my family and a pleaser-type.

I entered first grade with this confidence, but was shattered when we started reading. There were three groups: the A group, the B group, and the C group. One of my best friends was in the A group. I was in the C group. The book I was reading (from the old "Dick and Jane" series) did not inspire my wondering about what those words were all about. I could read a little bit, and I was slow. I had to look at each word very carefully and think about it. If someone would *tell* me a story, I got it fast and I loved telling stories. The words in "Dick and Jane" just didn't mean much. I preferred doing activities outside to sitting down to read.

I distinctly remember feeling that I was dumb because I was in group C reading this stupid, little, baby book. The A group was reading interesting ones. I also noticed that I didn't hear sounds properly. When my second-grade teacher corrected my pronunciation, I couldn't tell the difference between her correction and what I said. I wanted to be a straight A student; I wanted to do it right.

I loved to draw, but I found handwriting difficult. I recently found a picture—my first drawing from kindergarten that my mother had saved all these years. It was a drawing in red crayon that filled the whole page with intricate lines. I put my name on it and reversed a number of the letters. In second grade we started the Palmer writing method, and I had to work hard at my handwriting; I couldn't stay within those lines for anything. My writing is still irregular. It reflects my moods; it's very free. People often joke that it's so illegible, I really should have been a doctor

In my artwork, I now recognize that I draw lines from a feeling place rather than, "It has to look like this." An exciting line has lost and found qualities to it; it's heavier, it's lighter; it tells a story in one line, one sweep. You may never do that same line again, and you don't really want to. In penmanship, my hand couldn't conform to one kind of line.

I also have difficulty with spelling. I can still spell the same word many ways and not know which is right. I had nightmares when, further along in school, teachers made many corrections in red in the margins because I had all these misspellings. As an adult, I started calling it "creative spelling." My school taught the memorization of words. It would have been wonderful to have the rules and learn how words work.

I Found These Little Ways I Could Really Excel

My reading picked up when I was in fourth grade, and I experienced the joy of discovering books in the library. I was enchanted. One summer I read explorer stories. I can still see some of the books in my hands. I was excited and for the first time enjoyed reading.

I had an ongoing joy about painting. My mother always made sure we had art supplies. One Christmas my grandmother gave me two paint-by-numbers oil painting pictures. One was an ocean scene and the other a horse. I sat down in my polka dot, Christmas p.j.'s after everyone had left, and I began painting. I got up the next day and painted all day in my polka dot p.j.'s. I remember the thrill of seeing these colors that were so intense in comparison to the children's watercolor sets I had been painting with. I loved the smell of oil paint. Here were all these little lines and all these colors coming together to make a picture. I didn't stop or do anything else until I had completed the two paintings. Those paintings are still present in current paintings in the way I draw and paint the image. I can take separate shapes and colors and know how they will work together.

I discovered a love of writing poetry also on my own. When writing my own poetry, I could spell any way I wanted. Something in me was trying to get free, and exploring the meaning of words in poetry felt freeing.

I began doing B+ work in elementary school with very little effort. I realized that I certainly wasn't dumb. There wasn't anything that I absolutely couldn't do, but when I connected to something I really loved, learning was effortless. When something didn't make any sense to me, however, I had to apply a lot of effort.

I loved theater. In fifth grade we had a pageant, the story of Martha Washington, that was put on for the whole elementary school. On the day of the big performance, the girl who played Martha became ill, throwing up just a few minutes before the performance. I was very shy, but I went up to my teacher and said, "I think I can be Martha." I had been so fascinated by the whole theater thing, that I realized I knew all of Martha's lines as well as her stage movements. My teacher looked at me with this great sigh of relief. She picked up Martha's cotton batten wig and put it on me. I was Martha and I was flawless. It was just so wonderful that I had the courage to go and say I could do that! I found these little ways I could really excel.

Oh No, I've Got It Too!

Around age 11, I started having prophetic dreams about events that would sometimes happen. I also began to sense what someone was going to say before they said it. I had known by that time that there were beings or energy present around us that we couldn't see, but it would terrify me. I had a diagnosed schizophrenic grandmother, and all I could think was, "Oh no, I've got it, too." I was very careful not to let on that this was happening. I had started feeling as though I was handling the schoolwork pretty well, and I was well liked; I fit in. I had theater, and people liked my creative stories, although teachers would give me A's on my composition and C's on the mechanics and spelling.

I also had what I now know is a past-life remembrance. I often made my father come up and check the attic by my bedroom, because I thought I could smell smoke. I was always sure there was going to be a fire. That turned out to be a past life. Later these experiences made much more sense.

I Probably Would Have Done Well With Home Schooling

Meanwhile, on my own time, I loved the outdoors. I built tree houses and walked to the woods. I had special places where I'd go and write about how beautiful things were. I was not yet expressing my feelings; that came later. At this earlier point it was just descriptive. I loved colors and shapes, and I was hungry to look at things. More and more of my creativity was coming forth. I drew (though I never visited an art museum or gallery until I was in nursing school) and loved writing poetry and stories.

We left school four to eight weeks every year from first through seventh grade to vacation in Florida. My father owned a seasonal business and got depressed in the winter when he wasn't working. Our family doctor knew that he liked Florida and fishing and suggested that he go there for his health. The school principal believed travel was more educational than school. It was a gift.

In Florida, I did my schoolwork easily. I finished all of the assignments I was given in about one-half hour every day. Back home, if the assignment was not something I wanted to do, it would take forever and feel terrible. But in Florida I thought, "If I do this, I can get on my bike and go down to the beach, to the lighthouse and look for shells." So I focused. That freedom also gave me more time to write and draw. I probably would have done well with home schooling.

I loved doing research. If I knew I had a certain topic to write on, I'd watch for information in the Sunday papers and library. One year in Florida, when I was around eleven, there was a book on the shelves of our rented apartment, *Comparative Religions*. I put away my comic books and I read. What fascinated me was that I believed that if there was Truth, then it went through everything, and I started looking for that Truth. I knew about Zoroastianism (a Persian religion founded in the sixth century BC by the prophet, Zoroaster) when I was eleven years old. My spiritual passions were really starting to come alive. I was a little kid when I put down *Little Lulu* and began reading about religions. And from that time on, my mother couldn't get me to go to Sunday school, because it just didn't equate with what I was learning on my own.

I'd Zone Right Out

Junior high school had seven ability tracks. They put the smartest kids in track 7 to try to fool everyone about the leveling system, but everybody knew that track was the highest. My sixth grade teacher had recognized that I was really bright, that I could apply myself, and that I was a storyteller. He thought that I could make it in the top track. I loved being there. A lot of my friends were there, too. However, they dropped me in the middle of the year from 7/7 down to 7/3, because I just couldn't understand diagraming sentences or develop a report properly; I was humiliated.

In eighth grade I was still in the middle track. My teacher had me stay after school to help me with diagraming sentences. Before her help, English grammar was like a foreign language. Working one-on-one enabled me to understand it. She said she knew I could do it. First, we started with very simple sentences—including a verb, noun, an object and a couple of articles. Well, that was okay. She gave me some more, and then it clicked. I could visualize what these words were doing, and there was a name for what the words were doing. She had me work with her for one hour and the next day I had no problem. I could not only diagram, but I wanted to diagram the most difficult sentences I could find.

The reports for classes were deadly for me, because they were dumb, uncreative, and I knew the teachers were going to make corrections all over my paper, because I made so many mistakes in spelling and grammar; it was a drag. History was boring facts, and I'd zone right out, unless it was a story. The tests were about spitting back facts and dates through multiple choice, and that was awful for me. Essays were great, though, because I was allowed to write my thoughts without the teacher counting my spelling and grammar.

Although I could remember general information like crazy and apply it, I had difficulty memorizing specific things. For example, we were required to memorize poems, and that was hard for me. I'd have to push to do it. I could, however, memorize something if it captivated me (like Martha Washington's part which, while it had a few lines, was mostly about attitude and action, including a dance minuet). I was better at doing more of a performance piece, than sheer spoken memorization.

I continued to enjoy creative writing. In eighth grade I wrote something that my teacher liked and had me make into a play. This teacher was highly creative also and recognized and encouraged me. She took another piece of mine and got it published in a national scholastic competition.

"You're Not That Smart, but You're Nice. You'll Make a Good Nurse."

I was in a real hurry to finish high school. I knew life had to get better. I dreamed of finally finishing high school for years.

A major disappointment with high school was that I wanted to take art and was told I couldn't, because I was college bound. Art was only for the slow students. For years I had been doing art at home. I took riding lessons and I had to earn my own money, so I went around the neighborhood selling drawings of kids' pets for fifty or seventy-five cents. I was always doing something with watercolors; it was easy. My eye would constantly find things that were interesting. I doodled in class and dreamed, oh did I dream! I would be looking at the board and thinking about going canoeing. I couldn't wait until summer came. How I loved the summers!

In high school, I was brilliant in chemistry. I don't know why. I was invited to a small after-school group where we did more advanced chemistry problems. I was the only girl. I was so good at it, my mother said, "Don't let the boys know you're this smart in chemistry, because they won't want to take you to the prom."

Physics didn't make as much sense. I remember at the year's end the physics teacher went around the class asking students what they were going to do after high school. I replied that I was going to nursing school. He said, "That's good. You're not that smart, but you're really nice. You'll make a good nurse." The year before, the chemistry teacher wanted to help me get a scholarship to go to college. If quantum physics had been taught, the story might have been different . . .

One course I loved in high school was a wonderful bullshit course. We sat in a circle, not at desks, and the teacher said he was training us for college. He had us read books, like Machiavelli's *The Prince,* and asked us what we got out of that. I found my hand going up, because I understood the concepts. We didn't write papers; it was all verbal. He taught us to think. That was easy for me. I could make connections, and other kids, who usually got A's, weren't really connecting.

"You Want To Do Your Art, So Do It!"

I wanted to go to art school, but because of finances it was either state teacher's college or nursing school. My mother said I had always fixed little animals (I was this little nature bug, who went out and found injured birds and maimed or orphaned baby rabbits, took them in and fixed them). She said she thought that I would make a good nurse. I went to nursing school.

I had two semesters at the University of Buffalo included in my nursing degree. During that year, I started to like literature. Later I took Chaucer in old English and Survey of African Literature. The nursing part of my program went well, and I did a bang-up job because I found it interesting, but it just didn't feel creative. All I could think about was how much I wanted to go to art school. However, coming from a very practical family, I had been told I could not make a living at art. I didn't know whether I'd be good at it or not. I just wanted to do it.

A resident I dated while in nursing school said, "You want to do art? So *do* it." He gave me the courage to turn in a portfolio. I had no idea how to create a portfolio. I had no art training, and I was competing against kids who had gone to professional art schools in New York City. I turned in my portfolio and forgot all about it. About two months later my brother called me about a letter that had arrived from the University of Buffalo. I asked what it was about. He read that I'd been accepted into art school! So I began art school, moonlighting in nursing on the weekends for tuition and rent.

Art school was wonderful. When I was taught things in specific ways, that didn't bother me, because I knew I had to learn the techniques. I saw it as a challenge and not an insult to my art form (because I hadn't developed an art form yet); I soaked it up. I knew that the more tools I had, the more ways I would have to express what I wanted to convey. I wanted to know all the options, so I could figure out my own voice.

The Children Learned to Look at Things in a Different Way

I finished my art degree part time over four years because I had married and had children. We moved to Houston, and I combined finishing my degree with teaching art at a private school. I was fascinated that the kids who were not A students were the best art students.

We did a wonderful variety of things including animation, sculpture, and performance pieces. It was wild, and they loved it! The results were phenomenal. At the time I thought it would be interesting to put together an art book for teachers with many of my ideas.

One of the things I taught over those years was perspective drawing. I called it "eyeball perspective" for the first through third graders, though books said perspective drawing can't be taught to that age child. Some first graders still drew the sky in a line at the top of the paper. The first thing I did was to have everyone go to the window, come back, and on their paper point to me how far down the sky goes. I'd ask, "Does it come down to here? Just put your hands up." Some put their hands up. "Does it come all the way down to here." A few more hands would go up. Then I'd have them go to the window and look at how far down the sky came. You could hear kids saying, "Oh, it comes down all the way." I helped them see. That was very exciting.

I worked with some kids who weren't doing well academically but were *really* creative. These children glowed. I taught them a new vocabulary. Within my own family one of the best compliments you could have was, "Wow, *that's weird*," or "*That's wild*." I shared the same compliments with these kids. I loved teaching, I absolutely loved it; I could see these kids responding.

I Don't Understand It, but I'm Just Going to Do It

I divorced a regimented marriage, and, after that, my creativity *really* started to come alive. I then found a way to make a living with my art to support my two children. I had studied printmaking at the University of Houston (where I finished up my last half of a BFA) under a master printer from Czechoslovakia. It was like a European apprenticeship. For four years I took every single course offered in printmaking, and he created study courses for me. It was wonderful. I turned printmaking into a business of silkscreening and made a living.

I continued to write. I was journaling, writing children's stories, and I took writers' workshops. I got into writers' groups, published a piece in Pageant magazine, and did graphic design. Then, I realized I had other funny abilities.

It happened one day when I was sitting outside, writing in my journal. All of a sudden, I realized that I was "hearing" another voice. I caught myself; people who did this were crazy. I feared that maybe my grandmother's schizophrenia was catching up with me. Then I remembered being able to do weird stuff when I was younger. What reassured me was that the "voice" felt good, and I thought, "I don't understand it, but I'm just going to write it." The "voice" (intuition) spoke to my art and helped me, because I was getting ready to do a show. The "voice" was saying that what I feel and express will come through my brush and my colors—allow it to flow.

I began journal writing in my garden every day, carving out my personal time around my studio, business time, and two children. I received a series of "channelings." There were themes, like "the human condition," and "responsibility." One theme about guilt ended up being about joy. I thought, "Oh, this is going to be heavy; it won't be any fun." At the very end, I could hear and feel the joy.

I would write fast, sometimes for a full hour or more, and my arm felt ready to drop off. Someone watched me write once and said I really was "channeling," because there was no way a conscious mind could be spilling out stuff that fast for that long. The writing was in very poetic, heartsongy words.

I didn't know what to do with that piece of my life until, out of desperation to better understand a relationship, I had a session with a psychic. After our session, she insisted I had to come to her workshop on the weekend. I wanted to say, "No," because my background was scientific, practical; I was too skeptical. However, I was afraid to say that I wouldn't be there, because she was about six foot two and had these "woo-woo" eyes that seemed to look through me. I went, but I thought it was going to be a waste of time.

Right away she had us line up in front of a man who was really sick. She said, "What do you feel? Imagine that you are wearing Max's body. What doesn't feel right?" It was obvious to me that his sinuses were yucky. At first I was quiet, because I was a newcomer. Nobody was saying anything, so I said I was feeling this, this, and this and the sinuses are . . . The facilitator with a great big grin said, "Yes. And?" I said that I was feeling this pressure in the chest; now I'm feeling . . . and she was laughing at this point, saying, "See, I told you, you had to be here." And I thought, "This is weird but exciting."

Then I was put in front of a woman I didn't know. "I want you to sit here and tell her what's wrong with her." I said, "How do I do that?" "Just do it," she said. I sat there, and all of a sudden I saw a vertebrae (I knew it was a vertebrae from my anatomy studies) that was twisted and had this s-shaped black mark in it. I described it, and the teacher said, "That's it! She fractured one of her vertebrae. What are you going to do about it?" I didn't know what to do. She suggested that I give her back the image of painting it with coral. That's a natural substance and it's strong. She said to use strengthening images.

Later that afternoon I was sent to another woman. I saw people putting their hands up in the air over her. I thought, "Okay, then I'll put my hands there." All of a sudden my hands came up over her kidney area, and I said, "Ooh. I'm seeing your kidneys, and they're red and inflamed." I asked a professional healer, who was paid to do this work, to double-check my reading. He did it in a different way, but he said I was right, and asked, "How long have you been doing this?" I looked at my watch and said, "Four hours." He said, "You're *really* good."

I didn't know what to do with this "woo-woo" stuff, but I kept taking workshops, and later joined a study group. Soon I was assisting in teaching, because I could do it so easily. I did not have a term for what I was doing until I heard the term "medical intuitive" from Carolyn Myss (medical intuitive, author of *Energy Anatomy*).

People Started Figuring Out That I Was Doing Something Different

My professional work changed dramatically when my eighteen-year-old son had a terrible head injury, resulting in much reduced functioning. I had no time to do big paintings and art shows although I did continue somewhat in my business. Mostly, I took care of my son. Friends and some of their friends would have me do "intuitive readings," and they gave me lots of practice. I finally sold my house in Houston and moved to Maine with my son where I reestablished my art business. The economy had a big decline in 1991. When the economy gets bad, art-related business suffers. I had been working with three publishers around the country who closed at the same time.

It was time to change my work. The only thing I could find to do to support myself, my son, and house mortgage was long-term care nursing (I hadn't been a nurse in a quarter of a century). After a couple of years, co-workers figured out I was doing something different. I began to teach staff about holistic nursing and intuition.

I continued learning more about holistic nursing and found out about others around the country who were "woo-woo" nurses. I also took courses in holistic nursing. I worked very hard for certification. The course required a year long practicum and academic writing that was not easy for me.

In one course, we learned about taking care of the caregiver. This was a vital piece for me, because I was so focused on taking care of everybody else. "You mean I'm supposed to take care of myself and listen to my own intuition?" We learned about the ripple effect. The gist of it is this: if we take care of ourselves, are true to ourselves, listen to our hearts, that energy is going to ripple out into our family. From there it ripples out into community, community to nation, nation into the world and so on. Everything we choose to do has this wonderful ripple effect.

I learned about Reiki (hands-on channeling of healing energy) and realized others were doing unusual things, like I was doing, but they were doing it professionally. So I began a part-time medical intuitive and Reiki practice. A year later I opened a private practice full time.

If Someone Is There Validating Us, We Can Recognize What We Really Know

My intuitive/energy work is fun, and the people I have worked with have said they've had real life changes from learning about themselves. What I actually do in these sessions relates to abilities I had when I was little, things I just knew. For example, I see energy fields around people. The energy I pick up around people is translated in some form for me through a metaphor or an image or maybe a word. When I work like this, I have learned to step aside of who I am; I'm there to serve this person, to be a translator. While I'm doing it, I'm not really that aware of being me and set expectations to the side. That took a lot of practice.

"Channeled" information comes from my inner guidance or clients' greater wisdom. Humor is often there. The awareness gives me some guidance, like a direction to go in, a question to ask, or, sometimes it's guidance about how to phrase something so it comes out in the clearest way.

Validating intuition is important for me in terms of my self-validation. Trusting intuition is more important than any teacher I've had in the physical plane. Intuition validates my art and wisdom.

Every session with clients is unique. It's about seeking universal truths, like those I sought as a child reading about the world's religions looking for the thread of truth that went through them all. If there is a thread of truth, it is love at a high level. I think everything is healed with love (perhaps not cured but healed). When people love themselves, they can heal and become empowered to manifest their inner knowing and potential.

We are all so much wiser than we think we are, and if someone validates us, we can easily recognize our wisdom and direction. I had talents, I wasn't a freak, I wasn't schizophrenic, and I wasn't stupid.

I have also returned to my art. I did a commissioned painting of pink river dolphins based on a woman's spiritual questing. My psychic teacher in Houston had said that when I went to Maine, I would find my people, do healing work, teach, and paint "soul paintings." At the time I wasn't doing any of these, and I thought that she was really off the mark. The painting about the pink dolphins is a soul painting about visions, dreams, and personal myths.

The strands of my life have all come together—my writing, art, psychic ability, subtle energy healing work, and holistic nursing. These are all beautifully intertwined. If I'd consciously orchestrated it, I couldn't have done it any better.

It really does all come together—all those little talents. So many people are so miserable and depressed, because they feel that dreams at soul level cannot be brought forth. The majority of people requesting "energy readings" are using their creativity at a tiny amount of their potential. Other demands on their time drain them. I want to bring that creative spark to the front.

Addendum

At the time of the editing of this interview, I have returned to my own writing and painting full time, and I have created a small retreat center for others to reconnect to their creativity. Embracing my native creative expression feels like a long-held dream coming to life. Once found, my commitment has been relentless. Sharing my joy of this creative reality will encourage others to follow their dreams and expression.

Linden's story shares the journey of an artistically creative individual with sensitivities of acute perception and energy attunement. Her journey towards living her life creatively, true to her light, documents her triumph over disempowering obstacles in aspects of her schooling and pervasively in her family life. Initially, while Linden's refined sensitivities engendered an astute understanding of and appreciation for her varied childhood living circumstances, these same sensitivities overwhelmed her, stymying her creative expression. As an adult, Linden developed a creative life process which empowered her sensitivities to be the gift of expression, not just perception, that they were meant to be. Today, both her art work and her art process facilitation invite hope and personal empowerment for others. Linden's story offers inspiration to all who yearn to free their inner spirit.

There is the risk you cannot afford to take
(and)
there is the risk you cannot afford not to take.
—Peter Drucker in The Artist's Way

Linden's Story

Everything Was Very Magical In Appearance

During the first eight years of my life in California, Alaska, and South Carolina I think my parents were in the idealistic stage of being a family together. Everything was very magical in appearance. My mother made my two sisters, our dolls, and I beautiful dresses and pinafores, and we visited places like Fairyland wearing our Alice in Wonderland look-a-likes. Everything was picture perfect. My mother did all the housemaker's things very beautifully; she was an artist and perfectionist in whatever she touched. We modeled the things that my mother sewed for us, and we represented our family image as we were the small images of what our family was doing. It was rather typical of the fifties—lots of show.

I loved all the things my mother created and fed from those quietly, but I didn't create on my own. I was the helper, always standing by for what needed to be done. My dad was handy with tools, so I brought him his requested tools. While I never used the tools then, I did learn all about them. Similarly, with my mother, I got to know all the art materials. I would assist her in getting her pictures out; I would model for her, but I didn't actually do the creative work. I was the fetcher, supporter, observer. My creative expression was not looked for or encouraged.

Up until the tenth grade, we lived in tight-knit neighborhoods where I was able to visit others freely and would find ways in which to be useful in order to belong. As well, I loved the hands-on experiences. For example, if someone were building a brick patio for their pool, I would help lay the bricks. I loved actually doing the work. Despite the roaming I was allowed to do, however, I lived in an authoritarian family and was highly controlled in my choice of activities, beliefs, and what feelings to have.

I Was a Very Sensitive Observer

Being a navy family, we moved a lot, and when I was nine we moved to the Philippines. We lived eight miles up a mountain in the jungle in a cleared off space with a chain link fence all around it. The compound included a hospital and eight homes. Right outside the fence was the jungle with Howler Monkeys, Fruit Bats, Pythons and wild boars which were as much a part of our day as song birds are here. I loved the stark contrast to the U.S.

I was very interested in everything about this new culture and my mom was too. She actively took us on adventures outside the fence. One time we went to a place where they used to have the beautiful summer resorts, but the pools had become overgrown with vines. I was fascinated by the idea of what used to be there, imagining what the life was like. Another time we went up some falls in boats to where there were bamboo foot bridges flung across the large ravines that we walked across; it was very exciting. After that we continued walking up to where the Pygmies lived, and I gave a woman, the size of myself, three of my dresses that we had brought to give away. When we came down from our climb, she was wearing all three dresses. That image has been very powerful for me through the years. I remember thinking about what that meant to her to have them and thinking about how different my own life was.

Now I marvel about how willing my mother was to take us exploring beyond the fence. However, despite the exotic adventures she exposed us to, my mother and my father, as well, still dictated our choice of activities, what we wore, what we did, and how we breathed. However, looking back, I realize what a sensitive creature I was and how astutely I observed the world through my own lens. However, I kept my knowings to myself.

My thirst for international experiences was planted in the Philippines. Following our stay there we went to Japan for two weeks. Again, my mother immersed my family in the culture. In my adult life I went back to Japan for two years and later lived in Norway for two years as well as traveling in many other countries. My international experiences opened up for me a perspective on life which permeates how I live and everything I choose to do. It has an influence on my smallest to my most important choices regarding my philosophies, perceptions, and desires. It sculpted me.

Because I've lived so many places, I developed a way to provide continuity and structure to my life's unfolding by gathering what was magical and wonderful about each experience. I loved living by the river and what that meant; I loved living on top of a mountain and what that meant. The gift of this way of processing life has been that I continue to seek the magical and wonderful in all my experiences even those that are sorrowful or impoverished. Also, I realize, looking back on the many restrictive walls my parents constructed, I was driven to find a light within those parameters.

I Shut Completely Down

In the Philippines in fourth and fifth grade, however, I had experiences in school that shut me down completely. When I look back on my three years of schooling before that, I have no sense of being unhappy or discontented. I also have no sense of whether I was a good student or not, of whether I struggled—I just remember jumping rope and being a kid. I also remember being Cinderella in my class play, being up on stage, the center of attention, and I would not have been able to do that after my fourth grade experience. There were fifty kids in my class, and I didn't know anybody; I felt invisible. I had no idea how to make friends within this environment. I sat and looked out the windows for two years.

Mrs. Irons was my fourth grade teacher, and she ruled the class with an iron hand. There was a little boy in our class who was always in trouble, and she would twist his ear and take him off to the corner. If he misbehaved, we all missed recess. I was so frightened, I didn't ever say anything; I just held my breath hoping to fade from view. I never learned to read beyond whatever I learned through third grade, and I would cry and cry over my homework. That year I had piano lessons with a lovely Philippino teacher, Aurora, but I resisted the lessons in order to exercise some say in my life. I remember wondering to myself why I was being mean to my piano teacher who was just lovely.

The one light during those school years was my music teacher, Mrs. Z. She was an abrupt person, kind of scary, but she was dynamite! She really loved what she taught, and if you were interested in the subject and participated and learned, that was all that she asked of you. I felt safe with her, because her agenda and mine were a match. She taught us Tinikling (a bamboo pole dance) and songs which I loved and still sing to children today. She gave me what I wanted—not facts, but experiences. Her classes were very hands-on;

we sang the songs and danced the dances. I participated with my own voice and movements within her structure and felt the beginnings of some joy. However, other than the rich experiences I had in the music class, I felt that I learned nothing those two years. At this juncture the oppressiveness of my school life matched that of my family life.

Exciting the Light

For my sixth grade we moved to Long Island, New York, and I went to a really top notch school with terrific teachers and a great program. The teachers were exciting and the kids were exciting, although initially I remember feeling positively pale. On my first day of school I wore an organza pink dress my mother had selected and everybody else was in play clothes. This set me apart (along with my shyness and innocence), for even though I had had unusual experiences abroad, I had led a very sheltered life in many respects. I also felt apart from the other kids because I couldn't read well.

My teacher, Mr. Dunham, was also new to the school. He was a big, tall man with a nice manner, and he took me under his wing—I was the new one, and he was the new one, so we had a bond. I had a special reading program with a boy named Glenn, and our reader was three grades below the level of everyone else in the class. Being in the same reading group with Glenn gave me the feeling of being unrecognized and misunderstood by my classmates. The school had a big science program, and I was amazed with the concepts I learned—like the particles of matter—that my classmates had been learning about since second grade. These concepts opened up a world to me that I had never known existed.

Because my education had been so lacking, I couldn't do a lot of the grade level work, so Mr. Dunham tapped into what I *could* do. I remember making huge brown paper maps of all of the continents. I had a project and liked making something for the class; I gained acceptance and found an active role. Also doing the maps felt therapeutic and was the kind of hands-on experience I craved. I love maps and the sense of adventure they spark in me, and I thought at one time that I might be a cartographer.

That year with Mr. Dunham, I became a reader through the augmentation of experiences at home. My father listened to me read every word of *Pippi Longstocking* which confirmed to me that I *could* read. Subsequently I found *The Secret Garden*, my favorite book to this day, and the first book I read to myself. I identified with Mary and Colin who were both restricted by the adults in their life and had to find their way out of a foggy and sorrowful place into their secret light—which they eventually felt safe to bring forth into the world.

We stayed four years on Long Island, and my experiences there held the best part of neighborhood and school life in memory and the worse part of family life for me. It was here at the age of 13 that my innocence fell away and one more layer of darkness dampened my sense of self. It was safer to be invisible.

In the ninth grade I had a gifted English teacher, Mr. Kopp, who offered fascinating titles in a literature-based program like: *The Good Earth* by Pearl S. Buck, *Raisin in the Sun* by Lorraine Hansberry, *The Nectar in a Sieve* by Kamala Markandaya. Our book discussions were fascinating. Once again my light was sparked by these powerful descriptions of cultures that I could identify with, augmented by my own sensitive observations on our family travels. Similar to Mrs. Z.'s music class and my map experience with Mr. Dunham, I felt gifted by an experience which gave me an opportunity to shine forth to myself.

We moved to Florida for my last three years of high school. I was always in honors math and in the low English class with kids who had lots of problems and often ended up dropping out of school. I imagine that my placement in English classes had to do with my inability to perform on timed tests. I would look great in these classes, because I would do my work and I was interested.

While I love the ideas in books and I love the language, it takes me a long time to read. I like to read books that give me information and stories set in other cultures. I particularly enjoy reading about people's journeys to finding their light. In reading aloud to my own three children, I have found that I also love young adult books because of their healthy values and and strong descriptions of healthy families. Growing up, I had a longing to experience healthy family life. So, I basically read for inspiration.

Along with some difficulties in reading, I also had difficulties with writing. I remember in eighth grade sitting there with an assignment to write five hundred words. After what seemed like two hours, I wrote my first sentence, and I felt like I said all that I wanted to say. And that's the way it has always been with me and writing. I did take a spontaneous writing class weekly for four years during the time my son Brennen was sick with Leukemia, and I was able to break through to write for myself. I can do that if I want to, but I think that I gravitate towards brevity in expressing my ideas—a distillation of my thinking, often in combination with art.

Searching Out of the Fog

There was a part of me that has always been very orderly and organized. However, it took me years to acknowledge and develop my creative side. My older sister was seen as the highly creative child in my family, and I was seen as being organized and orderly. She ended up going to art school and I, because I didn't understand myself well, trained to be an elementary teacher.

My college experience at the University of Vermont was depressing, although I loved Vermont. I was overwhelmed by the number of students, the generic course work, and lack of hands-on learning or practical application. I felt very unsuccessful and shut down again. The only parts of my teacher training program that I loved were the creative parts—like an art course on the techniques of color and children's literature. I also vividly remember a talk that Joseph Campbell (author of *The Power of Myth*) gave at our school. I found his ideas so exciting, but I wasn't ready to integrate them into my life, because I had not validated or consciously invited forth that mystical piece of myself. It was, though, the beginning of my later conscious development of a spiritual life, a seed planted years before I could nurture it.

For the next twenty-two years, I was married and divorced two times, had three children and lived in Vermont, Japan, Illinois, Indiana, Norway, and Maine. During this period, I was searching out of the fog, trying for the consistent lightness of spirit and joy that I can experience now which then dappled in and out of my life only occasionally. With the birth of my third child, I developed a blood clot and during the eleven days that I lay in the hospital, I vowed to change how I lived my life. The challenges of this change become the risks that I could not afford not to take. I vowed to nourish that which brought out my gifts, my joy, my light.

> To find what is worth keeping and with a breath of kindness blow
> the rest away.
>
> —Robbie Robertson

This took time and evolution of self.

During the next ten years of my life I focused on healing and nourishing myself and my family. I went to psychotherapy, dance therapy, acupuncture, and an astrologist. I took classes in yoga, African dance, visual arts, writing, and began dancing again. I also began taking my art work seriously and joyfully. I single-parented my three children and helped my son to live his life to the fullest during his six year struggle with Leukemia. I was his cheerleader, the one to help him find "the cake" when there was no sweetness to be seen. I began embracing, creating, and integrating a new belief system and spirituality.

Nine months after my son died, I began to unfold and live life more fully from my authentic core. From the expanded consciousness that I allowed myself, my son, in spirit, supported this journey. I energetically felt the "good job mom" pat on the backs as I took greater risks to live my life to my fullest.

During the past five years I took a workshop, "True Heart/True Mind," which led me learn Reiki (healing light energy). I met with a talented intuitive monthly for four years who became my creativity cheerleader. I joined a dance community that became a lifeline of social life and fun and energized me to meet the responsibilities in my life with light. This also gave me the opportunity to dress up and sparkle. I was in my passion and I was glowing. Dance remains a gift to myself; if I forget to dance my whole life bogs down. During this time also, I went to "The Gift Retreat" during which I healed and let go of that which is not useful to who I am, inviting forth that which I want to be.

I So Love Awakening Joy Through Embracing My Creative Process

Regarding my work, during this time I left my "safe" jobs and created my own home business which initially consisted of offering Reiki and art process work (self-exploration through art), and doing my four modes of art work: collage, inspirational water color cards with writings from my life experiences, lamp shades, and a wide variety of painted creations (like mirrors, boxes, chairs, etc.). I have since added mural work, family care, children's book consulting, gallery work, and catering. I continually rebalance my business asking for "good work" to do. Staying in touch with purposeful work has allowed me to further let go of attachments around securities like money, health insurance etc.

Reiki is a perfect energy modality for me. People have often commented to me over the years that my energy field of calmness and presence was of great benefit to them, moreso than what I said. I have so often felt that I have struggled with speech and communication, feeling tongue-tied when under pressure to respond to a topic (then later thinking of all the things I'd really wanted to say). Reiki has that element of silence, and yet through transmitting healing energy, you're doing something for somebody. Also my fine sensitivity to energy fields supports this work.

My visual art work explores the theme of moving from sorrow to joy and celebration. It is spiritual and whimsical. I have drawn upon my observations of life, and after pondering them, have transformed them into poetry and images. My art invites hope and personal empowerment. In my art process with my clients, I listen to what people are saying or asking for, and I open to what the situation is intuitively asking of me; I provide the service organically from that insight. I open to the light in myself and others.

Through my own struggle to free myself to recognize and express who I really am—to "follow my bliss" as Joseph Campbell says—moving beyond the confines of the physical and psychological barriers created in my family and in some of my schooling (and consequently my self-created barriers), I am able to perceive the stress in other people's lives and offer wisdom from my own growth experiences. I look for each person's personal power. I so love awakening joy through embracing my creative process with my own work and with others.

My unusual sensitivities from an early age opened me to worlds within worlds, astute understandings of human nature, light within darkness. My awarenesses tapped from these very sensitivities, which often felt overwhelming to me, led me to tune out and shut down in many circumstances, hiding my wisdom and my creativity from others as well as myself. Today I have learned to creatively manage this sensitivity in how I take myself out in the world in order to keep open to all situations I choose. For example, I arrive early at an event allowing me to process each person's energy field in small doses as they arrive. My sensitivities have become the gift they were meant to be, and living my life from my creative core has enabled me to move into increasing easement and flow. To a great measure, I have found peace.

In the following story, my son Matt talks about his growth into empowerment. However, in this case, rather than focusing on the influence of teachers and mentors, Matt focuses entirely on his internal creative process. He explores the internal experiences of a highly sensitive, creative individual, who, despite his brilliant mind and many talents, struggled against self-annihilation. Matt's journey of learning to channel his creativity in a healthy and fruitful manner is an inspiring model for all who struggle with the challenges of demanding creative forces.

> To live a creative life, we must lose
> our fear of being wrong.
> —Joseph Chilton Pearce

Matt's Story

I Was Haunted by Those Images

My earliest learning memory, at age four, is very clear. I was sitting at our study table scribbling all sorts of different colors on paper with crayons, and then, right out of the blue, a circle came, right there on the paper. I' d been doing zig zaggy lines that looked to me like a bunch of colored streamers. But all of a sudden, right in the middle, was this perfect little circle. I was very impressed by that, so impressed that I showed everybody. From that circle, I started making circle people, typical of children's drawings with the arms and legs growing out of the head.

My earliest form of self-expression was definitely drawing. I remember learning how to make triangles, and with triangles I could draw swords and heroes with swords. I could also make letters. I could make the letter M for Matt, my name, and turn the M upside down making vampire teeth. I remember getting *very* excited by my drawings. My two older brothers, Michael and Adam, had some pictures displayed on the refrigerator door to which I proudly added my own budding art work. Michael, at age 10, had some pretty advanced artistic skills, so I worked like crazy to try to get up to his status.

At age five and six my passion for drawing became based around the children's books my father read to me—and he read to me a lot. The best thing about those children's books was the illustrations, particularly those of Steven Kellogg and Chris Van Allsburg. I loved Steven Kellogg's illustrations for his ability to create lots of images on one page; you would always have something to look at. I loved Chris Van Allsburg's illustrations, because he created drawings that looked like photos, and I couldn't believe that some artists could draw so well, that they could trick the eye into believing there were objects that were closer to you and objects that were further away from you that cast shadows. I fell in love with those books. My two favorites were the *Island of the Skog* by Steven Kellogg and *Jumanji* by Chris Van Allsburg. I was haunted by those images.

I Had These Intense Personal Standards

Throughout my schooling, I was tormented by runaway anxiety episodes. The sensation I had at these times was that the world is a very heavy and frightening place, and that you don't want to push it too hard, or it will swallow you whole and put you in a place of darkness. I remember an experience in fourth grade when the teacher was at the blackboard writing information about narrative techniques in the book we were reading. I remember thinking, "My God this is so heavy; this is *real school* here." I felt like I was all of a sudden taking a college course, and a huge fear ran through me as I wondered, "Am I up for it? There's gotta be a trick here, there's gotta be something that's deeper and more complicated than what I'm picking up on. How can I even begin to approach this?" In fifth grade we had question and answer assignments about the reading in our social studies textbook. I spent about four pages on each question just to make certain that there was a competent level of seriousness. Every single time that these worries came up, I would get reality checks from the teachers that actually what I was producing was ten times more intense and thorough than the questions required.

In my sophomore year in high school I'd been lauded time and time again for my intelligence and my depth of insight. So I think I pressured myself to get to the heart of things, and I had to get to it perfectly and cleanly, otherwise it was counterfeit—cheating. For example, I'd write pages and pages and pages of notes about different elements of a short story we had to analyze, but I could never organize a paper because the whole thing seemed so huge.

It's About Coming Into Balance

Eventually I broke down under this self-imposed pressure, and I couldn't get any school work done at all. After my breakdown, I began a process of learning how to proceed with my work in manageable sections. I learned how to let go of taking huge things on, swallowing them whole and attempting to come out with divine creations that were either despicable or miraculous. I learned how, actually, to contribute a little bit of something every day and to be satisfied with the doing and building of it, as opposed to the miraculous "pregnancy and birth" of it.

In my sophomore year of high school, I had a term paper to work on that felt monstrous. It was only ten pages, but at that time the idea of writing ten pages of analysis felt enormous. How was I ever going to do such a thing? I had a tutor, Ann, who constantly reminded me that it was about the doing of things that was important, not worrying about if the divine touch was going to come down and explode through this paper, or not. Ann would also ask me, "What would you be able to live with if it got done? Would you be able to live with a C paper?" "Yes, of course," I answered. "Are you sure?" she'd ask. That's where I really had to step back and say, "Yes, I'm willing to get a mediocre grade if I can get this thing done." That was the really big step for me, consciously allowing myself to be imperfect.

For challenging projects, I've developed a system of working on the parts where I give myself a limited amount of time—literally putting in my hours as if I was doing a manual labor job and leaving it when the time is up. Despite this containment, however, at some point, there comes a moment when the ball really gets rolling and ideas start flowing. That's a moment that I've worked very hard to try and temper—not necessarily to control or quench or ignore, but to temper. The reason for that is that the moment I get an inspiring idea, my first instinct is to run with it and run with it and run with it. But that gets me into the very same energy that makes me run with negative ideas—go with it, go with it, go with it until the whole world is colored with this dark thing dominating every element of my life.

Instead, I've developed a very helpful belief in embracing "the dull." I'm defining "dull" in the sense of something that is *completely unmiraculous*, something that makes so much sense it's like breathing. I read an essay once, about the human body's ability to adapt, in which the author used jogging as a "dull" example. If you jog every night, you'll go from being in extreme pain from your first jog, to, perhaps a month later, jogging the way you'd walk and feeling the same way. What I find so useful about that idea is that it puts you in a process where miraculous things are within your day-to-day control dependent only on your dull, daily actions. Although it is certainly not a glamorous approach, it allows me to get remarkable things accomplished without crashing.

The creative process is such a scary one in so many ways; it is a leap into the unknown. That's why it's so important for me to have those parameters of focused, structured time to say, "I'm going off the deep end, but the life preserver is right over there—we'll do a piece of work and let it go." You just give yourself a nice parameter, and then you get to dive into it, giving intuition a nice, safe place to play. If you do that enough times, then amazing new things form—they just happen. I have done piece after piece of writing, that is far more developed than the original idea that I came up with, through allowing myself on a regular, healthy basis to open and then seal, to process and then digest.

A Director Has to Let Go and Trust

Theater directing, which is where I choose to focus my creative energy for the foreseeable future, is such a huge challenge for an independent, creative individual who likes to feel in control. Pre-production work is completely gratifying, because I can sit down and set things out all on my own. That process is just delightful. I get to interpret the play—drawing little comic book versions of all the actions and the choreography; I do my research, and I establish my own angle on the play, I frame certain events, I begin to put music to it . . .

The challenge of directing is that, to a certain extent, you have to give up that control and security when you go into rehearsals. A director has to let go and trust. The director has to let go of being the solidifier and manipulator of the situation and become the source of inspiration for the other creators who are the actors, musicians, technicians, and stage managers. And the giving over can be uncomfortable.

I remember on Show Night for a theatre piece in Spain that I was acting in and directing (during a college jr. year abroad), one of the cast members, Jesus, came up to me and said, "You look nervous," and I said, "I am. I just want everything to go O.K." Jesus said, "Don't worry; you'll do great." I thought to myself, "I know I'll get through it as an actor—I've been there, done that." Then Jesus—who I originally didn't think was going be the kind of guy that I could connect with—put his arm around me and said, "Hey listen. Great leaders know how to distribute the work load. Trust us." And I remember at the time thinking that if I had to put a pile of bricks in my backpack and jog up a nine mile mountain, I would do that if I knew it would make the show come out perfectly. But I had to do something *even more challenging* ; I had to let go.

It Just Bloomed

The joy of directing is learning to first scaffold deadlines and focuses then to let go in ways you never dreamed possible. That's an enormous challenge, because I do want the show to be good, and I do have ideas that are *so good*. However, I say to myself, "You know, as good as it is in your head, you've got to let it become theirs and let them reinvent it." Of course the risk you run is that they will take it in a direction that doesn't have anything to do with anything, and all of a sudden you lose the thread of the show, and the show doesn't have direction. So the director *does* have to establish limits and become the voice of "more of this and less of that, within this amount of time, try it this way."

I remember another insightful point in my Spain year. I was directing my American classmates in a Thanksgiving pageant. We were trying to work out the first bit—how the Pilgrims landed on Plymouth Rock and how difficult it was for them to find food and then how the "Indians" saved them from starving and showed them how to plant. In discussion, we seemed to be getting nowhere when a moment of perfect directing manifested, a moment that I almost think was just handed to me so I could remember it in future directing projects. I was walking in a circle saying, "Just walk, get your body moving, get your blood flowing." And they were saying, "Matt this is stupid. What does this have to do with anything?" "Just do it," I said. So they got moving and at some point one of them said (joking around), "We should do something like in our Flamenco class," and they spontaneously did this dance routine in front of me. Now if my attention had been elsewhere at the time, I could have said, "Okay, enough fooling around; let's get on with what we really have to do." But that very second I saw great energy coming towards me, and I said, "Sounds great; let's use that." And they said, "What? We were just fooling around." I said, "No, what you were doing was great. It was energetic, lively. You guys do it really well. Let's use it somehow." They said, "How?" I said, "What if when you turned around on this movement, you mimed having a gun in your hand. When you're marching forth on this number, you are marching forth looking for food." Within twenty minutes, we had the first moments of all the first key events of that piece choreographed. It just bloomed.

The Director Becomes a Navigator of Energies

That's something I need to be doing more of as a director—looking for those moments of energy and saying to myself, "This is not necessarily fitting into your masterplan, but let it go and see where it takes you." The director becomes a navigator of energies. The director sits in this little sailboat and the cast provides the winds and the waves. It's the director's job to say, "This wind is really strong, so I turn the sails this way to get us going in this direction. How do we harness this particular energy force to our advantage, so we can get to where we are going faster?"

A directing project I did in college, consisting of two completely different shows, one experimental and one traditional, illustrates these challenges. Both were leaps into the unknown, because with a traditional piece, you're talking about the challenge of professionalism, whereas with an experimental piece, you're talking about literally trying to pull a form out of nothing. While I wish I had been able to be even *more* flexible in my directing, I do appreciate the challenges I was up against. With the experimental piece, I was working with ten extremely enthusiastic minds, and there was the challenge of taking this bubble bath of energy and trying to channel it into *something*. So I had to impose very strong limits. I had to consistently say, "O.K. We're going in this direction and we're going to leave this behind. Does anyone have any serious objections to that?" ("Please don't," I thought.) But little bit by little bit, the piece became something truly original; it was just wonderful. We did it by allowing ideas to come in pyramid fashion. At the beginning you're at the base, and you're scattered in all these different directions, and then you get to the next level and there are fewer directions in which you can go, which inspires the third level where you've canceled out all of the other options, and you have a really tight nugget of a piece. It came together, one step at a time within a give-and-take process of, "We are now within this chamber with these options, give me your ideas." And then onto the next chamber.

With the traditional piece, it was more about problem solving, because it was more concrete from the start. So I encouraged the actors to just experiment. For instance there was a moment in the piece where a wife had to be comforted by her husband, and we needed to establish a close relationship. I told the two actors involved to play with finding positions that were comfortable. First they tried cuddling standing up. I said, "O.K. That's an option. Is it comfortable?" No it wasn't. So I told them to keep trying, and eventually they just sank to the ground so that the husband could really cradle the wife in his arms. That felt just great to them, so we needed to find a way to include that. We eventually established a dramatic sequence in which the wife fainted, and the husband had to come down and scoop the wife up in his arms which added a whole new twist. When you open yourself up, you allow for happenings—even better than what you could have imagined—to come and solidify themselves. And that happened again and again in that process. I think the audience got to see what was largely a product of every single cast member's inner brilliance being let out and then bottled in a certain way. That's the goal every single time a director directs, and hopefully with each process the audience gets to see a glimpse of that inner brilliance more and more with each show that I put on.

CODA

In just about every book or article I've read on directing, different masters tend to agree on two points: a good director is extremely organized; a good director is gentle and positive with the actors. If you are not organized, then all the energy drains out of the rehearsal. If you are not gentle and positive with the actors, they will hide within themselves, and their performance will be a brittle shell.

The same goes for the way I treat myself if I want to get good work done. Without specific goals and limits, I feel like a slave to whatever work I do. Without a gentle and positive attitude towards my efforts, I will procrastinate, produce safe, dull work and hide under the covers when I sense that Feedback is nearby.

I've listened to people who talk about their creative process as if it can only have integrity if it is informed by agony. I've come to a couple of conclusions about such an idea:

1. The agony in a creative process is not in the doing, but in the *anticipation* of the doing. Doing a project may sometimes be scary and tiring, but I've never been in as much pain as when I'm anticipating the pain. And as soon as you realize that THIS MOMENT of sitting on your couch, biting your nails and projecting three hours ahead of time, that THIS is as bad as it gets, then you will notice that most of the heaviness vanishes. You can just go to work and leave your work when it's time to stop. Dull. Wonderful.

2. People who openly frame their creative process as some sort of self-martyring, are usually just trying to impress you. They want validation that it can be difficult and frustrating. They want their efforts made tangible through the degree that you are intimidated by the description of the process. Ya know what? When you peel back all the big, scary layers of responsibility and expertise, this tortured artist is still operating from the child's impulse to *play.* We do our creative projects because fundamentally, it is GREAT FUN.

*   *   *

My fellow creators, here is my wish for you and myself: Let's be peaceful and productive. Let's set parameters for ourselves and play within them. Let's be so gentle and positive with ourselves that positive and critical feedback have the same effect on us. And through this dull approach, let's behold, on a daily basis, the extraordinary richness that flows forth.

PART III

Implications of Education for Creatively Gifted Learners: Awakening Passion and Authenticity in All Learners

The sole concern of learning
is to seek one's original heart.

—Mencius

In my introduction to Section II, "Heartsongs: The Struggles and Triumphs of Creatively Gifted Learners," I discussed following the throughline of each learner's story, noting what passions and abilities were seeking development. Highly creative learners feel compelled to be true to their authentic callings. We all, however, have a unique calling. Teachers who are listening to and living their inner guidance are in a position to awaken Self-awareness in all of their learners.

Educating for Wholeness

Many programs are trying to effect educational reform
from the outside in, but the greatest immediate power
we have is to work to reform from the inside out.
Ultimately, human wholeness does not come
from changes in our institutions, it comes
from the reformation of our hearts.

—Parker Palmer, *The Courage to Teach*

To foster authentic learner empowerment, teachers must discern and cherish wholeness in themselves and others. Wholeness includes the personality, but is beyond that personality; it includes the consciousness of the inner being, the wisdom of the heart. Dr. Rachel Naomi Remen (1999), a holistic medical educator, writes in *The Heart of Learning Spirituality in Education:*

> *Educare* the root of the word *education* means "to lead forth the hidden wholeness," the innate integrity that is in every person . . . And, as such, there is a place where "to educate" and "to heal" mean the same thing. Educators and healers both trust in the wholeness of life and in the wholeness of people. Both have come to serve this wholeness. (p. 35)

Parker Palmer (1998), a writer and traveling teacher who works independently on issues in education, community, spirituality, and social change, writes in *The Courage to Teach,*

> In classical understanding, education is an attempt to "lead out" from within the self a core of wisdom that has the power to resist falsehood and live in the light of truth, not by external norms but by reasoned and reflective self-determination. (p. 31)

These definitions differ radically from the intent driving much education policy and practice today. As holistic practices evolve within our education systems, practices which honor the integrity of individuals and their right to self-determinism, traditional education practices continue to focus exclusively on training students to *fit into* predetermined cultural ideals. Steven Glazer(1999), cofounder of the Naropa Institute School of Continuing Education and Living Education: Place-Based Living and Learning, writes in *Spirituality in Education The Heart of Learning:*

> Contemporary education is teaching us to succeed in this world as it is, rather than to heal this world into what it might become. Yes, we are learning to read, to write, to program computers, to find jobs; but the way we are teaching and learning—the way we are learning to see, to act and behave—is undermining the life and the life force that ultimately sustains us all. (p. 259)

Development of full selfhood is the birthright of all. Clark Moustakis (1972), an existential therapist, wrote in *Teaching is Learning:*

In the transformations of the individual, biological and otherwise, certain persistent characteristics remain. These inherent qualities of the organism are the potential basis for creative expression and original behavior. The individual is born with personal integrity which can be stifled and weakened but never completely destroyed. To the extent that this intrinsic nature of the individual is honored, nourished and cultivated, the person maintains his integrity. The intrinsic qualities become more distinct and lead to originality of attitude in all significant or crucial human endeavors. Though unseen, the intrinsic nature of each individual affects the nature of his growth and development. (p. 5)

We are being increasingly called to develop our full potential as we awaken to an expanded understanding of our true nature. Responding to this awakening will transform our culture and the purpose of education. This is not a time for narrowing consciousness by focusing on measurable, objective learning goals related to our surface personalities; it is a time to open up to a deeper wisdom sourced from within. Commitment to developing our full potential can confront and transform the reductionist mentality which has limited us. Creatively gifted learners are driven to explore their inner depths. The education philosophy that supports these highly creative learners to flourish in their self-empowerment can inform education practice which supports authentic learning empowerment in all.

The Teacher As Catalyst for Holistic Growth

No printed word, nor spoken plea can teach
young minds what men should be. Not all the
books on all the shelves—But what the teachers
are themselves.

—Anonymous

As we explore the conditions of educational transformation that foster authentic learning empowerment, we need to research the qualities within individual teachers which encourage or disparage against this. Teaching is sourced from the inherent, lived philosophy of each teacher, not from a prescribed philosophy. Carl Rogers (1983), an existential educator, wrote about empowered learning in, *Freedom to Learn For the 80's*:

We know—and I will briefly mention some of the evidence—that the initiation of such learning rests not upon the teaching skills of the leader, not upon scholarly knowledge of the field, not upon curricular planning, not upon use of audiovisual aids, not upon the programmed learning used, not upon lectures and presentations, not upon an abundance of books, though each of these might at one time or another be utilized as an important resource. No, the facilitation of significant learning rests upon certain attitudinal qualities that exist in the personal *relationship* between the facilitator and the learner. (p. 121)

Teachers whose living is not sourced from their inner knowing are not likely to reach out to support authentic empowerment in their learners. Teachers whose self-definition is limited to the parameters of personality alone are not likely to to feel comfortable fostering creative self-intiative. Parker Palmer (1998) asserts, "Deep speaks to deep, and when we have not sounded our own depths, we cannot sound the depths of our students' lives." (p. 31) Individuals devoted to the call to be true to their own awakening can awaken others.

In *Freedom to Learn for the 80's,* Carl Rogers (1983) lauded Sylvia Ashton Warner, author of *Teacher*:

> . . . who took resistant, supposedly slow-learning primary school Maori children in New Zealand, and let them develop their own reading vocabulary. Each child could request one word—whatever word he wished—each day, and she would print it on a card and give it to him. *Kiss, ghost, bomb, tiger, fight, love, daddy,*—these are samples. Soon they were building sentences, which they could also keep. "He'll get a licking." "Pussy's frightened." The children simply never forgot these self-initiated learnings. (p. 122)

Rogers goes on to say:

> But it is not my purpose to tell you of her methods. I want instead to give you a glimpse of her attitude, of the passionate realness that must have been as evident to her tiny pupils as to her readers. An editor asked her some questions, and she responded: a few cool facts you asked me for . . . I don't know that there's a cool fact in me, or anything else cool for that matter, on this particular subject. I've only got hot long facts on the matter of Creative Teaching, scorching both the page and me. (p. 122)

Teaching that is passionate and fully alive comes from living that is passionate and fully alive, ever expanding as consciousness grows from unlimited depths. Following are the anecdotes of nine teachers who bring forth an exciting vision of teaching and learning. I celebrate these teachers and many like them who have the courage to step out and follow their hearts, both in their personal and professional growth, who strive to be true to the core of their belief in the potential of authentic empowerment in all. They can inspire us to create a new definition of the purpose of schooling.

Engendering Compassion
Lisa

> Through the offering of genuine engagement to our
> students they can begin to experience interconnection
> and wholeness, and experience the interior energetic
> non material quality of life.
> —Steven Glazer

You can't teach students compassion, but you can give them an environment in which they can experience it. You can take them out into the field. For thirteen years I took seventh and eighth graders to Sonogee Nursing Home. It was always a bittersweet experience. Kids experienced the ill health of their friends and sometimes the dying and the death of their friends, but they also experienced the cheer and the warmth of true bonding. When I switched to teaching fifth graders, I thought, "Great! Fifth graders, age 10, it will be just as beautiful." And I was told it wasn't age appropriate.

The following piece is from an "age inappropriate" student who went to this nursing home on her own time:

Bound By a Wheelchair

> When I see you lying there bound by a wheel chair, I can't help but
> wonder why. It's so hard for me not to cry to see a friend suffering
> and bound by a wheelchair. Sometimes I turn to God and say, "If she
> could just live one more day, I would love her more than ever before,"
> but now you have passed away it is clear to see that you and I will
> never be apart from one another deep inside.
> —Brandi Smith

I talk with my students about human rights, followed by animal rights and earth rights. When we share common vocabulary and thoughts about these issues, I show the students the documentary of Jane Goodall, "A Reason For Hope." It touches them completely. I give them the opportunity to join "Roots and Shoots," the organization Jane started in Tanzania in 1991. It is now in fifty countries. "Roots and Shoots" encourages young people from all around the world to make the environment a better place for animals and humans alike.

One of my students got a letter from Jane Goodall. She had been really inspired by Jane's "Root and Shoots" program and had just done a report on her for our Explorers unit. I suggested that she send her report along with her thoughts and feelings about the program. She sent Jane her report and included a really nice letter about what she felt about Jane's work for the past forty years. Jane wrote back to her on beautiful stationary telling her about how important it is for all of us to have a reason to hope and to be part of projects like "Roots and Shoots." When I saw my student come into the classroom with her letter, I got goosebumps.

On the documentary, "A Reason for Hope," Jane talked about carrying pieces of hope with her—for her a piece of the Berlin Wall and the leaf from a tree in Hiroshima. When I talk to the children about it, they share their own pieces of hope: a shell from a vacation etc. And it's important for them to realize that adults have these symbolic pieces. There is a part in the documentary where chimpanzees are gazing at a beautiful waterfall with great pleasure. After watching for a while, the chimps do dances of celebration. I pause before I show that scene, and I ask the children, "How many of you living on our beautiful island visit a favorite spot and are so excited you have butterflies, and maybe dance around. Then maybe at the end of the day when you're a bit tired, you might sit back and listen to a loon, or watch the waves come in?" And, of course, they all put their hands up. Then I say, "Just watch these primates and see if you see a similarity with your experience." And they all see that similarity.

I show the kids the PBS special on KoKo, the chimp, when discussing the importance of language and how it's not just our species. And how, perhaps, if we tried harder, we could communicate with other species. There is a scene in the special where KoKo's friend witnessed his mother's death of decapitation by poachers. And he was able to not only able communicate the story through the sign language he had learned from KoKo, but he was able to express his deep sadness. By seeing that the students realize that sadness is not just a human expression. I happened to mention the experience to some of my colleagues in case they wanted to show the program to their students and discuss language and the interconnectedness of all beings, and they were horrified that I showed it. But no one in my classroom had been horrified. They showed empathy.

I have books in the classroom about a young Canadian child rights activist, Craig Kielburger, who, when he was in the sixth grade, started "Free the Children." He was the type of boy who didn't ask his parents, "May I go down to the store and get an ice cream?" He asked, "May I go to India and interview the children, so the rest of the world can know what they are experiencing?" I also taped an interview of him on Oprah, a program whose theme was "Making a Difference," and showed it to the children. When they realized that this young man started thinking this way in the sixth grade, and started a group at his Canadian school which spread and spread and spread, I didn't have to do anything more. The students automatically said, "Well, we can do something." And I didn't have to give them possible projects to become involved in. Each year students come up with different ideas. This year they raised money for the elephant sanctuary in Tennessee. In the past they have raised money for an awareness about "Roots and Shoots," the local SPCA, and a multitude of other wonderful organizations. You don't teach that kind of commitment. That would be artificial. Sharing inspiration from my core is what touches theirs.

Meeting the Standards Through Inspiration and Fun
MaryAnn

Genuine learning and genuine growing, whether in terms of
one's own self or with one other person or groups,
require awareness and freedom to be. Once these
conditions are present it is essential that the learner
commit himself on the basis of his own desires and preferences
and that he actively participate in life both as an initiator
and in response, in solitary projects and activities and in
joint efforts and communications. The commitment, involvement
and active participation of the learner make the difference between
a real learning process and the motions of learning that typify
too many school activities.

—Clark Moustakis

As a public school teacher, I am required to show how my lessons are meeting certain standards of achievement, but I don't teach directly to these standards. I create units that are interesting to the students and interesting to myself and then show how they meet the standards. And I'm excited about what I'm teaching!

One of my favorite units is about the Iditarod. I teach this unit because the participants in the Iditarod accomplish incredible feats after much training, practice, and perseverance. They show that people can accomplish things they set out to do, even when they're a huge stretch. We have available to us now daily updated pictures of the dogsled races, as well as live radio reports. The children really get into it.

I have a whole "across the curriculum" unit that goes with following the race. In science we study Arctic animals, and in reading I provide related books that my students (third and fourth graders) choose from. Together we read *Balto* by Cindy Chang (the true story of a dog who participated in a dog sled relay, transporting diphtheria medicine from Anchorage to Nome, going through the town of Iditarod) and collect facts from each chapter. Then we read the book *Stone Fox* by J. Gardiner. We engage in literature circles to discuss it which gives every student a chance to talk and a chance to lead a section. I post a map of Alaska, and we each follow a musher and learn about them. Every day a different student prints out the standings of where each participant is and then reads the chart (they have to learn about what all the different aspects mean) to find out where to move the little sleds along on our map. We also have the Iditarod reading challenge. I put the children into groups of three to five and the first team to read 1,049 pages (the Iditarod is approximately 1,049 miles long) wins something special, but every team who finishes wins something. They read a lot! When all of the reading teams "cross the finish line" we have a celebration. One year we had a waffle party in the morning, and this year the students wanted a play time in the gym for which they made up all kinds of games.

I cover a lot of different standards in this project, all through inspiration and fun. In the units I teach, I leave room for the students to diverge and flow with their interests. While I want my students to have the tools they will need for lifelong learning, I know that it's the compelling experiences they will really remember.

I Am a Witness to Miracles
Jane

> We had found a way of being with students that was
> sharply different from conventional education. It did
> not involve teaching so much as it involved us in a process
> that we came to think of as the facilitation of learning.
> It involved a deep trust of students, rather than the distrust
> prevalent in most classrooms. It involved an attempt to be
> with the learner in a number of ways. It meant being with
> the student in a sensitive understanding of his or her own
> interests, desires, directions. It involved being a real person
> in the teacher-student relationship, rather than playing a role.
>
> —Carl Rogers

I have been a teacher all my life. You start early when you're the second in line in a family with seven children. I dreamed of being a scientist, and I was one for a time. The calling to be a teacher is a powerful one, however, and one not easily ignored. I found myself in the classroom 13 years ago. Since then, I have been a witness of miracles.

If you are a teacher, you know what I am talking about. We all have a thousand stories. After a challenging first year of trying to impart my scientific wisdom to four sections of biology students and feeling like I was getting nowhere with them, I made a commitment to project-based teaching. If we couldn't engage in a purposeful piece of work while learning a concept, we moved onto something that did provide context and meaning for the students.

Parents often requested that their child be placed in my class. The special education department moved many of their students into my biology sections. Needless to say, my classes were packed with a diversity of students, student aids, classroom observers, and witnesses to the miracles I am about to share.

Jeremy

Genetics—my passion, but a challenging subject for high school sophomores. My familiarity with the subject sometimes prevented me from seeing what they could not see. So I brought in some new teachers to help out. These teachers were small white-eyed, yellow-bodied, or vestigial-winged flies, *Drosophila melanogaster*. You know them as fruit flies in your kitchen pantry. "Combine any of these types with the wild type fruit fly, and their offspring will tell you what you need to know about the laws of inheritance," I told them. And I showed them how to care for and respect the gift that these small creatures had to offer them.

In order to challenge the students, I let them choose what type of genetic cross they would like to make. I ranked the difficulty in analyzing and understanding the outcome of each possible genetic cross. I strongly suggested that students follow one trait through two generations (like eye color or wing shape). Trying to follow two traits like eye color *and* body color would require more work, more data, extended analysis, and a more complicated explanation of inheritance in a final class presentation. As I expected, one or two top students took the challenge and decided to follow two traits. And then there was Jeremy.

Jeremy wore a big puffy jacket. He never took it off. He was small for a sophomore. I was to learn that years of Ritalin had left Jeremy looking more like a sixth grader than a tenth grader. I think he compensated with the big puffy jacket. Let me tell you about how Jeremy was in our classroom. He was either in shut down mode or disrupting the class. No one wanted to work in a group with him and he didn't care. And so I was taken off guard when he chose to study the most difficult genetic cross I had to offer. For the first time, I saw Jeremy focus. Each student group needed to produce a poster with the genotypes of the expected offspring of their cross. Most groups produced a table with four squares (depicting four expected types of offspring). Jeremy had chosen to do a two-gene cross, and so he had to produce a table with sixteen squares (one for each of sixteen different expected types of offspring). He had to figure it out for himself, and he did. He spent the next several weeks setting up his crosses, counting types of offspring, comparing them to his table with sixteen squares, and calculating how close his observed numbers were to his expected numbers. The amazing moment was when he presented his results to the class. He was so clear about what had happened with his genetic crosses. He spoke as if inspired by the father of genetics himself, Gregor Mendel. He explained Mendel's Law of Independent Assortment as if he had always known it.

The other students in the class were impressed, really impressed. Their expectations of Jeremy shifted. He felt it, we all did. It was palpable. I learned to keep my mind open about which students might choose to accept an intellectual challenge. You don't really know a fifteen-year-old when he walks into the classroom. He has a whole lifetime of experiences that he brings with him. The importance of giving students options inside of expansive projects, and time to explore and reflect, is that it becomes possible for miracles to happen.

Kelley

Integrated hydroponics: growing tomatoes and zinnias with fish waste . . . hmmm . . . if we floated the plants in fish tanks, pumped fish tank water through gardens, divided tanks—half aquarium/half terrarium—we could make it happen in our biology classroom. One student could be chief engineer, another student the water quality expert, another the botanist, and another the zoologist in charge of animal health, monitoring changes in behavior, feeding the fish. Herbs, strawberries, corn, peas, pole beans . . . we grew these in December . . . a miracle in Maine.

Hydroponics open house: If you hold the open house the hour before the winter concert, the students have to arrive early anyhow to tune up, and parents have to wait for the concert to start—offer Christmas cookies and coffee, and they will come and see the gardens, winter gardens, designed with enthusiasm and tended with care. Students will bring them upstairs to room 200 and show them their hydroponics system and everyone else's system. Students seemed to have intimate knowledge of every detail of every system operating in the room, although I'm not sure when they acquired all of this detail. Some parents and their children stayed a long time in the room. Some never left for the concert.

Kelley and her dad stayed and stayed. I took a picture of them. Kelley had a lot to share with him. I thought I'd never get home that night to my own children. But I let Kelley and her dad linger. It seemed to mean a lot to both of them. For two hours they watched the water drip in Kelley's garden and talked about things. Kelley's group had designed a rainfall system. Each day they filled a soda bottle tower with fish tank water. Gravity forced the tank water through a series of perforated hoses strategically placed over fragile seedlings. All day the water rained onto the fledgling garden.

When I heard about Kelley's death, I wept. I wished we could go back to that night, warn her about speeding up. Encourage her to linger. Linger with those people she loved. As I reflect on times when students hung out in the classroom, talking after school, showing me things they'd brought from home, sharing a poem, a song, a piece of artwork, an "A" on an assignment in another class, I know that each afternoon was a gift of time. High school doesn't offer many opportunities for this to happen in the context of a fast paced day where we teach our children to move fast, eat fast, communicate briefly, where we send them the message that life is what happens after high school, and they hurry up to get there, graduating a semester early, a year early, if they can get there. Kelley wasn't the only student from our school who died in that car, but still we didn't take a day off from school. We kept going. Teachers were asked to refrain from attending the memorial service if they didn't know the students well. Not enough substitute teachers could be found to cover classes. I didn't go. I wrote a poem and set it to music and sang it to myself that night. My teenage son heard me linger with it. He made it through high school without a car accident. He was fifteen. She was seventeen. Now he's twenty and she's always seventeen. I don't teach high school anymore. How many miracles can you find in this story?

Matt

I no longer teach in the public school system. But students find me. And we travel together for awhile. Seeking purposeful work. And learning things worth knowing. A boy named Mattie came to me. "Matt" he wants to be called now. He has a thousand ideas in twenty minutes. He's flying. Beyond our ability to develop curriculum or lesson plans, beyond our imagination. He's our next best hope. Kept captive for too long in our educational structures. Go Matt!! Go!! It's okay—I know you notice me here. Trying to keep up with you. You looked me square in the eye yesterday and told me I'm a good teacher. You're fourteen. I'm forty-four. And I needed to hear it from you. And you knew that I did. You know how to help me help you. You are the guide. You are the teacher. How come no one else sees this? How did we find each other? Go Matt! Can you see that I am a witness of miracles. I am here to bear witness.

The Power of Positive Relationship
Cathy
Special Education Teacher

> To respond creatively to a pupil, to enter into
> a creative relationship with him, to be able to empathize
> with him, and to recognize and acknowledge his potentialities,
> a teacher must genuinely know him. Seldom do teachers
> stop to think what it means to know a child.
> —E. Paul Torrence

I know that for myself my relationship with my teachers definitely influenced my learning, so I know now my relationship with my students influences their learning. What I'm thankful for is that it's possible to develop a relationship with most of my students. It doesn't seem as magical, in a way, as it used to, because if I ask the teenagers I work with about themselves and strike up a conversation, it's pretty likely that will establish the relationship—it's so easy. It seems so sad to me, that as a student myself, I so rarely had that connection with a teacher, because it takes little effort from the teacher to do it. Also, my energy to do a good job teaching comes from the students' inspirations, so I have to get to know them as people. I'm not interested in just imparting knowledge.

This year one of my students at the start of the school year found a red pen in the hallway. He was really happy about it, because he doesn't like to waste his money buying pens, and at the same time he doesn't want to be hassled by the teachers for not having a one. For three days in a row he told me about finding the pen on the floor. He really liked it because it wrote really smoothly, and he used it until it completely wore out. For about three days before the pen ran out of ink, he pointed out to me, "My pen's getting low, my pen's getting low." And then one day he didn't have it anymore, and I said, "The pen's gone." He said, "Yeah, it ran out during math class." It seems so minor, but I felt so pleased about how special it was to him. He had it with him every single day; he doesn't ever take books home, but he took the pen home and brought the pen back again every day.

A lot of the high school students I work with struggle most of their school days. They feel bad about themselves, because they get so much negative feedback. A lot of the time the students walk into the special education resource room saying, "I'm dumb," or "I can't keep track of anything." And I like to point out what they are so good at. I've always seen their strengths, but I try consistently to share those with them. For example, some students can entertain a whole roomful of us, and in the process, they can help a roomful of people avoid doing anything productive for eighty minutes. It's not ideal for a school setting, but it's an amazing interpersonal strength. They're able to entertain both the students and the teachers equally—a stretch. It's such a great skill it pains me, because sometimes their strength gets in the way of what other students need to do or even want to do. But most of them do respond it you say, "You really need to stop entertaining us right now." Still it's sad that they don't have a lot of opportunities to practice their talent.

I like to engage my students in conversation about how they spend their weekend time. I remember what they say and follow up with, for example, "Did you make more scrambled eggs this weekend?" I'll listen to their advice about movies and books they did or didn't like.

I brought a book that I have loved as a teenager, *Walk Through Cold Fire*, into a class. It's a simple and compelling story about the discovery of first love. One student asked me what it was about, and when I told her it was one of my favorite books, she decided to try it. It was a little bit harder than what she could read on her own, so she read it outloud, and we talked about what it meant. She really understood it. It was so much fun to read and discuss that book with her.

One of the required portfolio tasks of sophomore year is writing on a specific topic for eighty minutes. In the end, the writing piece is supposed to be relatively well organized and free of errors. One of my students wrote a passionate piece about regret and how we all have things in our lives we regret. She went into into detail about how she regretted a lot of things about her relationship with a former boyfriend. And then she jumped around and talked about regrets she thinks that her parents have. I knew that her piece didn't really fit the organizational requirement of the assignment, and she was resistant to reorganizing; she was adamant about leaving it as it was, although she had in the past been open to revision on other pieces. So I said, "This is great as it is. It's too good for us to change. It seems like you really like it as it is, and I really enjoyed reading it as it is. Let's keep it this way and in a few days you can do this assignment again." I was honoring that the piece she wrote, sourced from her passion, was more important than assigned school work.

It's hard to ask students to "turn themselves off." I have to point out what certain requirements are for particular assignments and for getting through high school. If a high school diploma is a goal for the students, there are hoops they need to jump through. I think that students, to accomplish this goal, have to compromise themselves a lot. They have to spend a lot of time in classes that are uninteresting to them, classes in which they are not learning anything helpful. Some of the students learn enough to get by. They can write a mediocre paper, or they can answer some test questions, but they act like it's just guessing, and I think that in a way it is. They may know a bit of information about the topic, but it's not something that they're integrating in any meaningful way.

Students have lifeskills that don't show up on the test. Who's to say what are the most important things to know?

Bound by the Heart
Sherri

I am certain of nothing but the holiness
of the heart's affections and
the truth of imagination.
—John Keats

As a speech therapist, many years ago, I remember watching the lining up of students, and I remember how teachers were always shushing the kids. After I got my elementary teaching certification I thought, "These kids are mine, and we don't have to do that," and, of course, it was wild. I thought, "Oh, I get. That's why they do it." So there ensued a stretch of time for me trying to find a place of balance.

Throughout my years as a third and fourth grade teacher, I explored how to empower my students within a structure. An example is my folk tale unit. I began our unit by sharing a magical inspiration. At the start of every lesson I told or read or performed (with puppets) a new folk tale. Charlotte Huck's *Children's Literature In the Elementary School* has a wonderful section on traditional literature. In her introduction she talks about how stories came to be and how a people created the stories as a way of trying to understand themselves, their lives, nature etc. They told these stories over and over passing them down through generation after generation, polishing them to a fine sheen like a very polished stone. That polished stone was the image we used as we carried on the tradition of the telling of these folk tales. Every time I read a story or they read a story(individually or in small groups), the kids removed a stone from a colorful fabric bag and dropped it into a jar honoring that, "You're part of continuing the tradition of polishing the stones." They just glowed.

I read or told my stories from my rocking chair. I came into the room wearing a shawl made from a old lace curtain. The children said, "Where is Ms. Clixby?" and several said, "We *know* you're Ms. Clixby; you have the same dress on." After "she" got finished, I went out the door again. I began the unit with *The Story of Stories*, an Anunsi tale. In this tale the king owns all of the stories which he keeps in a trunk. Anunsi wants to make them accessible to the people. The king tells him, "Twa, twa, twa." Anunsi has to do three impossible tasks before the king will release the stories. With magical help Anunsi succeeds. The king was therefore forced to open up the trunk, and the stories flew out and went all around the world.

After we experienced the magic, I introduced the structure of the folk tales. "Look at this," I said, "threes and sevens. Let's think about all of the tales that have threes and sevens in them." There were three little pigs and seven brothers and there were seven tasks. They were discovering the motifs woven through, and they loved it! We'd be reading and one child would say, "Ms. Clixby! It's the youngest," or "It's the stupidest!" or "It's that one that does like snow does, the cumulative!" They became masters at being able to see the structures within stories.

We talked about and read examples of five different kinds of classifications: Cumulative (*The Gingerbread Man*), Realistic (*Stone Soup*), Fairy Tales (kings and queens and magic), Pourquoi or "why" stories (*How the Elephant Got its Trunk*), and Beast Stories (*The Three Pigs*).

I had tons of books on all levels for the children to choose from. The children had a chart in their folders to document the stories we all read. We also had a chart on the wall. The children went up to the chart on the wall after they finished a story, and if nobody else had put that story up under a category, they took a piece of rectangular paper, put the title on it, cut it into a circle (polishing it) and put it on the wall. The children were thrilled as they watched the chart grow.

Sometimes I had a worksheet like "What's the name of your story, what country is it from, how did it begin and how did it end, what kind of story is it?" Some children had a bit of trouble keeping up with the documentation, but in general they loved it, because it felt like detective work. They felt so proud using sophisticated words like "pourquoi" and "cumulative." All of the children were joyfully engaged on many levels. Later on, the children wrote folk tales of their own choosing.

When the children tackled writing their own folk tale, they drew upon the richness of knowledge and inspiration of many weeks of exploration. They knew all the different kinds of folk tales, the motifs like threes and sevens, and traditional beginnings and endings. Sometimes we took turns reading first lines of the beginning of our books and discussed similarities and differences. Then, all of the ways of beginning were put up on a chart for the children to draw upon for their own writing.

For a final performance of their stories, I offered many choices. I modeled puppet shows with stick puppets, slide shows (using transparencies on which I put squares which could be blocked off to show one image at a time using the overhead projector), skits, pop-ups, animations with video cameras (I could only handle a couple of these—they were pretty intense), and fractured folk tales (taking a tale like *The Three Little Pigs* and changing the characters into three little wolves etc.). They could perform their own stories or work in a group with someone else's. All of the children were really involved. They bound their hearts to those folk tales.

Authentic Communication
Jill

> When the facilitator is a real person, being what she is,
> entering in to a relationship with the learner without presenting
> a front or a facade, she is much more likely to be effective.
> This means that the feelings that she is experiencing are available
> to her, available to her awareness, that she is able to live
> these feelings, be them, and able to communicate them if appropriate . . .
> It means that she comes into a direct personal encounter with the learner,
> meeting her on a person-to-person basis.
> —Carl Rogers

Today, my sixth grade students finished up their book talks, and there was a lot of good conversation between the presenters and their classmates. I acted as facilitator and sometimes asked genuine questions—I did not control the discussion. And that's a wonderful thing to watch. Children love to be "on stage," but I was seeing more than that. I was seeing them deeply involved in conversation about their own thinking, about what they were learning and the connections they were making.

Children are so quick to realize when learning isn't authentic. In canned programs, there just isn't the potential for making the connections learners can make when they choose what they study and are invested from the beginning. Real learning *requires* personal investment. However, public schools are run by the expectations of society. They hire teachers to follow certain steps to insure that certain facts deemed necessary are acquired. However, genuine inquiry, connecting what you are learning to what you know and want to know, can only happen under certain conditions. And it can't happen if someone else is always writing the prescription.

I am required to have the next year's language arts curriculum mapped out the previous year. In a spread sheet, I have to list the learning results and projects that I will be working on the first, second, and third trimesters. But I make the planning broad enough to leave the door open, so that wherever the students take me I can go and keep the learning real. I set up projects that I feel will work well for the children, and then I look for the standards that relate. For example, I can prove what my children know and don't know about punctuation just by showing a final copy of their writing. I also encourage my students to be able to say, "OK let's look at my project. What standards did I hit? And what standards are still out there that are expected of me?" If children are going to meet their potential, they need to self-examine what they know, what they want to know, and how they learn.

I recognize my students as fellow human beings. I have to be the protector, the leader, the person who sometimes has to make a decision. But I do that at times when they know I have to do that, and they want me in that role. Outside of those situations, we're just people speaking and sharing with each other. My students come to realize that I learn as much from them as they learn from me. And they're amazed when I say, "Wow, do you realize that I never knew that before. Thank you; you taught me something today." This kind of communication certainly evolves as the year progresses, because for some children authentic communication is a brand new thing for them. Some children have never really been listened to; they've not been talked to, they've been talked at, and so they have a much more difficult time responding to my invitation.

I do specific things to show the children that I'm not just a teacher. I ask them before a vacation what they're looking forward to during their time off, and I tell them what I'm looking forward to. I also kid around with them. Today the music teacher interrupted our class to ask about a lost pencil. He stood at the door while we were involved in a book talk. Finally we all stopped and looked at him, and he said, "Did any of you take my pencil?" I looked at him as I put my hands on my hips and said, "You're interrupting my class for a pencil! Do you need a pencil? I've got a pencil!" He said, "This is a very special pencil, and your students were taking a test and somebody borrowed my pencil and didn't return it." I said, "I'm sorry about that. Does anybody here know what he's talking about?" And nobody did. So I went to my desk, and I got a pencil and gave it to him. After he left I said, "Hmmm, I'll fix him. When's the next band rehearsal?" The kids looked puzzled, and one boy said, "What have you got on your mind, Mrs. Farley?" I said, "Well, I'll tell you what I'm going to do. I going to wait until band rehearsal, and I'm going to go in and wave my arms and say, 'I want all of you to stop playing.'" And then I'm going to look at Joe and say, "Somebody in here has my pencil." A student said, "Oh, he'll get so angry." I said, "Well we'll see. Something tells me he's not going to get so angry." They love that kind of joking around. It helps them to see me as a person.

Kids love to be zany. Last year a student said, "Can we do something that just our homeroom does? Can we have a pajama day?" I said, "Why not!" So the next day they all wore their pajamas, and I wore my bathrobe. And, of course, you can't just wear pajamas without having a cuddly—perfect for the extended SSR (sustained silent reading) we do on Fridays. And some of the children said, "You know, I read better in my pajamas." To me this is not fluff; it's about authentic connection. And it's part of genuine community that we build in the classroom.

I love what I do. The way I teach is something that I discovered within myself. I didn't adopt a particular training to wear as a teacher cloak. That was already within me and going to college drew it out.

Critical *Feeling* Skills
Phyl
Teacher Education Professor

> Unless the self is free to express itself, to respond
> with uniqueness and distinctiveness in every situation
> which is significant, meaningful, and a challenge
> to one's potentialities, the very capacity for growth
> is stifled and denied. Expression of the self is the
> individual's way of asserting his own yes-feeling,
> emerging from his own root system.
> —John Dewey

Teaching for me is all about showing up as a real human being, as whole as I can be in the moment. I think I've always done that, but I'm becoming more and more intentional. I always tell my students personal stories about my life, right from the start. I tell them how old I am, and in the first couple of days, they find out about my sons, Jeff and Chris. From the very beginning my behavior, for a lot of students, appears pleasantly shocking.

In my teaching, I encourage my students to follow their hearts and to trust their intuition. So many of them are heartfelt—they really care. But when you scratch the surface, they have been deeply wounded, so they're afraid to follow their heart. Thus I've been doing a lot more with social/emotional curriculum, looking into personal differences and diversity to enhance greater understanding of self and others. Almost everyone is drinking it in, which gives me the validation that they do operate from their hearts, even though their hearts may have been confined. Also, so many of the young women I teach have been given the notion that they are to be perfect from before they even start. I say to them, "Be sloppy, be messy, make mistakes, and enjoy learning from them."

As a way to encourage authentic communication with my students, I have them journal weekly, and I write back to them. I tell them it's a conversation, and, of course, I don't put a grade on their writing or even a checkmark. In the 32 years I've been teaching at the college level, I've *never ever* dealt with grammar and spelling or grading, because I know many students have been deeply affected by the red-pen scourge. I attempt to invite the deepest level of personal response, outside of any judgment; I'm relentless in this. And as I pour my heart out to them, I experience more and more of a heartfelt response from them.

I structure our course "The Teaching Process" with essential questions. The essential question we are exploring in my class right now is, "Who are you as a person/teacher?" I tell my students, "The whole idea is to bring yourself into your classroom, and if you are unconscious about who you are, there is the very real danger of excluding some of your students." I give my students the Kiersey Temperament Sorter, built on the Meyers Briggs Personality Style Inventory, during the first class. This tool offers sixteen different personality profiles to enhance personal understanding and to heighten awareness of individual differences. I have my students write down the qualities of the personality style that is the opposite of them and ask them how they respond to those qualities. Usually they recognize annoyance or worse. I tell my students, "When you open your doors as a teacher and the students come flooding in, there will be some folks in that class who will annoy you or worse. Why? What is it about that particular student and you and your relationship? If you're more conscious about who you are and who you are not, you'll be able to make a more positive connection."

I think that education is truly life; it's our individual, unfolding, life's journey. And I'm there to be a catalyst to my students' fullness of being. My whole life has been about being as invitational, relational, and non-threatening as I can possibly be, so that I can invite forth the potential in another person. Through being that way with my students, I'm encouraging them to be that way with their students. In this, I am going against the tide. The power structure within Colleges of Education is tightening down in every arena. The tenure and promotion process now is even more structured and confining than previously and is against collaboration of any kind. Teacher educators are also required to follow the same increasingly rigid evaluative procedures and standards that are dictated to the public schools. There may be no way for me to do what I'm doing within that context, and I may have to find other venues (at least for awhile) outside of the institution I'm in. Meanwhile, in the private conversations I have with a number of the education faculty, I hear that they're dying to try more relational teaching.

Much of the educational change these days is just tinkering and is not grounded in discussions about what education is really for: personal empowerment. There is a huge emphasis on rubrics for each project which define what work is good, what work is mediocre etc. related to specified standards. Intuitively, my stomach goes into knots when I participate in discussions about that, because that focus on measuring up to predetermined standards is the antithesis of the way I live my life. My students and I are in each other's lives for a purpose, and we live that purpose together. I focus on how I can support my students' life journeys versus evaluate how they measure up to artificial criteria. And I know that in the process of supporting their journeys, they are supporting mine. I see myself as planting seeds with my students of unconditional trust and acceptance. And their experience with me will need a lot of nurturing in the face of the educational realities that they're in. However, I trust that, if their intentions are strong, they will continue to grow both in their own beingness and in their ability to support their students' becoming.

There is a lot of emphasis in education now about critical thinking skills. Well, what about critical *feeling* (or intuitive) skills? Although so many of my students say they make their decisions through their hearts, they have so many fears that skew them toward being guardians of their egos rather than guardians of their souls. And I am humbled by how few people have had any opportunity to move beyond regimentation, conformity, and uniformity to be in a space in which they are honored for being fully who they are. I am often a beginning for my students, creating a first time space of nonregimentation, nonconformity, nonuniformity, helping them see that there are windows in their boxes, and helping them become lifelong "flinkers"—people capable of simultaneously thinking *and* feeling.

Awakening the Heart
Megs

It is only with the heart
that one can see rightly;
for what is essential
is invisible to the eye.
—Antoine Saint-Exupery in
The Little Prince

I believe that we all have this wonderful goodness within us, and that we have the capacity to access this God power. In my teaching, I have devoted myself to honoring and facilitating the awakening of the heart's power where this goodness resides. I first explored this concept with kindergarten children in a preschool where I used to teach. The process soon took on its own natural evolution.

Age five is a time of a big "moving out" transition, which can feel fearful, but has the potential for great empowerment. I wanted my children to know that, however they were feeling, they had this wonderful power always inside them to help them through the hard times. I created the following visualization to guide our process. I had the children visualize a tree that was in their heart always, any kind. I'll never forget the detailed descriptions they came up with: fall, winter, spring trees, some had leaves, some were Christmas trees, some were fir trees. I told them that they had that tree always planted in their heart. Then I asked the children to tell me a really good feeling that they had, and I heard about the smell of new tennis shoes, sitting on their mother's lap, learning to tie their shoes . . . I told them to take that good feeling and wrap it in a package. They all did that, describing to me what their packages looked like. Then I told them to put their package under their tree. I told the children that their good feeling was always there in that package under their tree in their heart, and that when something in their life felt not good, the good feeling has the ultimate power—just open the package and feel the good feeling. The bad feeling that you don't like then becomes smaller. Then you wrap the good feeling back up, because it's always there, always wrapped just the way your would like it to be, sitting under that powerful tree which is always in your heart.

Next we explored Heart Mapping, a way of solving problems through the heart. We wrote down (I transcribed) and drew about our feelings, about what felt good and not good, and what seemed to work well and not well about a situation. Then we would go to our hearts and explore ways to find solutions to our problems. I told the children that sometimes thinking can lead us astray. Our minds are extremely creative and love to make up stories, and once we believe that our minds are wise, we believe all the stories that we make up in our heads. We begin to live those beliefs, to live those stories, and we may not be living in our highest potential. By listening to our hearts, we can access a deeper wisdom, and then we can go to the brain for information to fulfill our new beliefs. I tell the children, "Let's be servants to our hearts, not to our heads."

The next evolution was the creation of pause buttons. I told the children that they all had a pause button available to them at all times through which they could access their high heart feeling. One little boy had the idea of drawing a pause button, so many other children, of course, drew pause buttons as well—beautiful buttons that looked like sunshines. They wrote "pause" on their buttons in bright colors. We hung these buttons around the room, and often, when the children were having a hard time, they would run over and touch their button and stop and move into their hearts.

*   *   *

One day, *I* was having a hard time. One little guy at lunch time was spilling his food everywhere, and I started losing my patience. I would sometimes tell the kids, "My patience is taking a trip on a spaceship. That means it's not here right now, so I'm going to take a deep breath, but I might be a little short with you." When I spoke these words on this occasion, a little boy looked at me and said, "Megs, I think you'd better pause and go to your heart." And I looked down at him and said, "You're absolutely right. And it's not as easy as it sounds, is it?" Talk about eating crow!

Being Real
Adam

Not all experiences lead to growth. Experiences
must relate to one's potentialities and individuality,
be consistent with what one wants to do, must involve
the real person before they can be true or significant.
They must touch the person in his being and in his
course of becoming. Then intrinsic nature, being, and
becoming merge and unify into the self.
—Clark Moustakis

The alternative program where I teach, Jewel City Community Day School, is set up semester by semester. Ideally students only stay for a semester, and then they go back to their former school. In the real world about half stay for a year and a small portion may stay for three semesters. The program serves kids seventh through tenth grade. The students have a choice between doing the program or being expelled from their high school. The population consists mostly of kids who are falling through the cracks: kids who aren't crazy or violent gangsters, but who are flunking out or doing stupid things to get kicked out (like bringing a knife to school which they don't use). The school is just one classroom.

The reputation of the program is that it's analogous to jail. I've never met a student who came happily, except a few who were so tripped out that they misbehaved right away and were booted right out. The newcomers usually have no sense of how to interact with peers or adults and are both angry and fearful. Because there are around nine students in a class with two teachers giving them a lot of attention, it is hoped that their problems, skills, and needs can be addressed. I know, however, that the only way I can possible be of benefit to them is to try to figure out who they are, to treat them like a person instead of a label, to be cool with them and also firm with them about boundaries and discipline—while at the same time being really human. The following is a case history of one of my students.

Steven mysteriously came into our program from a really rich school district. He was involved in a trial, so neither he nor his parents were talking about what had happened. All that we knew was that he had pulled a knife on someone, and so he had been booted from his district which needed somewhere to put him. I took one look at him and thought, "This is an artistic kid." He reminded me of myself when I was a student. He wasn't dangerous or macho-looking. His shoulders were sloped inward; he was quiet. After a couple of months my first impression bore out. He was totally creative, totally interesting—therefore a complete misfit. From what he was saying in class I could tell that he was already a free thinker.

I set up a Rock and Roll journalism class based around him, because I found out that he was really into rock music (which is unusual for his age, fourteen, because most kids were into Hip Hop). I was concerned that if he was really bored by what was going on, he was going to get into more trouble or become more detached. A small group of us read classic Rock and Roll journalism together. We'd talk about what we read and talk about music. The experience was creative, expressive, fun, and relaxed. Steven began to open up.

I can't give you any slick teaching tricks. I'm not really interested in teaching; I like to share stuff that I'm interested in. My students and I just hang out. It really didn't take much for Steven to really open up. He started sharing his music, bringing his guitar in for our Poetry Slams. I made a deal with him that if he did his homework for a month, I would bring in a friend who had recording equipment, and he could record a CD. He was all over that. We recorded the CD and that was the springboard for him. Steven then made a deal with his father (because he had saved some money) to get his own recording equipment. He was launched.

Whenever I hung out with Steven, I affirmed how interesting he was. I told him that he was messed up, but that he was working it through in a very artistic way. I told him, "You're an artist, and you've got to deal with it. You *really* have to learn to make better decisions so that you can create your art the way you want to." Steven began to figure out who he was and what he wanted to do and how to make his life work.

I got a letter from his father a year later saying that he was at a new school, he had a lot of friends, and he was digging his life. His father said that it was just amazing to them, because up until his experience at the Jewel City Program, all of his teachers had thought that he was retarded. I knew exactly what was going on with Steven when he wrote his first Rock and Roll journalism paper for me, because it was just like that papers I did and still do. Instead of having artificial introductions and an artificial thesis followed by five reasons, he had one hundred million ideas which he tried to put down on three pages. I told him, "Steven, your problem is not that you don't have anything to say, it's that you have too much to say, just like me, and this is how you can try to control these ideas and focus on just one thing, so that it is more understandable to other people." I think that I was able to support a part of him that no one else was either seeing or supporting; I played him as an artist. I talked about what you do when you're an artist and how to live and what your life is about. Real learning is only going to happen from a sense of honest identity. He had done his own work, but he needed a role model to develop his potential.

The best I can do for my students is to be real with them. I'm interested in other people, so it's fun getting to know the students and where they're coming from and what their lives are about. A lot of the kids I work with are lost and freaked out, and just having an older man be real with them can be meaningful to them, even if there are no tangible results or rewards; often no one has wanted to relate to them. I try to engage my students in genuine dialogue. I run some of my film script ideas by them, and I challenge them to discuss why they like a certain Hip Hop artist.

My students have a real inability to discipline themselves and to focus, so they need to write about their lives and write songs and poetry about the street in order to make greater sense of their lives. I think that most standard writing instruction is about killing your own voice—how to make you sound like everybody else. So if a student writes me a paper and it's in broken English and it's filled with slang and their own vernacular expression, that's gold, and I want them to hang on to that. The tightest writing that is going right now in the literature field is where really smart people are trying to write like that, because they're realizing that it's all about voice and voice gives you authentic character development.

When I was a student, the only teachers who meant anything to me were those who took me seriously. Students may not always be bright, but they can tell a bullshit artist three miles away which causes them to check out and disengage. With my small group, I have the option just to hang out with them.

What keeps coming back to me as a goal for my students is to help them figure out what they really want and to talk about that. I tell them that their their dream doesn't have to be separated from their life.

References

Preface

Clark, E.T. 1991. "The Search for a New Educational Paradigm: The Implications About New Assumptions About Thinking and Learning," in *New Directions in Education. Selections from Holistic Education Review,* edited by Ron Miller. Brandon, VT: Holistic Ed Press.

Palmer, P. J. 1998. *The Courage to Teach.* San Francisco: Jossey-Bass Publishers.

Who Is the Creatively Gifted Learner?

Allende, I. 2000. "How I Create" an interview by Joseph Dumas in *Modern Maturity.*

Armstrong, T. 1995. *Myth of the ADD Child: 50 Ways to Improve Your Child's Behavior and Attention Span Without Drugs, Labels, or Coercion.* New York: Putnam Inc.

Barks, C. 1995. *The Essential Rumi.* New York: HarperCollins Publishers.

Brazee, P. and Salvage, J.G. 1991. "Risk Taking, Bit by Bit," *Language Arts* 68 (9): 356-366.

Briggs, D. 1967. *Your Child's Self-Esteem: The Key to His Life.* Garden City, NY: Doubleday.

Claxton, G. 1997. *Hare Brain Tortoise Mind. How Intelligence Increases When You Think Less.* Hopewell, New Jersey: Ecco Press.

Cramond, B. 1995. "The Coincidence of Attention Deficit Hyperactivity Disorder and Creativity," *The National Research Center on the Gifted and Talented.* Storrs, CT: The University of Connecticut.

Freed, J. and Parsons, L. 1997. *Right-Brained Children in a Left-Brained World.* New York: Simon and Shuster.

Gardner, H. 1983. *Frames of Mind. The Theory of Multiple Intelligences.* New York: Basic Books.

Gowan, J.C., Demos, G.D. and Torrance, P.E. eds. 1967. *Creativity: Its Educational Implications.* New York: John Wiley.

Hallowell, E. M., M.D. and Rately, J.J., M.D. 1995. *Driven to Distraction: Recognizing and Coping With Attention Deficit Disorder from Childhood through Adulthood.* New York: Touchstone.

Jenkins, P.D. 1986. *Art for the Fun of It. A Guide for Teaching Young Children.* New York: Prentice Hall Press.

Kneller, G.F. 1965. *The Art and Science of Creativity.* New York: Holt, Rinehart, and Winston.

Millman, D. 1993. *The Life You Were Born to Live.* Tiburon, CA: HJ Kramer, Inc.

Pirto, J. 1998. *Understanding Those Who Create.* Scottsdale, AZ: Gifted Psychology Press.

Schaefer, C. E. 1973. *Developing Creativity in Children.* Buffalo, NY: D.O.K. Publishers

Smith, S. 1991. *Succeeding Against the Odds: Strategies and Insights for Learning Disabled.* New York: St. Martin's Press.

Torrance, P.E. 1973. *Creativity.* San Rafael, CA: Dimensions Publishers.

Torrance, P.E. 1970. *Encouraging Creativity in the Classroom.* Dubuque, Iowa: W.M.C. Brown Company Publishers.

Vitale, B.M. 1982. *Unicorns Are Real. A Right Brained Approach to Learning.* Rolling Hills Estates, CA: Jalmar Press.

Weaver, C. 1994. *Success At Last. Helping Students with AD(H)D Achieve Their Potential.* Portsmouth, NH: Heinemann.

West. T. 1997. *In The Mind's Eye : Visual Thinkers, Gifted People with Learning Difficulties, Computer Images, and the Ironies of Creativity.* Amherst, New York: Prometheus Books.

Seeing Through a Different Lens: Facilitating the Creatively Gifted Learner

Atwell, Nancie. 1987. *In the Middle Writing, Reading and Learning with Adolescents.* Upper Montclair, NJ: Boyton Cook Publishers, Inc.

Beane, J. and Lipka, R. 1984. *Self-Concept, Self-Esteem and the Curriculum.* Boston: Allyn and Bacon.

Bear, D., Invernizzi, M., Johnston, F. and Templeton, S. 1996. *Words Their Way. Word Study for Phonics, Vocabulary and Spelling Instruction.* Upper Saddle River, NJ: Prentice-Hall.

Berger, B. and Cushman, N. 1970. "It's Mine! I Didn't Know I Could Do It So Good!" *A Statement of Philosophy to Accompany the Children's Art Exhibit at the National Association for the Education of Young Children—Annual Conference.* Boston, MA.

Brazee, P. and Salvage, J.G. 1991. "Risk Taking, Bit by Bit," *Language Arts* 68(9):356-366.

Cramond, B. 1994. "Creativity and ADHD: What is the connection?" *Journal of Creative Behavior*, 28, 193-210.

Dyer, W.W. 1998. *Wisdom of the Ages. A Modern Master Brings Eternal Truths into Everyday Life.* New York: HarperCollins Publishers Inc.

Gattin, John. "Samplings from the Naropa Institute Conference on Spirituality in Education." *Shambala Sun,* September 1997.

Getzels, J. W. & Csikszentmihalyi, M.1976. *The creative vision: A longitudinal study of problem finding in art.* New York: Wiley.

Goodman, Ken. 1986. *What's Whole in Whole Language.* Portsmouth, NH: Heinemann.

Graves, Donald H. 1983. *Writing. Teachers and Children at Work.* Portsmouth, NH: Heinemann.

Greene, M.1988. "Research Currents: What Are the Language Arts For?" *Language Arts* 65:5:474-480.

Holdaway, Don. 1979. *The Foundations of Literacy.* New York: Ashton Scholastic.

Kerr, B. 1985. *Smart girls, gifted women.* Columbus, OH: Ohio Psychological Association.

Madden, L. 1988. "Do Teachers Communicate with Their Students as if They Were Dogs?" *Language Arts* 65: 142-146.

Moustakis, C. ed. 1972. *The Child's Discovery of Himself.* New York: Ballantine Books.

Nash, P., Kazamaias, A., Perkinson, H. 1965.*The Educated Man: Studies in the History of Educational Thought.* New York: E. Krieger Publishing Co.

Norris, K. 1996. *The Cloister Walk.* New York: Riverhead Books.

Piechowski, M.M. and Colangelo, N. 1984. "Developmental potential of the gifted." *Gifted Child Quarterly,* 28, 80-88.

Ruiz, D.M. 1997. *The Four Agreements.* San Rafael, CA: Amber-Allen Publishing, Inc.

Rutter, M. 1989. "Attention deficit disorder/hyperkinetic syndrome: Conceptual and research issues regarding diagnosis and classification." In T. Sagvolden & T. Archer (Eds.), *Attention deficit disorder; Clinical and basic research* (pp. 1-24). Hillsdale, NJ: Erlbaum.

Smith, Frank. 1985. *Reading Without Nonsense.* New York: Teachers College Press.

Sternberg, R. J. 1988. "A three-facet model of creativity," in R. J. Sternberg (Ed.), *The Nature of Creativity* (pp. 125-147). New York: Cambridge University Press.

Torrance, E. P. 1970. *Encouraging Creativity in the Classroom.* Dubuque, Iowa: W.M.C. Brown Company Publishers.

Implications of Education for Creatively Gifted Learners: Awakening Passion and Authenticity in All Learners

Glazer, S. ed. 1999. *The Heart of Learning: Spirituality in Education.* New York: Tarcher/Putman.

Moustakis, C.E. 1972. *Teaching As Learning.* New York: Ballantine Books, Inc.

Palmer, P.J. 1998. *The Courage to Teach.* San Francisco, CA: Jossey-Bass Inc.

Rogers, C. 1983. *Freedom to Learn for the 80's.* Columbus, Ohio: Bell and Howell Company.

Warner, S.A. 1963. *Teacher.* New York: Simon and Schuster.